An Unsettled Conquest

Early American Studies

Daniel K. Richter
Director
McNeil Center for Early American Studies,
Series Editor

Exploring neglected aspects of our colonial, revolutionary, and early national history and culture, Early American Studies reinterprets familiar themes and events in fresh ways. Interdisciplinary in character, and with a special emphasis on the period from about 1600 to 1850, the series is published in partnership with the McNeil Center for Early American Studies.

A complete list of books in the series is available from the publisher.

An Unsettled Conquest

The British Campaign Against the Peoples of Acadia

GEOFFREY PLANK

PENN

University of Pennsylvania Press

Philadelphia

Published with the help of the
Charles Phelps Taft Memorial Fund,
University of Cincinnati,
and a grant from the McNeil Center
for Early American Studies

10 9 8 7 6 5 4 3 2 1

Published by
University of Pennsylvania Press
Philadelphia, Pennsylvania 19104-4011

Library of Congress Cataloging-in-Publication Data

Plank, Geoffrey Gilbert
   An unsettled conquest : the British campaign against the peoples of Acadia /
Geoffrey Plank
p.   cm. (Early American Studies)
Includes bibliographical references and index
ISBN 0-8122-3571-1 (alk. paper)
   1. Acadians—Nova Scotia—History—18th century.   2. Micmac Indians—
Nova Scotia—Government relations.   3. Micmac Indians— Nova Scotia—
History—18th century.   4. Nova Scotia—History— To 1763.   5. Acadia—
Colonization.   6. Great Britain—Colonies—North America—
Administration—History—18th century. 7. Nova Scotia—Ethnic relations.
I. Title.
F1038 .P59   2000
971'.6/01—dc21   00-041804
                                                                    CIP

For Ina and Sonja

Contents

Introduction   1

1
New England and Acadia:
The Region and Its Peoples   10

2
The British Arrive:
The Conquest and Its Aftermath   40

3
Anglo-Mi'kmaq Relations,
the French, and the Acadians   68

4
Anglo-Acadian Relations,
the French, and the Mi'kmaq   87

5
Ile Royale, New England,
Scotland, and Nova Scotia   106

6
The French, the Mi'kmaq, and the
Collapse of the Provincial Government's Plans   122

7
The Acadian Removal   140

Conclusion   158

Notes   169

Bibliography   211

Index   231

Acknowledgments   237

Principal Acadian settlements at the time of the British conquest, 1710. Smaller Acadian communities, closely tied to their Algonkian neighbors, inhabited the St. John valley and the southern peninsular coasts.

Pivotal new settlements and missions, 1710–1755.

Introduction

ANYONE approaching Annapolis Royal by water in 1725 would have first noticed the fort. By contemporary European military standards Fort Anne was a modest structure, often in disrepair, but it was situated on a high point on the river's edge downstream from the main settlement, and above it flew a large Union Jack flag. The fort served as the center of government for British Nova Scotia. During the spring of 1725 soldiers energetically patrolled the periphery of Fort Anne. Gunners manned the cannons at the corners of the earthworks and scouts kept a watch in every direction. The British were at war with the Mi'kmaq, the local native people, and especially in late May the men in the fort feared that they were vulnerable to a siege.

Continuing up the river, rounding a bend, and approaching the village, the traveler would have encountered a strikingly different prospect. Most of the civilian inhabitants of Annapolis Royal were Acadians, descendants of colonists from France. Nova Scotia had been a French colony (known as Acadia) before the British seized it in 1710, and very few English-speaking settlers had arrived since the conquest. And though the Mi'kmaq fought the British, they were not at war with the Acadians. During the Anglo-Mi'kmaq war most of the inhabitants of Annapolis Royal went about their business much as they had before the fighting started, and the villagers might have appeared from a distance as a people at peace with the world. But that impression would have changed if our hypothetical visitor had arrived on May 22 and looked toward the base of the fort on the side facing the center of the village, where a man hung suspended by his wrists in chains. The British authorities had put him there "in Order to terrify the other Inhabitants [of Annapolis Royal] from Clandestine Practices of betraying the English Subjects into the Indians' hands."[1]

The man in chains was a local Acadian merchant named Prudent Robichaud, and he was hardly an inveterate enemy of the British colonial government.[2] As early as 1711, a year after the British first took control of Fort Anne, he had offered his services to the men of the new garrison.[3] Over the intervening years he had volunteered to help the British on several occasions, and indeed he would continue to do so in the years to come. But the provincial council, the body charged with governing Nova Scotia, had issued orders prohibiting the villagers from trading with the Mi'kmaq, providing them lodging, or supporting them in any other way.[4] The councilmen (most of whom were military officers) heard reports that Robichaud had "entertained" a Mi'kmaq visitor in his house, and they punished him as a warning to the rest of the Acadian community to stay away from their Mi'kmaq-speaking neighbors.

Robichaud's experience illustrates several problems intrinsic to the putative British conquest of Acadia in the first half of the eighteenth century. The Acadians and the Mi'kmaq had lived side by side for more than one hundred years before the British took nominal sovereignty over the province. A web of friendships, family ties, and commercial connections linked the Mi'kmaq and the Acadians, and the pattern of interaction they had established proved resistant to change.

From 1710 through the 1750s the British colonial governors and the council of Nova Scotia consistently sought to sever the ties that bound the Mi'kmaq to the Acadians. The provincial authorities believed that separating the two groups would establish peace in the region; increase the political power, cultural influence, and economic position of English-speakers in Nova Scotia; and assist the government in its ongoing effort to recruit Protestant, English-speaking settlers. But from the time of the conquest at least until the late 1750s, British officials in Nova Scotia faced a set of interrelated problems in trying to accomplish their goals. They could not recruit English-speaking settlers without more forcefully asserting their authority over the land and its inhabitants. Given the weakness of their military position, they were seldom able to impose their will unilaterally. But when they sought the assistance of Mi'kmaq-speakers or Acadians, close associations between members of the two communities disrupted efforts to deal with them separately. Furthermore, the French imperial authorities retained considerable influence in the region, especially after the establishment in 1714 of a new French colony on Cape Breton Island, or "Ile Royale." The French presented the British with constant competition for the allegiance of the Mi'kmaq and the Acadians.

During the Seven Years' War in the late 1750s, several of the difficulties confronting the British would be alleviated, at least partially. The French military would be expelled from the area and Nova Scotia's provincial government would direct an operation to seize and relocate most of the Acadians, successfully separating them from the Mi'kmaq.

The British conquest of Acadia is best understood as a process rather than a brief event; decades passed before the inhabitants of the region felt the full impact of the British occupation. Nonetheless, whether speaking Mi'kmaq, French, or English, everyone in the vicinity of Nova Scotia was affected almost immediately by the arrival of the British military in 1710. The conquest altered nearly every aspect of life, including the languages the local peoples used, their economic lives and subsistence strategies, their manner of interacting with each other, and the ways they related to the religious groups, nations, and empires of the wider world.

Though the conquest changed the structures of community life in the region, it was almost impossible to measure its effect on the interior lives of individuals. The diverse inhabitants of Nova Scotia did not fit into simple categories according to religious affiliation, sense of group identity, or political belief. Furthermore, conflicting claims of loyalty, combined with coercive pressures, led men and women to act and speak in ways contrary to their inclinations. The British seizure of Acadia changed the words and behavior of almost all the local peoples, but one of its most important consequences was to complicate any effort to discern the personal leanings of one's neighbors.

These circumstances made Nova Scotia unusually difficult to govern. Nonetheless, most of the British administrators who came to Nova Scotia in the first half of the eighteenth century arrived with ambitious plans for what they could accomplish there. The men who led the expedition in 1710 came from outside the region, and thereafter until the 1750s almost all the members of the colonial administration were strangers to the region when they assumed office. Their unfamiliarity with the landscape and its inhabitants lent an abstract quality to their early policy declarations; after they encountered the physical demands of life in the colony and faced the Mi'kmaq and the Acadians, almost all of their initial projects had to be modified, renegotiated, or abandoned.

The first half of the eighteenth century was a time of widespread change in the ways communities on both sides of the Atlantic categorized themselves in terms of politics, religion, language group, and race.[5] Europe's increasingly dominant position in world markets inspired many Europeans and colonists to assume a heightened sense of their own "civilization," which contributed to a hardening of racialist ideas.[6] But even as they were placing more emphasis on the distinctiveness of Europeans in general, the inhabitants of Europe's rival empires were also defining themselves in opposition to each other. As historian Linda Colley has argued, "British" identity took shape in the eighteenth century in part as a way to distinguish the people of Britain from those of France.[7]

At the same time that the Europeans were redefining their own nationalities, in many colonized areas indigenous peoples adopted a reverse-image vision of the world and celebrated their local culture (in the process reinventing it) to distinguish themselves from the European colonizers.[8] In the long run, political discord within the European empires would lead some colonists to assert their own distinctiveness and, to borrow a word from Benedict Anderson, "imagine" themselves as members of new nations independent from Europe.[9]

These developments affected Nova Scotia's peoples in complex and unique ways, in part because of the influence the British, the Acadians, and the Mi'kmaq had on each other. Examined in detail, imperial history is always local history. But Nova Scotia's story is also part of a broader narrative of British colonization and conquest in North America and other parts of the Atlantic world.

Colley has argued in the context of Britain itself that a new way of thinking about "British" identity in the eighteenth century accommodated cultural and sectarian differences among the English, Welsh, and Scottish.[10] The transformation was still in process in mid-century, but similar trends were occurring in British North America, as New Englanders adjusted to the presence of Anglicans and Baptists, and English-speaking colonists throughout the North American colonies learned to live peacefully with Dutch, French Protestant, and German neighbors.[11] These developments encouraged individuals to recharacterize themselves and redirect their personal loyalties. Men and women began to sense that they belonged to a larger and more diverse political community, one tied together primarily by a common allegiance to the British crown and a shared commitment to the cause of Protestantism, broadly defined.

Early eighteenth-century British promoters of the conquest of Acadia claimed that they wanted to convert and assimilate the region's native population and deport the Acadians to France. By the end of the period those aims were reversed; the Mi'kmaq were violently excluded from British colonial society and the Acadians (at least those who could be captured) were forcibly relocated to the thirteen colonies and coerced into living in proximity with Protestant, English-speaking colonists in an effort to assimilate them. These projects, to "root out" the Mi'kmaq and to transform the Acadians into Protestant "faithful subjects," reflected a simple logic flowing directly from contemporary ideas about the nature of colonial identity within the British Empire. Nonetheless, the provincial authorities adopted these programs only after years of hard experience in Nova Scotia.

In recent years, many scholars analyzing the process of imperial expansion in eighteenth-century North America have examined intricate webs of relations between native peoples and colonizers in places where the interests of rival empires overlapped. Historians studying the Great Lakes region, the Ohio valley, Louisiana, and the Spanish borderlands have studied the ways representatives of different cultural groups in "borderland" regions struggled to coexist in environments where none of them had a monopoly on power.[12] Native peoples, French, Dutch, Russian, and Spanish colonists, Mexicans and other conquered groups in the lands that became Canada and the United States have generated scholarly interest for generations, but recently works examining the process of Anglo-American conquest have proliferated, grown in sophistication, and heightened our awareness of the complexity of territorial expansion. Much of the best of this work, whether dealing with native peoples or with conquered people of European descent, has centered on themes of cultural survival and adaptation, reminding us that North America has always been a place of many nations who have related to each other in ever-changing ways. Earlier generations of historians referred casually to "vanishing peoples," but most current historical work suggests that nations seldom disappear; instead they change and survive. But much of the new scholarship, to say nothing of recent events, has also reminded us how difficult survival can be and how important a conqueror's plan to eradicate a people can be, whether or not the plan fully succeeds.

There is a rich scholarly literature on Nova Scotia in the first half of the eighteenth century.[13] Over the years historians have written extensively about the articulation and development of Acadian culture, Mi'kmaq polity and lifeways, Anglo-Mi'kmaq relations and the position of the Mi'kmaq in the imperial rivalry between Britain and France.[14] Some of the best detailed work on the history of the province has focused on the experiences of specific individuals and families.[15] Another significant body of literature has examined the broad pattern of Nova Scotia's relationship to New England.[16] The colony has attracted the attention of legal historians and scholars interested in British imperial administration.[17] This book is distinctive in analyzing the experiences and actions of all of the region's peoples simultaneously, and it emphasizes, in ways previous studies have not done, the complex ramifications of the conquest for different groups of English-speakers as well as for the Mi'kmaq and Acadians.

Several factors combined to make the incorporation of Acadia into the British Empire uniquely contentious. In addition to the complexity of the relationships that already existed among the peoples of the region before the conquest, divisions among the newly arriving English-speaking soldiers and colonial officials made policymaking difficult for British imperial administrators. The men who promoted, organized, and led the expedition that effected the conquest represented a political coalition of diverse interests, including Tories and Whigs, English, Scots, and New Englanders. The partners worked together effectively in planning and executing the military campaign of 1710, but they had different plans for Nova Scotia's future. Because of local concerns, and their longstanding interests and experience in the region, the New Englanders in particular had trouble cooperating with the British colonial government in Nova Scotia after the conquest. Partly as a result, at least until 1749 the actions of various New Englanders undermined British efforts to bring order to the province.

Just as the proximity of New England unsettled Nova Scotia, so too did the presence nearby of a new French colony on Ile Royale. Operating from Louisbourg, their fortress community on the island, the French competed with the British for the trade and allegiance of both the Mi'kmaq and the Acadians. Long after 1710 most French colonial officials continued to think of the Acadians as French subjects, and they assumed that the Mi'kmaq would be aligned with French interests. As late as the 1750s some advisors to the French government thought that the British conquest of Acadia could be partially or wholly reversed, and that French authority should be restored over the Acadian villages along the Bay of Fundy.[18]

Another complicating factor in the history of Nova Scotia was that both the Acadians and the Mi'kmaq formally adhered to the Catholic faith. This disfranchised them politically within the British Empire and foreclosed any possibility that Nova Scotia could follow the course taken by New York, where the descendants of the original Dutch colonists participated in the full range of English colonial governmental institutions after the English seizure of their colony.[19] Many British colonial officials assumed that the Catholic Church exerted an insidious influence over the Mi'kmaq and the Acadians. Catholic priests served as emissaries between the two groups, and helped establish and maintain communications between the peoples of Nova Scotia and the French colonial authorities on Ile Royale and in Canada. The British exaggerated the power of the priesthood, but they worried that Catholic clergymen issued orders to the Mi'kmaq and the Acadian villagers and that the church functioned as a shadow government undermining the authority of the governor and provincial council, and furthering the imperial interests of France.

Especially in the 1740s and 1750s, British imperial policy debates concerning the Acadians tracked other contemporary discussions involving the status of Catholics and nonjurant Anglicans in other places within the British Empire, including Ireland and the Scottish Highlands.[20] But the unique geopolitical circumstances of Nova Scotia provided the British with the apparent incentive—and in the 1750s the opportunity—to implement proposals in Nova Scotia that had been debated and rejected in other parts of the empire.

Nova Scotia deserves special attention from historians of the eighteenth-century British Empire in part because its history reflects cultural and political developments occurring throughout the realm. The colony is also important to historians of North America, not only because of the complexity of its history but also because the British seized it so early. Acadia was the first French colony in mainland North America absorbed into the British Empire, and the policies the British adopted there had a wide-ranging influence on subsequent events elsewhere on the continent. In 1755, when the authorities in Nova Scotia sent thousands of Acadians to the English-speaking colonies, they initiated a series of migrations that scattered French-speaking, Catholic exiles across thousands of miles and altered the cultural landscape of much of British North America. With this and other actions the government of Nova Scotia also exported a set of ideas, policy goals, and tactics that would exert a discernible but immeasurable influence on the behavior of British and Anglo-American officials in the years to come.

The indeterminacy of labels is one of the principal themes of this book. Place-names in North America's eastern maritime region were constantly contested between different language groups in the eighteenth century and frequently changed as sovereignty passed from one empire to another. Thus the words "Acadia" and "Nova Scotia" referred to the same colony, and "Cape Breton Island" was also known as "Ile Royale" after the French established a new colony there in 1714. Similarly, the inhabitants of the region carried multiple identifications, and the words they used to describe each other changed over time. Intermarriage, migration, and occasional cultural conversion had the effect of challenging the fixity of any racial or national classification scheme.[21] Nonetheless, the categorization of peoples mattered; Prudent Robichaud, for example, would never have been hung by the wrists if his visitor had not been identified by the British as an "Indian."

As much as it is important to remember the malleability and uncertainty of place-names and group categories in Acadia and Nova Scotia, it is also necessary to retain a sense of their importance. Such labels provided structure to the lives of the inhabitants of the maritime region in the eighteenth century, and so they must inevitably guide the work of historians.

As far as place-names are concerned, for the sake of clarity I have chosen to employ the words used by the nominally sovereign colonial powers, shifting for example from "Acadia" to "Nova Scotia" in the discussion of events after 1710. In keeping with common practice I have avoided using the word "British" when referring to the period before the Treaty of Union between Scotland and England in 1707. But beyond that shift in terminology, I have not made any other historically specific adjustment in vocabulary when referring to the peoples of Nova Scotia. Recognizing always the indeterminacy of the words, I have used the label "Acadian" to refer to the French-speaking Catholic inhabitants of Acadia and Nova Scotia, "Mi'kmaq" to identify individuals who (as best as can be determined) used the Mi'kmaq language in their families and villages, and "British" to refer to persons who spoke English as their first language, regardless of their place of birth. (On occasions when I draw distinctions between "Britons" and "New Englanders," the word "British" obviously takes on a more specific meaning, but that should be clear from the context.) Similarly, I have used the word "French" to refer to the French-speaking inhabitants of France and the French-ruled colonies of North America, including Canada and Ile Royale.

The word "Nova Scotia" contains additional ambiguities; indeed in 1754 a dispute over the location of Nova Scotia's borders helped trigger the Seven Years War. Without intending to advance an opinion on the merits of the arguments put forward at that time, I have included the disputed territory, lands north of the isthmus of Chignecto in present-day New Brunswick, within the parameters of this study. On the other hand, Cape Breton Island or Ile Royale, though it is part of the Canadian province of Nova Scotia today, lies outside "Nova Scotia" for the purposes of this book. Nonetheless the history of Nova Scotia is in many ways inseparable from that of Ile Royale, and the French colony will figure prominently in my discussion.

The French on Ile Royale are important for this study for two reasons. First, they were continuously engaged with the Mi'kmaq and the Acadians as trading partners and often as political allies. The French were therefore players in the politics of Nova Scotia, just as the New Englanders were. Second, because the French employed, with varying degrees of success, distinctive strategies in dealing with the Mi'kmaq and the Acadians, their policies toward Nova Scotia's resident groups provide a valuable basis for comparison when assessing the approaches taken by the British in Nova Scotia.

This book is organized chronologically. It starts with a discussion of the peoples of the maritime region and the state of relations between them at the close of the seventeenth century, and it ends with an analysis of the events of the 1750s and the Acadian removal. Two chapters examine the period from 1718 through 1743, a time of significant change when the British struggled to define the nature of their authority over the Mi'kmaq and the Acadians. The evolution of the British-Mi'kmaq relationship and Anglo-Acadian relations are explored separately for two reasons: first, to highlight the role of cultural categories in shaping the life of the colony, and second, to facilitate ongoing analysis on the evolution of British thinking about the Mi'kmaq and the Acadian people. Chapter 4, in particular, examines shifts in thinking and patterns of interaction that would contribute eventually to the British decision to attempt the relocation of the Acadians during the 1750s.

Most of the English-speakers who appear in this narrative do so for only one or two chapters, because in comparison with the Mi'kmaq and the Acadians their careers in Nova Scotia were relatively short. By contrast, in order to emphasize the continuity of the Mi'kmaq and Acadian experience, I have followed events in the lives of two individuals from the start of the period under study to the end. These two figures, Acadian merchant Jacques Maurice Vigneau and Mi'kmaq leader Jean-Baptiste Cope, rose to prominence in the affairs of Nova Scotia in the 1750s. Their lives (especially Cope's) are better documented for that decade than for earlier periods but highlighting their experiences throughout their lifetimes humanizes the time scale of this study. Nova Scotia in 1760 was a vastly different place from the Acadia of 70 years before—the Acadians, the Mi'kmaq and the British were all significantly changed peoples. Nonetheless, it was possible for individuals to witness the entire transition firsthand.

Chapter One

New England and Acadia

The Region and Its Peoples, 1689–1704

IN the spring of 1690, when Acadia was still part of the French Empire and Annapolis Royal was still known by its original name, "Port Royal," a volunteer army from Massachusetts attacked. Some of the soldiers and officers who participated in the expedition were familiar with the Acadian village because they had visited before in friendlier times. Indeed one of them, John Nelson, had long worked as a merchant in Acadia and still maintained a warehouse in the village of Port Royal.[1] The military action marked the climax of a period of steadily worsening relations between the New Englanders and the French imperial authorities, and it helped inaugurate a new pattern of relations in the Bay of Fundy region.

From 1689 onward, warfare between the English and French Empires increasingly disrupted regional patterns of trade, diplomacy, and social interaction. The outcome and consequences of the New Englanders' siege indicate many ways in which the politics of the region was about to change. Nonetheless, old habits died hard and, in addition to providing evidence of change, the events of 1690 also reveal much about the ways the peoples of the region interacted earlier in the seventeenth century.

The period from 1689 through 1704 was a time of transition in the lands surrounding the Bay of Fundy. Large-scale imperial affairs affected regional politics more directly, but the local peoples—the Acadians, the Mi'kmaq, Acadia's colonial officials, and the New Englanders—retained a great deal of autonomy in conducting their relations. The authorities in New England, in particular, shaped their policy toward Acadia without specific direction from London.

The seizure of Port Royal in 1690 represented New England's most concerted effort to participate on the English side in the Anglo-French war that had begun in Europe in the aftermath of England's Glorious Revolution in 1688. That war began in part because France supported James II, the deposed Catholic king of England. Therefore, especially in the early years of the conflict, many of the English interpreted the struggle as a battle for the crown and believed that several elements of the English polity that had been affected by the recent revolution, including the balance of power between the king and parliament and the religious settlement in England, would be jeopardized if France won the war.[2]

Many colonists had similar fears. Prior to his overthrow, James II had consolidated English colonial government from Maine to New Jersey within a unitary "Dominion of New England." He and his appointees within the Dominion government had abolished several colonial assemblies and directed the colonists in New England to accept and support the activities of the Church of England. The Glorious Revolution resulted in the overthrow of the Dominion in 1689, and cast into question the legitimacy of all the English colonial administrations, whether they had survived the upheavals of the revolution or not.[3] A French victory in the ensuing war might have overturned the revolutionary settlement in America as well as in England, and many colonists concluded that the outcome of the imperial conflict would determine the fundamental structure of their religious and political lives.

Nonetheless, to understand the actions of the New Englanders in the Bay of Fundy region it is not enough to place them in a transatlantic imperial context. England's newly installed king and queen, William and Mary, had not yet decided to grant legitimacy to the new colonial administrations in New England that had been established as the result of a local uprising in the spring of 1689. Partly as a result, until 1691 the provisional government of Massachusetts met only silence when it asked the authorities in England for permission to take military action against the French. The New Englanders were left to pursue their own strategies, and therefore their actions often reflected regional and local concerns.

The complex regional dimension of the conflict revealed itself in the results of the siege of Port Royal. The New Englanders succeeded in taking the French fort, but almost immediately thereafter the project collapsed in apparent disarray. While ostensibly maintaining that they wanted to hold Acadia, the New Englanders plundered the countryside and alienated the local people. Then they left the province unguarded, and within weeks the French military returned. The project failed in large part because the men who organized the campaign differed in their aims. Some of the promoters of the expedition wanted to lay the groundwork for profitable postwar relations with the Mi'kmaq and the Acadians, while others sought only to punish them for their alleged complicity in recent attacks against New England. This disagreement reflected rifts in New England society. Religious, economic, and cultural constituencies within the colonies struggled with each other over the direction of intercolonial relations, and one result of their disagreements was a pattern of abrupt changes in policy, most dramatically reflected in 1690 by the abandonment of Port Royal.

This chapter examines cross cultural relations in the Bay of Fundy region from the 1690 expedition through the turn of the eighteenth century. A complex web of relations, marked by both animosity and interdependence, had long linked the peoples of Acadia with each other and with New England and New France. Tensions had been building in the region since the 1670s, but many aspects of the Mi'kmaq/Acadian/New Englander relationship had their origins in even earlier times. Indeed, the unique way the Mi'kmaq interacted with European colonists was derived in part from their collective experience in the sixteenth century, when fishermen from several European nations first visited their shores.

The period from 1690 through 1704 marked the end of an era of uneasy accommodation. The Mi'kmaq and the French colonial administration were increasingly antagonistic to the presence of New England fishing vessels and merchant ships in Acadia's waters. The New Englanders responded angrily to the new restrictions, but rather than simply wishing to oust the French government and conquer Acadia, especially after 1690 most New England colonists wanted to hold the peoples of Acadia at an ever-greater distance. Growing hostilities and a gradual escalation of violence, informed in part by moralistic Puritan doctrines of warfare, drove the peoples of the region apart. The period from 1690 through 1704 was the last time that New Englanders acted independently in formulating their policy toward Acadia, and in contrast to later periods, when other groups of English-speakers were involved in the relevant debates, the New Englanders could not sustain any long-term effort to conquer Acadia and made no effort to incorporate its peoples into the life of the English Empire.

On May 9, 1690, seven hundred New Englanders in warships and transports arrived at Port Royal, the French colonial capital of Acadia.[4] The next morning, using a local Catholic priest as an intermediary, Sir William Phips, commander of the New England expedition, entered into negotiations with Louis-Alexandre des Friches de Meneval, the governor of Acadia, and the two men quickly came to terms on a capitulation agreement. Meneval surrendered himself, his fort, and his garrison into the New Englander's custody. Though Phips refused to provide written guarantees, he orally agreed to allow the surrendering troops to march out of their fort fully armed, and to arrange for their transportation to Québec. He also promised to allow the local Acadian villagers to remain in their homes and continue to practice the Catholic faith. But the situation deteriorated within minutes of the conclusion of the negotiations. Brawls erupted between the men of the two armies, and soon the New Englanders decided to disarm the garrison and take the officers and troops into custody. Some of the French soldiers would be imprisoned in Boston for years.[5] Soon thereafter the New England soldiers received permission to loot. In a systematic operation they fanned out across the countryside, robbed the local farmers' houses, killed livestock, and dug up gardens. They stripped and destroyed the major buildings in the fort and showed particular enthusiasm in desecrating the chapel. Eventually they pooled their plunder and divided the proceeds.

After the New Englanders began destroying the local farmsteads, Phips ordered the French-speaking inhabitants of Port Royal to swear allegiance to King William and Queen Mary. According to the official report of the proceedings they complied happily, "making great acclamations and rejoicings."[6] If there is truth to this description of the Acadians' reaction, their happiness probably reflected relief. Though the looting continued after the villagers had sworn allegiance to the English monarchs, the tender of the oath was accompanied by a promise that the violence would end.[7] Phips also asked the Acadians to choose their own leaders. The inhabitants of Port Royal selected an officer of the old French garrison, Charles La Tourasse, to serve as the "president" of a new governing council, and six prominent Acadians to round out the council and take the title of "magistrate." Phips instructed the new president and magistrates to obtain oaths of allegiance from Acadians living in outlying regions, and to disarm and arrest any "Frenchmen" whom they identified as "enemies of the English Crown."[8] Then the New England soldiers returned to work stripping the village and demolishing the fort, and when they had finished Phips departed with his fleet, leaving no garrison behind.

After Phips left, none of the residents of Acadia were willing to fight for the interests of New England. La Tourasse immediately petitioned the French imperial authorities to reappoint him as one of their own.[9] His wish was granted. A few days after the New Englanders left, a French officer arrived with five soldiers, took down the English flag, and reclaimed Port Royal on behalf of France, without facing any local resistance. By the summer of 1691 the colony had a new French governor, Joseph Robinau de Villebon.[10] Villebon directed the repair of the fort at Port Royal and placed a small garrison there, but he established his base of operations across the Bay of Fundy on the St. John River in present-day New Brunswick. He did so not to facilitate the concerns of government among the Acadians—as late as 1697 only eight Acadian families lived on the St. John—but because the location served him strategically in the ongoing war against New England.[11]

Opponents of the Massachusetts government cited this sequence of events as proof that the New Englanders were unfit to govern themselves, to say nothing of a conquered colony. The temporary seizure of Port Royal had cost a great deal of money and achieved almost nothing.[12] Prior to the expedition the Massachusetts authorities had claimed that they intended to conquer and retain Acadia, but after the fall of Port Royal the army's actions seemed poorly designed for achieving that result. The soldiers and officers had antagonized the local people and then abandoned them, without making any substantial effort to supervise their activities in the future.

Unquestionably there was incompetence in the way the campaign had been carried out. The entire project had been planned in haste and its leaders may have been overly optimistic. Not only did they plan to conquer Acadia, they also intended to take the larger French settlements on the St. Lawrence River later in the year. Before the fleet left Boston one supporter of the campaign argued that the "great part of the French people," both in Acadia and along the St. Lawrence, would welcome the New Englanders as liberators.[13] Such hopeful expectations may have led the some of the expedition's commanders to misinterpret the Acadians' readiness to swear allegiance to William and Mary, and to place excessive trust in the villagers' chosen leaders.[14] But the larger problem facing the New Englanders was that they did not agree among themselves on their aims. The men who had taken the most prominent role in garnering political support for the military campaign were merchants and fishermen with longstanding connections to Acadia. Though they had wanted to oust the French colonial government, these men had long enjoyed profitable relations with the Acadians and the local Algonkian peoples, and they hoped that their profits would increase after the inhabitants of the region formally acquired the status of English subjects. But other participants only wanted vengeance against the Acadians and the Mi'kmaq. They had no interest in maintaining good relations with them, and indeed many of them did not want to grant the Catholic Acadians or the Mi'kmaq admission to the English Empire.

Phips almost certainly belonged to the second group.[15] He was from Maine, born in a rough-hewn house on the edge of what was then New

England's settlement frontier. Though he had few social graces and could barely read or write, through a combination of extraordinary ambition and luck he had risen to prominence in various circles within the English Empire. Phips had made a fortune as a privateer and treasure hunter in the Spanish Caribbean, and in 1687, after several years of searching, he found *La Concepción*, the most valuable shipwreck discovered in the seventeenth century. He brought such large quantities of precious metals from the ship back to his sponsors in England that according to some historians he altered the relative value of specie and currency in the kingdom. His rewards included a knighthood, granted by King James II in the summer of 1687, but in many ways Phips remained a child of New England's backwoods.

As a native of eastern Maine he was conscious of the violent resistance Algonkian warriors had offered against the encroachments of New Englanders, and he associated all northern Algonkian peoples indirectly with the Acadians.[16] In 1689 the fighting in Maine had escalated, and Algonkian warriors burned the New England settlement at Pemaquid. Phips, like most of his contemporaries, believed that the action had been timed to coincide with the start of the imperial war. Jean-Vincent d'Abbadie de Saint-Castin, a man born in France living among the Algonkians near Maine, figured prominently in the New Englanders' thinking. Though Saint-Castin lived far from the centers of Acadian settlement, seventeenth-century New Englanders did not draw sharp distinctions between varieties of French colonists. Saint-Castin's alleged participation in the northern Algonkian attack suggested that the "French" generally (a category that to New Englanders included the Acadians) were accomplices in the recent events in Maine.

Such logic was particularly common among the followers of the Reverend Cotton Mather, who served as the commander's pastor and promoted the Acadia expedition as a punitive action. According to Mather the destruction of Port Royal would strike a blow against a wide variety of persons who deserved to be punished, including the men of the French garrison, the Acadian villagers, all hostile "Indians," Louis XIV, the Pope, and the devil himself. Mather recommended no compromises, and he did not support efforts to negotiate or reach lasting accommodations with the French or the Acadians. Indeed, at his most effusive he suggested that destroying the French presence in North America would defeat the devil forever and usher in the "Chiliad"—the thousand-year reign of Christ.[17] Phips formally joined Mather's church in the weeks before the expedition.[18]

The semiliterate Phips left posterity no personal journals, diaries, or letters indicating whether he fully accepted Mather's millennialist message. But regardless whether he believed personally that pillaging Port Royal would serve a metaphysical purpose, Phips also had worldly motives for looting the Acadian village. He had made his fortune from plunder, and like many of his soldiers he took the wealth of Port Royal, such as it was, as his due. This stance pleased his soldiers (none of whom wanted to serve garrison duty in Acadia), but it poorly served the interests of the New England merchants and fishermen who had rallied support for the expedition in the first place.

During the 1680s several prominent and successful Boston merchants had accumulated grievances against the French colonial government of Acadia. In an effort to control local commerce and protect the local economy for the benefit of French traders, in 1684 the French tried to bar New England merchants from doing business with Acadians. Though these regulations were easily evaded, they increased the risks associated with trade in the region, and the danger grew after the arrival of Meneval as governor in 1687. Meneval tried to make the new regulations effective by negotiating restrictive trade agreements with the Dominion government in New England. The Glorious Revolution and the beginning of the imperial war in 1689 forced him to jettison that strategy, but it facilitated his use of military force—particularly the commissioning of privateers—as a method of restricting intercolonial trade. Under these circumstances New England merchants who sailed the Bay of Fundy had a strong financial interest in supporting the conquest of Acadia. Formally incorporating the colony into the English Empire would repeal all existing trade restrictions. Furthermore, the removal of the French military presence at Port Royal would deprive French privateers of a convenient base of operations.[19]

New England's fishermen had similar reasons for supporting the attack on Port Royal. During the 1680s Acadia's governors had tried to tax New Englanders fishing in Acadian waters.[20] The edict proved unenforceable, but it led to altercations and helped provide a legal pretext for attacks on New England fishing vessels after the outbreak of formal hostilities. The first fatal casualties of the war in America were fishermen from Salem, Massachusetts, attacked by privateers operating out of Acadia.[21] From that time on fishing was seen as an unusually dangerous profession, and as result several towns north of Boston entered into an economic decline that would end only after the British gained nominal sovereignty over Nova Scotia in 1713.[22]

Several Boston merchants joined forces with fishermen from Salem to promote the campaign to conquer Acadia in 1690. But in their effort to gather political support for the project, they confronted opposition from members of the Puritan clergy.[23] Among New England's clergy Mather was exceptional in backing the project so vigorously. To be sure, other clergymen supported the expedition and agreed that it would serve "Christ's interest," but they did not necessarily share Mather's millennialist understanding of the meaning of the conflict.[24] Most Puritan clergymen were willing to approve retaliatory military raids, but while they believed that it was appropriate for the New England colonies to defend themselves and punish adversaries who attacked them, they did not generally support actions designed to take territory from the French. According to the common Puritan view, retaliation and vengeance were justified by biblical precedent, but Jehovah never told the ancient Israelites to expand beyond the borders of the lands God promised to Abraham.[25]

This interpretation of divine law did not rule out military action. On the contrary, the clergymen endorsed the administration of punishment as a war aim, and providentialism (the belief that God directs world events) strengthened the New Englanders' vigor in inflicting pain on their enemies. Orthodox Puritans believed that God judged entire peoples communally in wartime, and they interpreted suffering as an indication of God's anger. The greater the enemy's distress, the more convincingly it proved that heaven favored New England. In her analysis of an earlier period, historian Karen Kupperman summarized the impact of these beliefs succinctly: "It was dangerous to be the enemy of these Puritans."[26] Nonetheless, the clergy seldom advocated conquering French colonies. They compared New England to Israel, but few if any believed that places colonized by other European powers, such as Acadia or the St. Lawrence valley, lay within New England's promised land. If they associated the French colonies with any territory mentioned in the Bible it was Babylon, a dangerous country that righteous people should avoid.[27]

Puritan strictures against expansionist warfare continued to exert an influence on the colonies' policymakers well into the eighteenth century.[28] But the colonies were changing, and even by the 1690s there were those who held a contrary view. Two generations had passed since the founding of New England, and thanks to a high birthrate and long life expectancies, the population of the colonies had risen sharply, from approximately 21,000 at the end of the first major wave of immigration in 1642 to at least 90,000 by the 1690s.[29] The younger New Englanders were more diverse than their grandparents had been, and the expanding size of their settlements altered their relationship with the wider world. Migrations west, north, and east had brought them into closer contact with French colonists, the Dutch, and a variety of English-speakers in New York and elsewhere. Furthermore, the expansion of transatlantic trade brought new immigrants to New England who felt no attachment to the Puritan tradition. Many New England merchants, particularly those trading in the north, were culturally more broad-minded than most tradition-bound New Englanders. A significant portion of them were men born in England who migrated to America following the restoration of the monarchy in 1660, and in the late 1680s many of them gravitated toward the newly legalized Anglican church.[30] Furthermore, trading with French colonists and native peoples widened the perspective of many merchants, making them more willing to associate with peoples of other cultures. This relatively cosmopolitan outlook had a complex effect on their view of territorial conquest. In general, merchants were more supportive than other New Englanders of the 1690 expedition to conquer Acadia, but they were also more willing to try to accommodate themselves to the French colonial government after the conquest failed.[31]

Almost all the factors that led to the New Englanders' decision to attack Acadia in 1690 contributed to a weakening of their interest in holding the colony after the initial military action succeeded. Cotton Mather's millennial expectations were disappointed, and particularly after the failure of the expedition against Québec later in the year, he concluded in retrospect that the Acadia project had been premature.[32] Other Puritan ministers had supported retaliatory action against the Acadians without ever wanting to see New England troops garrison the colony, a viewpoint that was almost certainly shared by most of the soldiers involved in the attack. For their part, the merchants and fishermen who rallied support for the expedition were interested primarily in maintaining unimpeded access to the maritime region. Both groups were happy to see the value of Port Royal diminished as a base for French privateers, but given the absence of a strong New England government in Acadia and the impracticality of deploying a constant, effective naval patrol in the open Atlantic, the merchants and fishermen knew that they would be best served by a return to the conditions that had existed before the recent outbreak of war. They still believed that a restoration of the old order of things was possible. In the immediate aftermath of the expedition of 1690, few New Englanders understood that the pattern of regional politics had been permanently changed.

For decades, indeed since the founding of Plymouth in 1620, New Englanders had found ways to accommodate to the Acadians' presence.

Acadia was older than Plymouth; French-speaking colonists had lived on the coasts of the Bay of Fundy continuously since 1604. In its early days the French outpost at Port Royal had been a military base, a trading post, and a headquarters for missionary work among the local Mi'kmaq people. Its initial population was small, only a few dozen, and predominantly male, but by the mid-seventeenth century a larger and more stable French speaking community had been established, with a core of native-born colonists and a more even sex ratio. As their numbers grew, many Acadian families turned to agriculture, growing wheat and other crops and raising sheep and cattle, in the valley of the river that passed Port Royal (see figure 1). Smaller Acadian communities were established along the St. John River and on the Atlantic coast of the peninsula of Acadia. The settlers in these communities lived in close proximity with larger groups of native peoples, traded with them, and occasionally intermarried. Fishing was an important source of sustenance for all the Acadians, but grain and livestock were their main products for trade.[33] In the second half of the seventeenth century Acadian villagers moved from Port Royal eastward up the Bay of Fundy, bringing with them a diking technology that made it possible for them to drain salt marshes and protect them from flooding by the sea.[34] By the 1690s the eastern settlements, including Minas and Beaubassin, contained populations that rivaled that of Port Royal, but overall Acadia remained a modest colony, with a population of approximately 1,200 French-speakers.[35]

Though Acadia was small, it seemed strategically important, at least from the appearance of seventeenth-century maps, because it lay close to New England, the mouth of the St. Lawrence River, and the North Atlantic fishing banks (see figure 2). The maps were deceiving; the difficulties of overland travel and the small size and remote position of the Acadian settlements along the coasts of the Bay of Fundy reduced the strategic importance of the colony except as a base for privateers. Nonetheless, Acadia drew the attention of imperial projectors from several empires in the seventeenth century. An English raiding party wrecked the first French fort at Port Royal in 1613, and a much larger Scottish expedition seized the colony and temporarily placed new colonists there in the late 1620s. Another English campaign resulted in the establishment of nominal English sovereignty over the colony from 1654 through 1667, and the Dutch attacked and held Acadia briefly in 1674. Despite the efforts of their rivals, however, the French were the only European people to settle in the region permanently. The Scottish, English, and Dutch campaigns had a few lasting effects. The Scottish project gave the colony a new alter-

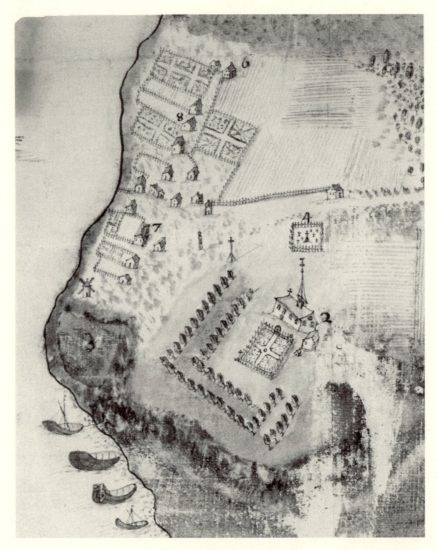

Figure 1. Port Royal in 1686. Detail of a map by Jean Baptiste-Louis Franquelin, "Plan tres exact du terrain ou sont sçitüees les maisons du Port Royal." Photograph courtesy of the Bibliothèque nationale de France.

native name, "Nova Scotia," which the Scottish and English used when they imagined they might reconquer the place.[36] But more important, the Scottish, English, and Dutch attacks on Port Royal reinforced a common belief among most of the peoples of the region that such expeditions mattered very little. Life in Acadia could continue after each attack much as it had before.

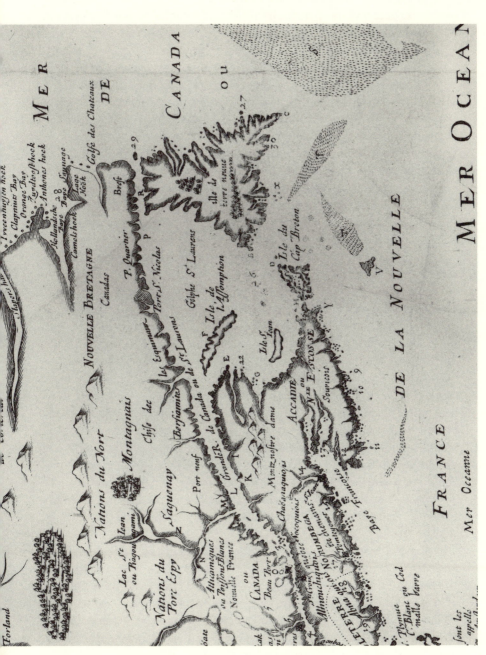

Figure 2. Detail from Samuel Champlain's map of Canada, published in 1653. Courtesy of the John Carter Brown Library at Brown University.

Acadia was the oldest successful French colony in North America, but within a few years of its founding France established another outpost at Québec, which would thereafter attract greater attention from Paris. Québec and the other French settlements further upstream on the St. Lawrence River gave the French access to a more promising fur-trading region than the one surrounding Port Royal and provided a larger stage for missionary work among native peoples. Furthermore, after the 1670s when hundreds of new French colonists began farming along the St. Lawrence, "Canada," as the St. Lawrence colony was known, had a significantly larger population than Acadia, and it figured much more prominently in the French government's long-range plans for North America. The exploration of the Mississippi valley and the establishment of new forts along its banks further increased the strategic importance of Canada at the relative expense of Acadia when French officials thought about North America on a continental scale.

In its early years Acadia was governed by proprietors, but after the reformation of the French Empire in the 1660s the crown of France assumed responsibility for appointing the colony's governors. The governors of Acadia officially held a subordinate position in relation to their counterparts in Québec, though the relationship between the two was never clearly defined.[37] The governors of both colonies reported to the Ministry of Marine in Paris, which oversaw French imperial affairs. Locally the governor presided over the military garrisons in Acadia, and he exerted his greatest influence in the villages closest to the largest concentration of soldiers, particularly Port Royal. In outlying regions many powers were devolved to persons with seigneurial claims, but most of the would-be aristocrats who held the seigneurial titles neglected their powers and responsibilities.[38] The Acadians outside of Port Royal, especially at the eastern end of the Bay of Fundy and along the Atlantic coast, resisted the claims of their seigneurs and usually governed their own affairs through local, hierarchical institutions such as the militia and the Catholic parish.

Especially in the second half of the seventeenth century, the Acadians were well connected to the wider Atlantic world. Despite the efforts of the French authorities in the 1680s, Acadian and New England merchants alike sailed the Bay of Fundy carrying goods, messages, and passengers between Acadia and Boston. An overland route linked the Acadians to the French colonists of Canada, and in Port Royal and other small military outposts, ships arrived at irregular intervals from France.

Of all the Acadian villages, Port Royal was the oldest and largest.

It was also ordinarily the center of government and the focus of much intercolonial trade. Acadian farmers, fishermen, and merchants lived side by side there in a diverse community. Soldiers and missionaries arrived regularly from Europe and elsewhere in the French Empire, and Mi'kmaq families visited often to meet with the missionaries, to negotiate with the governors, and to trade. Jacques Maurice Vigneau was born in the village in 1702.[39] His father was a fisherman who owned his own vessel.[40] During the summer, when his father left for extended periods, young Jacques lived with his mother and brothers in a house within sight of the French fort. In his ramblings he would have encountered Mi'kmaq children, the French sons and daughters of the men of the garrison, and perhaps some visitors from other nations as well. Vigneau was still a boy when the British seized Port Royal in 1710, but the arrival of a new contingent of English-speakers only advanced an educational process that had already begun. As an adult Vigneau spoke Mi'kmaq, English, and French, and he conversed easily and effectively with people from a variety of cultures.

Vigneau learned to read, but many Acadians did not, and most commercial transactions at Port Royal and elsewhere in Acadia depended on spoken words. Many Acadian villagers were engaged in commerce, sometimes on an international scale, but their commercial agreements were concluded without written contracts, and they seldom used documents memorializing the transmission of debt. Under these circumstances the rights and obligations of the villagers, in relation with each other and with outsiders, depended on mutual cooperation and communal memory, and merchants had to establish close ties with the Acadians to create a personal reservoir of trust. As a result, many of the travelers who did business at Port Royal became intimately involved in community life.

Mi'kmaq families also frequently visited Port Royal, but the pattern of behavior governing Mi'kmaq-Acadian relations differed significantly from that involving visitors of European descent. The Mi'kmaq had been in the region longer and the pattern of interaction they established with the Acadian people had its origin as much in Algonkian custom as in French or Acadian custom.

Approximately two thousand Mi'kmaq-speakers lived in the vicinity of Acadia in the closing years of the seventeenth century.[41] During the summer the Mi'kmaq lived in villages along the coasts of the Bay of Fundy, the Atlantic, and the Gulf of St. Lawrence, and supported themselves by fishing and gathering shellfish and other marine resources. In wintertime these villages dispersed, and the Mi'kmaq traveled in smaller hunting bands.[42] They could cross the Bay of Fundy and Gulf of St. Lawrence in large canoes, and even before the arrival of Europeans gave them added incentives to maintain intertribal contacts, the Mi'kmaq participated in a trading network that spanned hundreds of miles.[43] As hunters and traders they ranged as far north as Newfoundland and brought furs as far south as present-day southern New England, where they acquired wampum and corn.[44]

The Mi'kmaq may have been the first native people in North America to encounter Europeans. A well-known oral tradition surrounds the meeting, which cannot be dated precisely. On the night before the initial European ship arrived, a young Mi'kmaq woman dreamed that strange men would come to her people on a floating island. After the ship actually appeared the Mi'kmaq were profoundly affected by the woman's dream and its subsequent realization. They retold the story for centuries, and their account is the only one historians have of the event.[45] It is virtually certain the Europeans were fishermen (see figure 3). French, Irish, Basque, Portuguese, and English vessels were trolling the waters of the Atlantic maritime region early in the sixteenth century, and sometime before 1519 some of the fishing crews had already met the local people and engaged them in trade.[46]

Those early exchanges were not always easy. Mi'kmaq warriors attacked Portuguese fishermen in the 1520s after they tried to establish a permanent fishing station on the future Cape Breton Island. But overall the Mi'kmaq traded with the Europeans much more enthusiastically than other native groups, and indeed there is evidence that after the sailing ships began arriving the Mi'kmaq expanded the range of their hunts, perhaps because of overhunting in their original home territories in response to an expanding fur trade. Perhaps newly acquired European trade goods such as copper pots lightened the load of Mi'kmaq travelers and made greater distances easier to cover, perhaps diseases reduced rival hunting nations and made game in new areas available to the Mi'kmaq, and perhaps trade with the Europeans simply inspired within the Mi'kmaq a greater acquisitiveness.[47]

Though it is difficult to reconstruct the events of the sixteenth century in detail, it easier to discern the impact of those events on the founding of Acadia. Mi'kmaq leaders welcomed the French colonists when they arrived on the peninsula of Nova Scotia in 1605.[48] By contrast, every other French attempt to establish colonies in North America met armed resistance. Jacques Cartier and his men faced combat after they sailed up the St. Lawrence in 1534, as did French Protestant colonists when they tried to establish an outpost in Carolina in 1564. The founders of Québec in 1608 and the early settlers in Louisiana at the turn of the eighteenth cen-

Figure 3. Undated Mi'kmaq petroglyph depicting a European sailing ship, possibly from the seventeenth century. Kejimkujik National Park, Nova Scotia. One of a series of photographs by Olive and Arthur Kelsall, taken between 1946 and 1955, in the History Collection, Nova Scotia Museum, Halifax.

tury provoked a military response from at least some of the native peoples living in the vicinity of their new colonies. Most Spanish, English, and Dutch colonists had similar experiences. Thus the first Acadians were either smart to choose to settle among the Mi'kmaq or extraordinarily lucky to chance upon them.

A century of interaction with European fishermen and fur traders had convinced the Mi'kmaq that it was possible to benefit from engaging in exchange with the newcomers. Furthermore, because the Mi'kmaq were already familiar with Europeans, the arrival of the Acadians seemed less strange to them than it would have to other Algonkian or Iroquoian peoples, and the pattern of behavior established in the sixteenth century would have given the Mi'kmaq no indication that Europeans generally coveted large amounts of land. It was also fortunate for Acadia that Mi'kmaq was the only language spoken on the peninsula. Mi'kmaq bands did not fight one another, and north of the isthmus of Chignecto, where a variety of other Algonkian languages were spoken in addition to Mi'kmaq, by the seventeenth century an alliance network that historians have called the "Wabanaki Confederacy" maintained peace.[49] As a result, local diplomacy was less treacherous for the colonists at Port Royal than it would be, for example, at Québec. Around Québec and the other new French colonies in North America, violent animosities already existed between native groups before the colonists arrived, and when the French established alliances they found themselves engulfed in conflicts they had not started and barely understood.

Compared to other hunting and gathering peoples, the Mi'kmaq maintained an unusually intricate system of governance. In the summertime most Mi'kmaq families congregated in villages, usually along the coast, where elaborate hierarchies governed community life. By contrast, when they were inland hunting, they traveled in small groups with less formal social relationships.[50] Social organization varied with the season; this was true prior to the first arrival of the Europeans, and even more so after the expansion of the fur trade when Mi'kmaq hunting parties began to travel longer distances.

The summertime communities interested most European travelers, missionaries, and colonial officials more than the hunting parties, in part because the villages were easier to observe, but also because their social structure seemed vaguely familiar. As historian William C. Wicken has demonstrated through an exhaustive review of missionary records and censuses, the communities were very stable. Each Mi'kmaq family belonged to a specific village and the male descendants of the family remained affiliated with it through generations, as wives moved into the households of their husbands. Mi'kmaq men seldom moved from one community to another, but their social position within the villages was subject to change. Male elders assumed authority on the basis of their age, dignity, and ability to preserve social peace through a process of careful negotiation and consensus building.[51] They did not use force to maintain order, but French observers thought that they held quasi-military power over their neighbors. In the seventeenth century the French began applying military terminology to describe the Mi'kmaq leaders, most commonly calling them "captains" and suggesting that they ruled over clearly delineated sections of coast.[52] By the eighteenth century Mi'kmaq leaders had begun to describe themselves as "captains," and gradually they adopted a wide array of military titles to designate influential members of their communities.[53]

The use of these words reflected a shift in the ways the leaders presented themselves outside their home villages. Especially in the context of negotiations with colonial officials they sought to legitimize their position as negotiators by assuming a status comparable to that of officers in the colonial garrisons. The titles also played a role in Mi'kmaq relations with other native groups in the seventeenth and eighteenth centuries, as the Mi'kmaq affiliated themselves more closely with the Wabanaki Confederacy. Nonetheless, there is strong evidence that eighteenth-century Mi'kmaq leaders exerted authority in ways very different from those of European military officers, and that they could hold their positions only if they retained the support of those who sought their direction and advice. As one nineteenth-century observer put it, "whatever power [the Mi'kmaq leader] may possess, arises more from the ascendancy acquired by his mild and conciliating manners, than from any respect which the Indians pay to the office itself."[54] The village leaders would never have called themselves "captain" if the Europeans had not arrived, and the adoption of the title mattered, if for no other reason than that it gave the captains a way to command respect from colonial officials. But it is difficult to assess how much the adoption of a new vocabulary reflected a fundamental change in common Mi'kmaq patterns of thinking.

Similar questions arise in connection with Mi'kmaq spiritual life. In the early seventeenth century several prominent Mi'kmaq individuals began to identify themselves as "Catholic," and by the end of the century most families had accepted baptism and adopted Christian names, which they used when dealing with missionaries and colonists.[55] But conversion to Catholicism seldom involved a thorough rejection of traditional Mi'kmaq beliefs or practices, and many eighteenth-century observers, French and British alike, doubted that the Mi'kmaq shared their pastors' understanding of Catholicism (see figure 4).[56]

The personal names the Mi'kmaq adopted often reflected the ambiguities of their religious conversions. Jean-Baptiste Cope, for example, was born on the peninsula of Acadia sometime around 1698, and when he was

still a young child his parents took him to a French Catholic priest for baptism. The name he received at the ceremony (which he would eventually use in his negotiations with French and British colonial officials) carried religious and political significance. "Cope" is a shortened form of the Mi'kmaq word for beaver, and Cope's male ancestors had identified his family with the beaver for generations. The priest transformed the Mi'kmaq word for "beaver" into a European surname and assigned Cope a first name that evoked the Christian gospel and the project of evangelization.[57] The name "Jean-Baptiste" also meant something important politically, because John the Baptist had been informally designated the patron saint of New France.[58] There is no way to know who decided that Cope would receive these names — it may have been his parents, the priest, or Cope himself, depending on his age at the time he received baptism. It is also impossible to know whether Cope used these names in his daily life as a child. But years later, when he became a leader among the Mi'kmaq, he assumed an identity that confirmed many of the implications of the name that had been assigned him. He called himself a Catholic, settled near a mission, and worked intermittently to promote a political program that he thought would promote the interests of Catholicism.

Nonetheless it is difficult to assess Cope's inner spiritual life, because we do not possess documents privately written by him or any Mi'kmaq individual in the seventeenth or eighteenth century. Many contemporary observers were impressed by the apparent piety and devotion of Mi'kmaq converts, but others interpreted the Catholicism of the Mi'kmaq as strictly political. From the time of the first Mi'kmaq baptism on, the ceremony carried multiple meanings; diplomatic and economic considerations mixed with the spiritual in the calculations leading to the Mi'kmaq embrace of the new faith.

The first prominent Mi'kmaq-speaking person to accept Catholicism formally was a man named Membertou, who in the early seventeenth century was a respected elder among the Mi'kmaq living in the region where the Acadians chose to establish the fort of Port Royal in

Figure 4. Drawing purportedly by the missionary Chrestien Le Clerq or one of his contemporaries in the seventeenth century, showing Le Clerq providing religious instruction to the Mi'kmaq using a special writing system he developed for this purpose. The writing system, later elaborated upon by the missionary Pierre Maillard, created a special language of religious instruction comprehensible only to the missionaries and their charges. Drawing reproduced in Chrestien Le Clerq, *New Relations of Gaspesia*, translated and edited by William F. Ganong (Toronto: Champlain Society, 1910), 28.

1605. In 1610 a Catholic missionary came to the new colony, and within two months of the priest's arrival Membertou and his family had consented to receive baptism. At the ceremony he received the name "Henry," perhaps in honor of the reigning French king.[59] Conversion to Catholicism may have seemed to cost very little, and it pleased the colonists enormously to see the native people formally accept the teachings of the church. Two Jesuit missionaries arrived in 1611 to replace the original priest, and they paid particular attention to Membertou because they believed that he could set an example for the rest of the Mi'kmaq people. If he supported the church, they hoped his neighbors would do so too. Soon after the Jesuits arrived Membertou fell ill and went to the missionaries for a cure. The priests arranged for him to receive medicines, but they were unable to restore his health. After nearly two weeks in the missionaries' care, in anticipation of dying, Membertou indicated that he wanted to be buried with his ancestors in accordance with traditional Mi'kmaq practice. Church rules prevented this, however, because Catholics could be buried only in consecrated burial grounds that could not contain the bones of non-Christians. Membertou pleaded with the missionaries to make an exception in his case, but they refused. Physically backed into a corner in the shelter where he lay dying, he eventually relented and agreed to a Catholic burial, but the Jesuits' report makes it clear that he died afraid that the church had permanently separated him from his ancestors.[60]

Membertou lost the ability to reconcile a Christian identity with his allegiance to Mi'kmaq tradition. Perhaps he heeded the priests' warnings of hell or promises of salvation. But it is also possible that he chose to comply with the priests' wishes only for the sake of promoting the economic and political interests of his people. Most other Mi'kmaq individuals lived farther from the missionaries' scrutiny and found it easier to combine Mi'kmaq and Catholic traditions. Even after most or all of the Mi'kmaq had received baptism, their spiritual life often remained distinctively Mi'kmaq. Many formal converts continued to believe, for example, that immortal spirits animated the creatures of the woods.[61] Religious conversion meant something unique for each individual, but for villages, bands, and the Mi'kmaq nation as a whole, allegiance to Catholicism represented a social and political bond as much as anything else. By embracing Catholicism the Mi'kmaq signaled their willingness to work closely with the colonists of Acadia.

Membertou succeeded in establishing a Mi'kmaq-Acadian alliance that long outlived him. The alliance brought benefits to the Mi'kmaq at little cost, especially in the early years. Acadians were valuable trading partners, and they took up very little space, at least in the first half of the seventeenth century. Though they would occupy much more territory later, especially after the 1670s when they began to move to the eastern end of the Bay of Fundy, even then the settlers occupied only a small part of the peninsula, and much of what they took was coastal marshland claimed from the sea. The long experience of good relations with the French-speakers, combined with a local diplomatic tradition that discouraged shifts in alliances, maintained peace between the Mi'kmaq and the Acadians. Furthermore, by the 1690s the two groups had a common enemy in New England.

The New Englanders and the Mi'kmaq coexisted amicably for most of the seventeenth century, as fishermen from Massachusetts plied the waters off the Atlantic coast of Acadia without significantly affecting the lives of the native people. Occasionally the fishermen landed to dry their catch on the shore, but they did not construct permanent facilities, dispossess the Mi'kmaq from their villages, or otherwise compete with the native people for resources. On the contrary, fishermen and others from New England engaged the Mi'kmaq in trade, and as late as 1677 one historian of Massachusetts wrote that the Mi'kmaq had never committed any act of hostility against a New Englander.[62]

Things were changing quickly, however. In 1675 an Algonkian leader named Metacom, who was known to the colonists as "King Philip," led an armed coalition of native peoples against New England. It was a bloody conflict, and one of the costliest in terms of casualties as a proportion of population that the New Englanders would ever face.[63] The Mi'kmaq did not participate in Metacom's War, but at the height of the conflict the New Englanders as a group became hostile toward almost all native peoples, and some refused to make distinctions between members of different "Indian" nations.[64] In the spring of 1676 a New England ship captain named Laughton landed near Cape Sable, at the southernmost tip of the peninsula of Acadia, captured a group of Mi'kmaq individuals, sailed to the Azores Islands, and sold his captives to the Portuguese as slaves.[65] Responding in accordance with Algonkian customs of diplomacy and warfare, the Mi'kmaq held the New Englanders communally responsible, and in 1677 they launched a series of retaliatory raids against Massachusetts fishing ships.[66]

These events soured relations between the New England colonists and the Mi'kmaq, and although the violence subsided after 1677, mutual suspicion increased, in part because of a growing unease within New England over the closeness of relations between the northern Algonkian peoples and the French.[67] During Metacom's War the New Englanders took notice that many of the Mi'kmaq and other northern Algonkian peoples had formally converted to Catholicism. Already repelled by what they saw as the native peoples' "savagery," the New Englanders now also denigrated the Catholic converts as heretics. One Massachusetts clergyman in 1676 described the native peoples who had formally converted to Catholicism as "twofold more the Children of Hell."[68]

Such opinions were expressed most commonly in wartime, often by men and women who had little contact with native peoples outside a context of tension and violence. New England colonists who had interacted in peacetime productively with the Mi'kmaq and other native peoples were likely to hold more conciliatory views. After 1677 traders from New England resumed a profitable commerce with the Mi'kmaq. Throughout the 1680s, New England fishermen visited the Atlantic coast of the peninsula of Acadia without interference from the local Mi'kmaq bands and without disturbing them. Nonetheless, as the decade progressed and new, ambitious French governors were appointed to bring order to Acadia, the groundwork was laid for the creation of the tenuous political alliance within New England that supported the seizure of Port Royal in 1690. Merchants and fishermen who wanted peaceful, profitable relations with the Mi'kmaq and the Acadians joined forces with militant Puritan ministers and others who wanted simply to punish them.

The aftermath of the 1690 expedition was unlike that of any of the earlier seventeenth-century military campaigns in Acadia. The violence of that attack and subsequent raids alienated many of the Acadians from the New Englanders, broke their trust, and made it difficult for them to deal amicably with English-speakers. The war in Europe, in which a predominantly Protestant alliance was arrayed against the forces of Louis XIV, increased the sense of gravity associated with the fighting and made it more difficult for both the Acadians and the New Englanders to justify a local reconciliation. Violence between Algonkian groups and settlers in northern New England, combined with the ever-greater proclivity of New Englanders to associate Algonkian peoples with the French, heightened the New Englanders' sense of danger and solidified their belief that the Acadians were appropriate targets of retribution. And at least equally important, the French imperial authorities paid greater attention to Acadia after 1690. The colonial governors of the 1690s were determined to defend it and promote French military interests. Their actions served to strengthen the arguments of those New Englanders who believed that the French and the northern Algonkian peoples were coordinating their actions, and furthermore that all people associated with the French imperial interest, including the Mi'kmaq and the Acadians, deserved punishment.

By 1691 the French had repaired the fort at Port Royal and established a small garrison there. For the duration of the imperial war French privateers used Acadia as a base of operations. The colony also served as a conduit for equipment, news, and directions sent from France to French troops and Algonkian warriors operating north and east of the New England settlements, and French patrols worked vigorously and often effectively to bar New England merchants from the waters of the Bay of Fundy.[69] The French were unable to close New England's Atlantic fishery, but privateers operating from Port Royal intimidated fishermen. So too did the Mi'kmaq, who after 1690 worked vigorously to bar New England's fishing ships from approaching Acadia's coastline. New Englanders who landed even briefly to search for fresh water or to gain shelter from storms were subject to attack.[70]

Increasingly, retribution became New England's primary war aim in the region of Acadia. The Acadians at Port Royal were punished in the initial attack, but other groups on the peninsula, including Acadian settlers in the eastern part of the province and Mi'kmaq communities throughout the region, would be targeted later.[71] In the spring of 1696, confronting escalating tensions in Maine and an increase in French privateering activity, the Massachusetts General Court resolved to offer bounties for the scalps of "Indian" men, women and children (see figure 5).[72] Responding to the offer, a man from southeastern Massachusetts named Benjamin Church, himself a member of the General Court, raised a private army and sailed up the Bay of Fundy in search of Mi'kmaq families who could pay with their lives for the alleged crimes of the northern Algonkian peoples generally, and the French. The scalp bounty policy had precedents in the colony's earlier "Indian Wars;" it represented one of New England's distinctive ways, in the seventeenth century, of answering perceived "savagery" in kind.[73] Church and his men disembarked near Beaubassin, but as it happened they found no Mi'kmaq. Instead they struck out against the resources of the area. They slaughtered livestock and left the carcasses in the fields, and perhaps in an effort to inflict pain on the Mi'kmaq by impeding their ability to hunt, they also killed dogs.[74]

The 1696 raid illustrates the extent to which the New Englanders believed that they were facing an alliance of enemies in Acadia. They saw the Mi'kmaq and Acadians as agents of French imperialism and considered both groups legitimate targets of retribution in response to actions taken by Algonkian warriors, French privateers, or other forces the New

Province of the Massachusetts-Bay.

By the HONORABLE, the Lieutenant

Governour, &c.
Council & Assembly:

Convened at *Boston*, upon *Wednesday* the 27th. of *May.* 1696.
In the Eighth Year of His Majesties Reign.

For better Encouragement to Prosecute the French *and* Indian *Enemy, &c.*

Ordered,

THAT if any suitable person or persons shall offer themselves to take the Command of a Company against His Majesties Enemies, and obtain a Commission from the Honourable the Lieutenant Governour, or Commander in Chief, with Orders to Raise a Company or Companies for His Majesties Service: such Officers and Companies (over and above the Encouragement given by an Act of this Court, of Fifty Pounds *Per Head* for every Indian man, and Twenty five Pounds *Per Head*, for any Indian Woman or Child, Male or Female, under the Age of Fourteen Years, taken or brought in Prisoner; the Scalps of all Indians slain, to be produced and delivered to the Commissioner or Commissioners for War, as the Law in that case provides, and the benefit of Plunder) shall be allowed and paid out of the Publick Treasury their necessary Provision, Ammunition and accustomed Wages, for so long time as they are seeking or pursuing said Enemy. But when they shall return to any Town, Fort, Garrison or Vessels for so long time as they stay in any such place, they shall be out of Pay : And the chief Officer and Clerk of every such Company, shall each of them keep a Journal of all their Proceedings from time to time, and return the same unto the Commissioner for War, and that they be further supplied with Vessels for Transportation, and Boats as needed. And in case of receiving any Wounds or Maihems in the said Service, shall be encouraged as to Cure and Pensions as is by Law provided for Souldiers that are Impressed, and likewise to be allowed a Chyrurgeon with them if it be procured under Publick Pay.

And for Encouragement of speedy Succours and Relief to be yielded unto the Frontiers upon an Alarm or Attack made upon them by the Enemy ; such of the Neighbouring Towns as move to their Relief and towards the Surprizal or Pursuit of the Enemy, by virtue of the Law of the Province, or by virtue of any Order of the Lieutenant Governour or Commander in Chief, or Commander of the Regiment, shall have the like Encouragement as aforesaid, if such persons shall have pursued the Enemy farther than they may reasonably return in twenty four Hours, otherwise to be allowed no Wages.

Provided, That this Order shall continue in force for the space of six Months next coming, and for no longer.

Isaac Addington, Secr.

William Stoughton.

Englanders associated with France. As the actions of the soldiers in 1696 demonstrated, if the New Englanders failed to make one group attached to the French interest suffer, they often believed that they could serve justice equally well by damaging the interests of another similarly implicated group. Failing to find the Mi'kmaq, they attacked the Acadians.

For most of the war the New England colonies were running their own foreign policy, trying to operate in ways that would promote the interests of the English government, but doing so without specific instructions. The violent, punitive behavior of the New England armies conformed well to common English understandings of the imperial conflict early in the 1690s, and in 1691 the English ministry listened to the pleadings of Increase Mather and retroactively approved of what the New Englanders had done.[75] The Massachusetts Charter of 1691 placed Acadia under the official jurisdiction of the colonial government in Boston. But as the war progressed the interests of the New Englanders and the English ministry diverged. By 1697 after years of inconclusive fighting, the ministers saw the benefit of compromise, and the Bay of Fundy region was a place where concessions could be made at what seemed to be relatively little cost. When French and English diplomats met to settle the conflict they acknowledged the situation on the ground. The French had already recovered Acadia, and so England officially conceded French sovereignty over the colony in the Treaty of Ryswick in 1697.

An uneasy peace returned to the Bay of Fundy region. Though it is impossible to quantify illegal commerce, the level of smuggling between Acadia and New England probably increased, and many Acadian and English-speaking merchants tried to expand intercolonial trade.[76] New England fishermen returned to the Atlantic coast of Acadia with a little more confidence, though everyone in the region remained wary, with cause. A new Anglo-French war—the War of the Spanish Succession—started in Europe in 1702, and soon the combat spread to North America, with a resumption of privateering on the Atlantic coast and a series of incursions by French soldiers and Algonkian warriors on New England's northern and eastern frontier.[77]

When the new war began in 1702 the authorities in New England responded very differently from the way they had in the 1690s, in large

Figure 5. Broadside published in Massachusetts in 1696 offering prizes of £50 for the scalp of an "Indian man" and £25 for the scalp of "any Indian Woman or Child, Male or Female under the Age of Fourteen Years." Courtesy of the Trustees of the Boston Public Library.

part because of the cautious stance of the new Massachusetts governor, Joseph Dudley. Instead of taking dramatic action independently and asking for retroactive approval from London, Dudley refrained from aggressive action pending ministerial instructions. This new posture on the part of the governor and his supporters eventually brought new players onto the scene, including Scottish and English political leaders, French Protestants and various other representatives of the expanding English Empire. But early in the war, in 1704, a series of events occurred that owed more to New England's older, insular political worldview than to the new era that was about to begin.

Even before his appointment as governor in 1701, Dudley had survived a long political career by negotiating a difficult path, staying close to local interest groups while maintaining ties to imperial officials in London. In the mid-1680s he had identified himself with a body of conservative New Englanders including Puritan ministers, long-serving magistrates, and others who opposed the reorganization of New England's government during the reign of James II.[78] But in 1686, when it appeared that the king would impose his will on the colonies, Dudley joined forces with his erstwhile opponents and served temporarily as governor in the autocratic administration of King James's Dominion of New England. Though he claimed to have taken this position in order to defend the colonists' traditions, the administration he served overturned many aspects of New England life, for example by abolishing the colonial legislature and other institutions of representative government, and by legalizing and supporting the activities of the Church of England in Boston. After the Glorious Revolution and the overthrow of the Dominion government Dudley shifted allegiance to William and Mary, moved to England, and remained active in politics. By 1701, when he secured his commission as royal governor of Massachusetts, he had obtained a wide array of political enemies in Boston who were waiting for him when he took office.[79] Cotton Mather took the lead in calling for Dudley's ouster.

The political crisis of 1704 began with a raid by a party of French soldiers and Algonkian warriors on Deerfield township in western Massachusetts. The attackers killed thirty-eight people, and took more than one hundred of the town's residents overland to Montréal.[80] The "Deerfield Massacre," as it was called, heightened the impatience of many New England colonists who were nurturing grievances with the French and their native allies and were increasingly eager to strike out against them. The militant colonists felt frustrated by Dudley's legalistic reticence and believed they could act without official permission from England. Though no Acadians had participated in the attack on Deerfield, and some Acadian villagers had recently declared their willingness to cooperate with the New Englanders, Benjamin Church, the leader of the 1696 expedition to Beaubassin, decided on his own that he would return to Acadia for a punitive raid. He began recruiting volunteers before he had obtained official sanction from the governor or legislature. Church enlisted five hundred men, most of them from fishing communities in and around Plymouth, where many families had suffered from Mi'kmaq and French attacks on fishing ships. During his recruitment effort he was also engaged in correspondence with Dudley, and he asked the governor for permission to take Port Royal.

Dudley said no—the New England colonies would not engage in any expansionist campaigns unless they received instructions authorizing such action from Whitehall. But the governor also knew that he could not restrain the angry New Englanders much longer. Instead of ordering an attack on Port Royal, Dudley told Church to march his army through the other agricultural villages of Acadia and "use all possible methods for burning and destroying . . . the enemies' housing, and breaking the dams of their corn grounds."[81] He warned Church to avoid Port Royal and refrain from engaging the French military. This would only be a punitive raid aimed exclusively at noncombatants. Church did as he was told. According to the official account, when his men left Acadia only five houses remained standing outside Port Royal. The sea walls were broken and most of the Acadians' farmland was destroyed.[82]

By identifying Acadian civilians as enemies, Dudley employed the logic of communal punishment that had informed Puritan discussions of warfare almost since the founding days of New England. His orders also reflected an understanding of regional political alignments that had gained currency in New England since the 1670s, one based on a pair of interrelated assumptions: that French military officials were in league with all French-speaking colonists and allied Algonkian peoples, and that all those groups were proper targets for retaliation if any of them attacked. The Acadians were chosen for retributive action primarily because they were the easiest targets. The dikes protecting their fields made them vulnerable—a small breach in one dam could inundate acres of cultivated land in saltwater. Finally, Dudley's warning to Church to avoid confronting the French army revealed the limits of what the governor believed the New Englanders could do on their own. Vengeance was the Lord's, but the colonists could serve as God's agents. Any campaign for military conquest, by contrast, had to be initiated in London.

From 1689 through 1704 various constituencies within New England held conflicting views on the colonies' policies toward Acadia. In 1690 merchants and fishermen were the groups who most actively supported annexing the province, but they were also the New Englanders who had worked most extensively in Acadia under the French regime, and for most of the seventeenth century they had found ways to accommodate themselves with Acadia's French colonial administration. Their primary interest lay not in changing the Acadians' or the Mi'kmaq's government, but in gaining safe access to local marine resources and trade. If a settlement could have been reached that restored the circumstances of the first half of the century, when the colony was governed by the French but New Englanders were allowed almost unrestricted access to its coasts and peoples, the interests of the merchants and fishermen would have been served.

The imperial wars that began in 1689 altered the pattern of relations between the region's peoples, however. Intermittent combat in Acadia, on the borders of New England, and in the coastal waters off Acadia produced ever-lengthening lists of grievances that made reconciliation between the New Englanders and the peoples of the Bay of Fundy region increasingly difficult. Furthermore, the policies of the French colonial administrators inhibited intercolonial contacts and drove the peoples of the region apart. As the 1690s progressed, retaliation and the exaction of justice against the Acadians and the Mi'kmaq became the dominant aim of New England's policy, as the peoples of Acadia were made to answer for the actions of the French privateers, military men, and Algonkian warriors allied to the French.

The New Englanders formulated their own policies toward the Mi'kmaq and the Acadians in the last decades of the seventeenth century. During the 1690s the colonial governments sought ministerial approval for their actions only retroactively, and though Joseph Dudley ruled out any expedition of conquest without prior approval from London, the effect of his stance was not to inhibit all military action, but to concentrate the military resources of New England on projects aimed at strengthening defense, exacting retribution against perceived enemies, and deterring aggression from the Algonkians and the French. Throughout the seventeenth century, and at least until 1704, one constant in New England's stance toward the peoples of Acadia was that no one favored any effort to transform or assimilate the Mi'kmaq or the Acadians into English-speaking colonial society. The merchants and fishermen were quite willing to reach accommodations with cultural strangers. The Puritan clergy and other conservative New Englanders only wanted to keep them at a distance. The eighteenth century would witness various drives to convert and absorb the peoples of Nova Scotia into the British Empire, but the inspiration for those programs came initially from Britain, not New England. In 1707, when Governor Dudley finally received instructions from the British ministry on the direction of his policies toward Acadia, the pattern of regional politics changed fundamentally.

Chapter Two

The British Arrive

The Conquest of Acadia and Its Aftermath, 1705–1718

A combined force of New England volunteers and British regular troops took final possession of the French fort at Port Royal in 1710 during the War of the Spanish Succession. They maintained a garrison there for the duration of the war, and in 1713 the French and British negotiators at Utrecht transferred sovereignty over Acadia from France to Britain. From that time on, "Port Royal" was officially known as "Annapolis Royal" in honor of Britain's Queen Anne, and Acadia as a whole was known as "Nova Scotia."

The 1710 expedition to Port Royal nearly suffered the same fate as the 1690 action. A loose coalition of British and American political figures had supported the project, and like their predecessors in the earlier campaign, they could not agree among themselves on their war aims. The most dramatic disputes divided the men who arrived from Britain to lead the expedition from the New Englanders who supplied a large part of the initial military manpower and most of the logistical support. Within a year of the seizure of Port Royal, the British and the New Englanders had almost completely divorced themselves from one another, and their inability to work together jeopardized the survival of the small British force that remained in place. The garrison's troubles were exacerbated by friction within its diverse body of British officers, as Scottish interests clashed with English, and Tory with Whig.

Nonetheless, the garrison at Annapolis Royal survived the war, and its continuing presence forced the local peoples to alter many aspects of their lives. Some Acadians refused to cooperate with the conquerors, while others tried to exploit divisions within the garrison by currying favor with officers who were willing to serve their needs. The Mi'kmaq were also divided in their reaction. A significant number of Mi'kmaq families permanently moved away from the vicinity of Annapolis Royal. Some went to Ile Royale, which remained officially a territory of France, while others stayed on the peninsula of Nova Scotia, though few if any of the Mi'kmaq recognized British authority over them.

For their part, the French imperial authorities took dramatic action in response to the loss of Acadia and the concurrent loss of the French settlement on Newfoundland, which was similarly transferred to Britain at Utrecht. The French spent a considerable sum of money establishing a naval base and fishing settlement at a place they named "Louisbourg" on Ile Royale. The fort they constructed at Louisbourg was one of the largest in North America, and the town they built around the fort became an important outpost for the French fishery and a trading center for the maritime region. As part of their effort to build a strong French colony on Ile Royale, the French tried to recruit Mi'kmaq and Acadian families to move there from the peninsula of Nova Scotia. They met with some success, but Acadian farm families as a group refused to move to the French-ruled island. The land was poor on Ile Royale, the farmers had invested too much in their fields on the peninsula, and they were not sufficiently devoted to the French imperial cause to relocate. Also, the weak position of the garrison in Nova Scotia gave the Acadians grounds for hoping that the British authorities would leave them alone.

The colonial authorities in Nova Scotia, however, had no intention of leaving the Acadians in the position in which they had found them. In this respect the political figures who promoted the conquest of Acadia and its retention as a British colony in the early eighteenth century differed greatly from the New Englanders who had previously dominated the formulation of imperial policy in the region. Whether they were English or Scottish, Tory or Whig, almost all the Britons who discussed Nova Scotia around the time of the conquest harbored plans for directing fundamental transformations in the cultural landscape. Through a combination of forced migration, missionary work, educational reform, and other measures, they planned to create a new colony of Protestants incorporating immigrant settlers and at least some of the peoples who had lived in Acadia before. Most of their early proposals focused on assimilating the Mi'kmaq and other native peoples into British colonial society, but opposition from the Mi'kmaq and political disorder within the colonial administration doomed their plans almost from the start.

This chapter traces these events in part by focusing on the thoughts and actions of Samuel Vetch, who, more than anyone else, inspired the British conquest of Nova Scotia in 1710. Vetch was a Scottish Whig, and his plans for Nova Scotia reflected a political program closely tied to the interests and ambitions of Scots and Whigs in the early eighteenth century. Like many of his contemporaries, Vetch wanted to play a part in the founding of a Scottish empire, but his prospects for establishing Scottish colonies changed fundamentally after the parliamentary union of Scotland and England in 1707. That union was juridically a union of empires, and it represented a challenge to would-be Scottish imperialists. After 1707, Scots had access to the land, resources, and trade of the original English Empire, but the union also meant that anyone hoping to found Scottish colonies would have to gain approval from agencies based in London. In order to gain such approval, Vetch recruited a wide array of English and English colonial allies who supported him in his immediate project of attacking the French in Acadia; but Vetch's political partners remained indifferent, if not increasingly hostile, to his ultimate aim of making the colony distinctly Scottish.

The early history of British Nova Scotia reveals the complexity of the process of imperial expansion. Disagreements among the conquerors impeded their ability to take concerted action following the success of the initial military campaign. Furthermore, conditions on the ground, and the stances of the various local peoples—the Mi'kmaq, the Acadians, and the French on nearby Ile Royale—undermined or transformed the plans of the imperialists. In the first few years following the British conquest the peoples of the region struggled to decide among themselves whether, and under what circumstances, they could coexist. No one in the region could avoid participating in these debates, and they would continue almost without interruption for the next forty-five years.

Samuel Vetch was born in 1668, and he acquired many of his political principles early in life. His father was a Whig who actively opposed the accession of James II. In the mid-1680s Samuel followed his father into exile in Holland, only to return to Britain in 1688 as a soldier in the revolutionary army of William and Mary. After the Glorious Revolution he remained in the English army and spent most of the 1690s on the continent of Europe fighting the French.[1] Upon returning to Scotland at the end of the war, Vetch joined a company of adventurers seeking to establish a colony for Scotland in North America. In 1698 they sailed to the isthmus of Panama and founded a small Scottish outpost named Darien, but the colony was wracked by disease and dissension, and continuously vulnerable to Spanish attacks. All the colonists, including Vetch, left within two years (see figure 6).[2]

Vetch first visited Acadia during the short interval of peace before the outbreak of the War of the Spanish Succession in 1702. By that time he had moved to New York and married into the Livingston family, thereby joining a clan of immigrant colonists from Scotland who were active in New York's mercantile community. Marrying into the family gave Vetch access to a commercial network linking the English and French colonists and Algonkian and Iroquoian fur traders. Before 1702, in partnership with

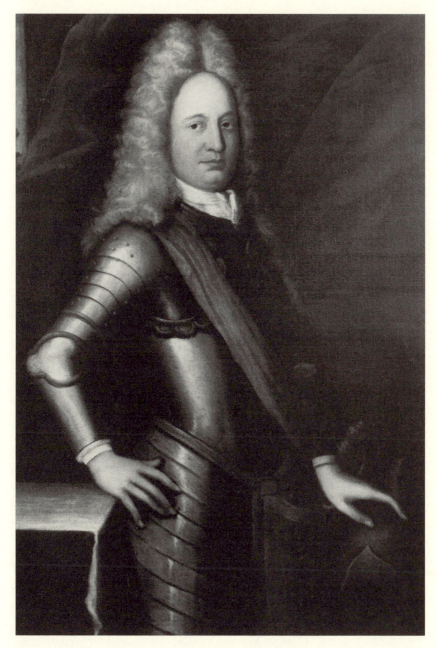

Figure 6. Portrait of Samuel Vetch in 1703, artist unknown. Reproduced courtesy of the Museum of the City of New York.

his brother-in-law Robert Livingston, he traveled to various French outposts in Newfoundland, Canada, and Acadia to trade. They offered the
French-speaking colonists liquor, tobacco, and other commodities in exchange for wine and furs, which they resold in New York and New England or shipped directly to Scotland.[3] These commercial ventures were
officially illegal, but the trade seemed profitable enough to justify the risk.
Though Vetch risked prosecution for his activities, his travels increased his
standing with some imperial officials because he became more knowledge-
able than most of his contemporaries about the French North American
empire. Over the next ten years Vetch cultivated his reputation as an expert on New France in order to gain the trust and support of ministers
and governors, and to justify his own increasingly prominent position in
the British imperial administration.[4]

After England and France went to war Vetch curtailed his contacts
with the French and the Acadians. He volunteered for military service, but
partly owing to the dubious reputation he had obtained as a smuggler he
was denied the commission he sought. Therefore he spent the early years
of the imperial conflict on the fringes of public service. In 1702 he joined
the governor of New York on a diplomatic mission to the Iroquois, and
in 1705, on behalf of Massachusetts governor Joseph Dudley, he traveled
(along with the governor's son) to Québec.[5] That second mission achieved
moderate success; Vetch and the younger Dudley secured the release of
some prisoners. Perhaps to reward Vetch for this accomplishment, in 1706
the Massachusetts governor gave him permission to revisit Acadia. The
resulting scandal provided the immediate inspiration for Vetch's project
of conquering New France.

Returning from Acadia late in the summer of 1706, Vetch arrived in
Plymouth, Massachusetts, with a quantity of furs he had purchased ille-
gally on his journey. The townspeople saw him arrive with the cargo and
reported him to the authorities in Boston. The criminal trial that followed
(Vetch was found guilty on reduced charges) received more attention than
most smuggling cases would because Vetch's activities potentially implicated the governor in treason.[6]

Dudley had enemies in Massachusetts, particularly among the local
clergy. But he also had powerful friends in England. Vetch sailed to London after his trial to talk to Dudley's associates and petition the ministry for exoneration. Cotton Mather, the New England clergyman most
hostile to the governor, opposed Vetch's errand with petitions and pam-
phlets he arranged to have published in London.[7] Sir Charles Hobby, a
prominent New England-born merchant, also appeared before the king's

ministers to demand the governor's ouster.[8] It was during this controversy that Vetch and Dudley began to petition the ministry for assistance in the project of attacking Acadia and French Canada. They had divergent motivations for advancing this proposal: Vetch wanted to serve Scotland by establishing Scottish colonies on the conquered lands; Dudley principally intended to silence his opponents who were urging him to adopt an aggressive stance toward the French colonies. Dudley would not take any decisive action without ministerial approval, and he thought that Vetch could serve as a useful emissary for him in London. The tactic was successful from the governor's point of view, since several of his critics, including Hobby, dropped their opposition to Dudley's remaining in office as soon as he announced his support for attacking New France.

Vetch secured the backing of the Whig-dominated ministry for an attack on Acadia in 1707. He stayed in England, however, and the operation in America was run by New Englanders. Dudley raised an army of one thousand volunteers, and, accompanied by a British warship, the troops sailed to Port Royal, where they disembarked on May 26 (see figure 7). A few of the men exchanged fire with small parties of French troops; others set fire to some houses and barns and one church. They burned crops and killed livestock, but did no further damage. On June 3 the officers decided to go home.[9]

When the fleet sailed back into Boston Harbor there was an outcry. Women and children heckled the general who had ordered the retreat.[10] Coming to the defense of his commanding officer, a chaplain on the expedition said that the attack had been called off because of the "mutinous disposition of the men."[11] Cotton Mather endorsed this theory. The men who enlisted had expected to burn Port Royal and leave. When they learned that Dudley intended to keep the fort, they threatened to revolt.[12] If Mather's account of the campaign is correct, the New England troops behaved in a manner consistent with their prior record of actions against Acadia. Hundreds of New Englanders had participated in operations against the French colony in 1696 and 1704 that were designed only to inflict damage on civilian property, punish the Acadians and Mi'kmaq, and gather plunder. Even the expedition of 1690, which had been launched ostensibly to conquer Acadia, had ended in a similar fashion.

Perhaps recognizing a pattern in the New Englanders' behavior, Vetch and Dudley concluded after the 1707 campaign that, if the British were to conquer Acadia and Canada, they would need a larger contingent of soldiers and settlers from elsewhere in the empire. And in any event, to

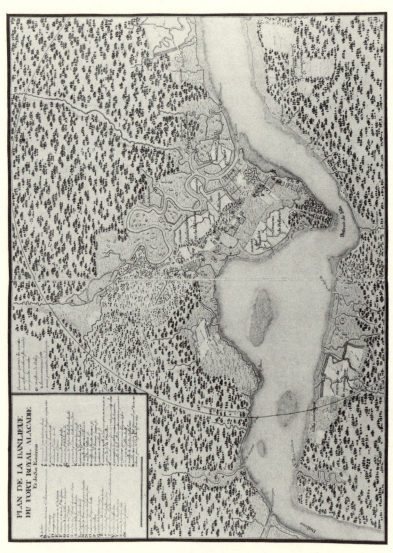

Figure 7. Jean Delabat's map of Port Royal in 1708. The fort, situated on high ground immediately down-stream from the center of the village, dominated the landscape visually, but its earthworks crumbled easily and most observers questioned the effectiveness of its design and construction. Photo courtesy of the Edward E. Ayer Collection, the Newberry Library, Chicago.

advance his full imperial ambitions Vetch preferred to employ Scots. For the next two years Vetch and Dudley lobbied the authorities in London for troops and naval support for an expedition against New France, as well as subsidies to encourage British settlement after the conquest had been effected.

In most of his letters and petitions, Vetch began with economic arguments for the conquest of New France.[13] He asserted that Britain's mainland North American colonies produced wealth for the mother country and the empire, not merely by providing products for the home market and for resale in Europe but, more importantly, by supplying the island colonies in the Caribbean with resources such as wood and food. Any action that served the interests of the mainland colonies, Vetch claimed, facilitated the production of sugar in the British West Indies. Sugar was one of the most profitable crops in the world, and increasing production would benefit the empire as a whole.

Vetch argued that the French presence in North America restricted the British colonists' ability to exploit their lands and supply the sugar islands, because the French hemmed in the colonists and forced them to divert their resources to defense. He furthermore maintained that the French, by exploiting the resources of Acadia and Canada, provided damaging competition to British concerns in various international markets, including those for fish, furs, and sugar. He predicted that the loss of Canada would weaken France's ability to supply its colonies in the West Indies, and in his most ambitious passages he suggested that the conquest of New France could serve as a step toward the seizure of extensive territories farther south in the western hemisphere.[14]

In making these arguments Vetch appealed to well-established mercantile interests. Most of his economic assertions were unoriginal, drawing on the writings of various political economists and colonial promoters who had been petitioning the Board of Trade for years.[15] The more creative, distinctive, and politically risky aspects of Vetch's and Dudley's petitions centered not on the economic benefits of the conquest of Acadia and Canada but on its cultural impact, specifically on the connections the two men drew between North America and Scotland. As early as the winter of 1706, before the final passage of the parliamentary acts in London and Edinburgh uniting the kingdoms of Scotland and England, Dudley suggested that the conquest of Canada would be an appropriate action to mark the anticipated Treaty of Union. The union of the kingdoms would grant Scotland access to the trade of the North American colonies and facilitate Scottish migration to America. Dudley argued that the

British government could enhance these benefits by conquering Acadia and Canada. Scots, he asserted, were accustomed to living in northern regions and therefore they would naturally migrate to the conquered territories and prosper once they settled there. "[U]pon the news of the union of the Kingdoms," he wrote, "I must humbly propose to your Lordships that a Scotch colony there of five thousand men would find their own Scotch climate and health, and a country far surpassing all Scotland."[16] In his own petitions Vetch advanced this argument more forcefully. He maintained that Scottish people, because of their intrinsic "constitution," were equipped for life in the northern reaches of North America. Canada and Acadia, he wrote, were "exactly calculated for the constitutions and genius of the most northern of the north Britons."[17]

Unlike much of New France, the places Vetch had visited most often as a merchant—the St. Lawrence River valley and the region surrounding Port Royal—had fertile soil and hillsides suitable for grazing. Especially in the summertime the landscape of those regions might have reminded Vetch of his homeland. Vetch knew that Canada and Acadia had colder winters than Scotland, but he had not seen the French colonies in their coldest months and he probably underestimated the severity of Canadian and Acadian weather.

It was an eighteenth-century commonplace that the nations of the world had adapted over generations to their specific climates; Vetch grounded his assertion that Scots were appropriate settlers for Canada and Acadia in contemporary ideas about climate and its influences on national temperament, health, and culture.[18] But the strength of his conviction stemmed also from his disappointment in Panama. He drew the contrast with Central America several times in his writings, emphasizing "how infinitely more agreeable this climate would be to our northern constitution than Darien."[19] His enthusiasm for importing a Scottish population into Acadia and Canada also drew from a well of filial piety and Scottish patriotism transformed by the Treaty of Union. Vetch believed that the time was right to create Scottish colonies, to symbolize Scotland's new role as a partner in the *British*, as opposed to English, empire. After 1707 Vetch used the new vocabulary self-consciously, crossing out the word "English" and replacing it with "British" whenever he inadvertently used the old terminology in labeling the Crown's overseas domains.[20]

In many respects, Vetch saw Acadia and Canada, together, as a new Scotland, but he did not intend that all the people of the provinces be Scottish by ancestry, nor did he expect that the Scots in Acadia and Canada would live exactly in the same way as in the home country. He wanted colonial soldiers detached from New York and New England militia companies to serve in the expedition against New France, and he hoped that a few of the colonials would stay in the conquered territories to help train the Scots in the skills they would need for settling on the frontier. He also, almost certainly, expected that English soldiers and Irish Protestants would participate in the conquest and settle alongside the immigrant Scots. And Vetch anticipated that Canada and Nova Scotia, after the British conquest, would have a substantial, permanent native population. One of his arguments for acquiring the French colonies was that they would provide the British queen with "hundreds of nations of new subjects, who will become intirely obedient to her laws."[21] There was a place for native peoples in Vetch's imagined future, but none for French-speaking colonists. Vetch saw the French in Canada and the Acadians as economic competitors and wanted to expel them from the continent.[22]

From the descriptions contained in Vetch's letters and petitions it is possible to construct a coherent picture of what he wanted Acadia and Canada to become. He expected large numbers of Scottish immigrants, along with a few settlers from the American colonies and perhaps a few English and Irish Protestants, to arrive in the conquered territories encouraged by parliamentary subsidy. The Scóts would immediately begin farming and, given their familiarity with the climate and the quality of the soil conditions, they would soon be self-sufficient, growing wheat "not only in vast quantityes, but the best of itts kind upon the whole Continent."[23] The immigrants would grow other crops as well and tend cattle, and if everything proceeded as Vetch hoped, within a few years of their arrival the new inhabitants of Nova Scotia would be mining copper, lead, and iron, opening marble quarries, cutting timber, building ships, whaling, and fishing commercially from bases on the Atlantic coast.[24] Along with the native people, the Scottish immigrants would be hunting and supplying the European and colonial fur trade.

Perhaps more than any other aspect of Vetch's petitions concerning the future of Acadia and Canada, his proposals for the fur trade reveal much about his plans for the immigrants and the native peoples of the northern provinces. When he petitioned the ministry for support for his project, Vetch asked for money to hire "country troops," including colonials and native warriors from the New England region, to help in the military expedition. He also wanted the ministry to provide incentives to encourage some of these men to stay in the north. He wanted them to train the regular British troops in the garrison (who would be deployed from Scotland) in the skills they would need to survive in the region, including "making and paddling birch canoes, as well as making and marching upon snow shoes (qualifications which are absolutely necessary to the troops who are to continue there)." He also expected the "country troops" (almost certainly native warriors and hunters) to teach the British "the forest exercises, as well as those of hunting the beavers and other creatures."[25] One possible interpretation of these statements is that Vetch expected his soldiers to be alone in the conquered territory after a short transitional period—that the native peoples who supplied the French with beaver pelts would not be available to trade with the British. But the more likely explanation is that Vetch imagined a future in which European immigrants would acquire some of the customs of the native hunters, who in turn would behave increasingly like the immigrants.

Especially before the conquest of Acadia in 1710, Vetch maintained that the conversion of "Indian" peoples to Protestantism was one of his primary goals. French Catholic missionaries, he said, promoted the interests of the French king, and therefore expelling them was a necessary precondition for making the native peoples British subjects. But Vetch and the other promoters of his project claimed that they intended to do more than separate the native peoples from the "french Missionaryes, who swarm among them" and convert them to Protestantism.[26] They also asserted that they would make the native peoples reject many of their "savage" ways. In his petitions Vetch declared that he wanted to introduce peace throughout the continent of North America and make all the native peoples subjects of Queen Anne. He predicted that one result of this would be to render obsolete many customs that Vetch considered violent or irrational, from ceremonial gift-giving to scalping. The political unification of the continent would transform many features of the native peoples' lives.

When he arrived in London in 1707, Vetch began to assemble as broad a political coalition as he could in support of his project of conquering Canada and Acadia. His strategy involved recruiting support from English Tories and Anglicans, two groups that would play a critical role in shaping British imperial policy over the next few years. Though few of them had reason to support Vetch's specific plan to establish Scottish colonies in America, or the project of evicting the French Canadians and Acadians in order to replace them with Scottish settlers, Vetch needed their support.[27] In 1708 Vetch established a political partnership in London with Francis Nicholson, who had worked closely with Dudley in the administration of the Dominion of New England. In that capacity he had involved himself briefly in New England's relations with Acadia, even visiting Port Royal at least once.[28] Nicholson was a lifelong Tory and an active member of the Church of England's Society for the Propagation of the Gospel. He was notoriously short-tempered, and his association with the Tory party had jeopardized his career at various times when Whigs dominated the English government. Nonetheless, he had served in various posts in the colonial administration on and off for nearly two decades, and his association with Vetch's project enhanced its credibility and expanded its political base of support.[29]

Early in the spring of 1709, with Nicholson's assistance, Vetch convinced the British government to authorize a summer campaign against Canada.[30] In a set of detailed instructions, the ministry granted Vetch a military commission, assigned eleven officers of the regular army to serve under him, and sent him to the American colonies to recruit troops for a late summer expedition against Québec and Montréal.[31] The ministers also instructed Nicholson to assist Vetch in his endeavors, and particularly to accompany him and advise him in his consultations with the colonial governments. Vetch, Nicholson, and the eleven officers sailed for America together after receiving these instructions, and for the first few months Vetch and Nicholson cooperated closely and effectively.[32] First in Massachusetts and later in the other New England colonies and New York, the two men gained the cooperation of several colonial governments and convinced hundreds of colonials to enlist for an invasion of New France. The New Englanders who volunteered were more interested in attacking the French than in taking their territories. They knew that this would be a Scottish expedition and they were willing to cede the conquered colonies to Scots if the French surrendered. As one soldier from Massachusetts put it, "The Scotch are to have Canada if they take it."[33]

Working with a sense of common purpose, Vetch, Nicholson, and their allies in the colonial governments raised a large army of volunteers, but nonetheless they had to cancel the 1709 expedition. Vetch and his supporters had succeeded in raising a sufficient number of troops for the attack, but they did not have the naval force they needed to sail up the St. Lawrence River against hostile fire. The warships the ministry had promised Vetch earlier in the year were detained in Europe, and therefore the conquest of Canada had to be postponed.[34]

In the following months, the Tories gained the upper hand in the ministry in London. In order to appeal to them and win approval for a renewal of the long-term project of conquering Canada, Vetch and Nicholson, along with their supporters within the colonial governments, agreed that Nicholson would return to London that winter to lobby for authorization to seize Acadia as a preliminary step toward the conquest of all the French North American colonies. Nicholson would be assisted in his lobbying efforts by four cooperative Iroquois emissaries, including a Mohawk leader who traveled alternatively by the names "Teoniahigarawe" and "Hendrick," who would remain prominent in Anglo-Iroquian relations for the next forty-five years.[35] The presence of Iroquois men in Nicholson's delegation strengthened the argument that the native peoples of North America would support the British conquest of New France.[36]

Prior to their departure for London, Vetch provided the Iroquois delegates with "fine clothes laced with true gold and silver lace, made as ours."[37] When the Iroquois emissaries arrived in London, Nicholson and the other men and women who greeted them gave them similar gifts and took them to elaborate events staged to dramatize the attractions of English culture. The Iroquois were escorted to puppet shows, Anglican Church services, cockfights, and banquets. The four men expressed gratitude for all that was given to them and seemed to exhibit interest in most of the cultural performances they were taken to. Public commentary in London after the arrival of the four Iroquois "kings" (as they were called) suggests that their visit generated a great deal of interest and debate about the project of civilizing and converting "Indian" peoples. Some tracts asserted that the Iroquois wanted to achieve a comprehensive "Revolution in Canada" and adopt most, if not all, of the cultural attributes of the British. Other tracts continued to emphasize the distinctiveness of the Iroquois as an American people, but almost everyone suggested that the local native peoples would be changed for the better following the conquest of Canada, in part because they would accept membership in the Anglican Church. The four emissaries' apparent enthusiasm for learning about the local brand of Protestantism and other aspects of English culture helped convince almost all of the commentators that the native peoples of North America would welcome a greater English presence in North America, and that they would willingly assist in the expansion of the British Empire (see figure 8).

The publicists who organized, promoted, and commented on the activities of the Iroquois in London tended to emphasize the attractions of English rather than Scottish culture. In part this was unavoidable, since the Iroquois were in London. But the domination of English cultural themes over Scottish had another cause beyond geographical necessity. By the time the emissaries began their tour, Vetch and Dudley had expanded their political coalition to include prominent English Anglicans and Tories. It was these men, newly recruited into the expansionist project, who planned the itinerary and presented the Iroquois men to the English public, most importantly, through the medium of the popular press.[38] Vetch was thousands of miles away in Massachusetts, and the

Figure 8. Illustration from a pamphlet entitled *The History of the Four Indian Kings from the Continent of America* (London, 1710), marking the visit of four Iroquois leaders to London, accompanied by Francis Nicholson. The publicity around the visit suggested that the native peoples of North America would welcome incorporation into the British domains. Reproduced courtesy of the Trustees of the National Library of Scotland, Edinburgh.

Anglicans and Tories, in general, did not share his vision of Scottish-dominated colonies in North America.

The delegation had arrived in London at a propitious time. Just days before she met the four Iroquois emissaries, Queen Anne had dismissed her Whig Lord Treasurer and appointed Tories to most of the positions of power within the British ministry. The Tories were anxious to demonstrate their effectiveness in prosecuting the war against France. There were also many figures within the party who viewed the conflict as an opportunity to use naval power to extend Britain's commercial presence to the far corners of the Atlantic world. It seemed that Vetch's plans could be modified to conform to this "blue water" strategy for imperial expansion, a common Tory vision of Britain's future role overseas.

Nicholson received new instructions in the spring of 1710. They differed from Vetch's 1709 instructions in three significant ways. First and most important, financial and strategic constraints limited the scope of the 1710 operation. Nicholson's instructions restricted the project to the conquest of Acadia, while in 1709 the ministry had directed Vetch to try to take all of northern mainland New France. Second, in 1710 Nicholson was made overall military commander for the expedition, with the provision that Vetch would be the conquered province's military governor if the attack succeeded. (Vetch's 1709 instructions had simply assigned Nicholson an advisory role.) Third, in a supplemental instruction the commanders received just before they entered combat, Nicholson was directed to "give all encouragement to such of the French inhabitants [Acadians] as shall come over us, or to make a timely submission, by offering them the continuance of all such lands, estates and privileges, as they do at present possess under the French Government."[39]

These supplemental instructions fit within a broad pattern of Tory policy for conquered lands. In many respects, the Tories' understanding of the empire was at odds with Vetch's. They did not endorse the dislocation of conquered peoples, partly because they did not want to incur the requisite cost to the treasury, but mostly because they considered almost all new subject peoples potential laborers and trading partners.

While party affiliations never simply determined the views of individuals, most Tories in the early eighteenth century had a strong belief in innate, indelible national characteristics. One of the major partisan issues of 1709 had been a Whig-sponsored General Naturalization Bill, which would have made it possible for Protestant immigrants from all over Europe to acquire the status of British subjects. Opposition to naturalization became a defining element of Tory ideology, as party members argued that foreign peoples would continue to be cultural "strangers" whether they moved to Britain or not.[40] This outlook inspired them to endorse restrictions on naturalization in Britain, but it also disinclined them toward any ambitious efforts to Anglicize conquered colonial populations. Instead they imagined that conquered colonies could continue to enrich the British Empire while remaining distinctly foreign. While many Tories professed to support missionary work overseas, they also generally encouraged the inhabitants of newly acquired territories to stay in their homes and retain their local traditions. For example, in 1711 the duke of Argyll, acting on behalf of the Tory ministry in Minorca, promised to protect the local customs and property rights of the Catalan-speaking Catholic residents of that newly conquered island, and in 1713 the Tory negotiators at Utrecht worked out similar arrangements for the French Catholic inhabitants of Newfoundland and the Spanish Catholic people of Gibraltar.[41]

In October 1710, when Nicholson negotiated the French surrender at Port Royal, he guaranteed that all the civilians living in the village (now called Annapolis Royal) would be allowed to remain. Vetch almost certainly opposed this concession, and for several months after he became military governor he petitioned the authorities in London for authorization to deport the Acadians living outside Annapolis Royal.[42] The ministry did not respond directly to Vetch's petitions, but in the summer of 1711 Vetch was issued binding instructions to extend the offer Nicholson had given to the inhabitants of Port Royal to all the Acadians, provided they swore allegiance to the British crown.[43] Without a formal reply, the Tory-dominated government in London had rejected Vetch's proposals for the Acadians' deportation.

Reluctantly, Vetch tried to comply with the ministry's orders, but his obedience gained him no political advantage. Though he tried to curry favor with Tory ministers, he never overcame the sense that he and the ministry were working at cross-purposes. In 1711 the British government funded a large-scale invasion of French Canada, an action Vetch had long advocated. But it is unlikely that the British government would have pursued policies in Canada that would have pleased Vetch if the operation had succeeded. Vetch did not have a prominent position in the chain of command in 1711, and during the campaign the ministry issued orders protecting the right of French colonists to remain. As it happened, a storm off the coast of the Gaspé Peninsula destroyed a large part of the invasion force, and the expedition had to be canceled. Its most important political legacy was to dampen enthusiasm, in the British colonies and in Britain itself, for further North American campaigns of conquest.[44]

Thereafter Vetch's alienation from the Tories, exacerbated by the physical distance between London and Annapolis Royal and the distractions of wartime, severely impeded communication with the ministry. By 1712, Nicholson was making Vetch's situation worse by lobbying for his ouster. Vetch defended himself by maligning Nicholson, and the two men sent repetitive petitions to the Board of Trade for years. Nicholson accused Vetch of incompetence and brutality; Vetch responded by claiming that Nicholson planned to deliver Acadia back to France. The dispute outlasted Vetch's term in office: in his angriest petition, written in 1714, he claimed that Nicholson was a secret Jacobite and that in a moment of indiscretion he had once drunk a toast to the exiled, French-supported, Catholic branch of the Stuart royal family.[45] Distracted by other matters, the ministers declined to resolve the dispute between Vetch and Nicholson as long as the war with France lasted. But they issued Vetch no detailed orders and sent him neither funds nor supplies.

As Vetch was losing contact with his Tory political partners in Britain, he was simultaneously becoming estranged from Dudley and the New Englanders. Vetch had never had a strong base of political support in New England, and the popularity he gained in 1707 when he first proposed an expedition to Canada had thereafter steadily declined, especially among the clergy. Though he used more florid language than others, Cotton Mather was in many respects typical in his declining support of Vetch. In 1707 Mather had given conditional support to the concept of creating a "Scotch Colony" on conquered lands in the French colonies.[46] A year later, after the failure of the 1707 expedition, Mather still supported Vetch's project, and preached from Hebrews 1:13, "Sit on my right hand, until I make thine enemies thy footstool," in order to promote, as he described it in his diary, "the great Expedition against the Idolaters of Canada."[47] But he did not support Vetch in 1710. After the troops disembarked from Boston he wrote, "the thing will go on, and you will foresee that it is like to be a Summer of extreme Distress unto us."[48] The New England clergy in general followed a path of disillusionment similar to Mather's. In 1709 a few local pastors volunteered to accompany Vetch's troops to Canada, but they blamed Vetch personally for the cancellation of that campaign and would not help him in 1710.[49] No New England-trained clergy accompanied the troops to Port Royal.

Failing to acquire clerical support for his expedition, Vetch had relied on economic incentives to get the New Englanders to enlist.[50] Some New England men were willing to serve the political and commercial interests of New England by attacking the French in Acadia, and those who enlisted were also happy to serve themselves by looting the Acadians. But Vetch's relationship with the New Englanders remained uneasy, and conflicts arose almost from the moment of the French surrender. When the colonials perceived that their own interests had been neglected, few if any were willing to make sacrifices to advance the imperial ambitions of England, Scotland, or "Britain."

Most New Englanders perceived a cultural divide separating themselves from the inhabitants of their ancestral home island. The increasing volume of trade and transatlantic migration had blurred the relevant distinctions, and as the eighteenth century progressed more and more colonists would identify themselves primarily as subjects of a large cosmopolitan empire.[51] Some New Englanders were already thinking of themselves that way at the beginning of the century, and indeed a few Boston merchants continued to support Vetch's project in Nova Scotia.[52] But they had a financial interest in taking the position they did, and Vetch's identity as a Scot placed him at a disadvantage in his dealings with New Englanders outside of the mercantile community. He had particular difficulty gaining the cooperation of the New Englanders nominally under his command.

After the fall of Port Royal the troops were surprised to learn that the capitulation agreement contained a guarantee that the French-speaking inhabitants of Port Royal could remain in their homes unmolested by the troops. This guarantee had been all but mandated by Nicholson's supplemental instructions, but those instructions had not been made public, and they seemed to contradict the promises the soldiers had received when they volunteered. Almost all the men expected plunder.

A larger controversy arose when Vetch ordered the New Englanders to perform garrison duty. Like their predecessors in New England's earlier campaigns against Acadia, most of the colonials had enlisted for short terms, and they planned to return to their homes and families immediately after the engagement ended. But after the French surrendered Vetch announced that more than two hundred New Englanders, along with an equal number of British marines, would stay in Nova Scotia until reinforcements arrived. The colonials protested and threatened to desert as a group if they were not placed under a New Englander's command.[53] In response, Vetch appointed one of his former political opponents, Sir Charles Hobby, to a high post in the garrison. Hobby's appointment prevented an immediate mass desertion, but it hardly placated the New Englanders. For the remaining twelve months there were constant disputes over the chain of command, as colonials quarreled with regular British soldiers and colonial and British officers struggled to assert the prerogatives of their ranks.[54] These problems intensified in the late summer of 1711, when the garrison was augmented with a new body of British and Irish troops.

Though relations between the different contingents of soldiers and officers remained difficult, by the time the British and Irish reinforcements arrived in 1711 the cultural and institutional divisions within the garrison had been overshadowed by other problems. Approximately 450 soldiers had been assigned to Annapolis Royal in 1710.[55] In the following spring disease struck, and by the summer of 1711 dozens of men lay dying. The numbers contained in Vetch's reports and other contemporary records do not exactly add up, but in June Vetch reported that 116 soldiers had died in the previous two months.[56] According to another estimate, 340 had died by July. Certainly a large part of the garrison had succumbed before the end of the year.[57] In the summer of 1711 Vetch went to New England to ask for new troops.[58] Given the likely fate of men assigned to the garrison, none of the colonial governments seriously considered his request. Vetch returned to Annapolis Royal in October 1711 only to discover that the New Englanders in his garrison had deserted; more than 150 soldiers had boarded a supply ship on its return trip to Boston.[59] Vetch responded angrily, and among other things dismissed Hobby from his position in the chain of command, which further alienated both him and his government from New England.[60]

When he originally conceived of the project of conquering Acadia, Vetch hoped that he would not have to rely on New England for manpower or supplies. He planned to recruit Scottish settlers, and he expected that they would become self-supporting within a few years. Immediately after taking command at Annapolis Royal, Vetch, along with the other officers involved in the conquest, petitioned the Board of Trade and other authorities in London for subsidies to encourage immigrants to come to Nova Scotia.[61] Vetch had originally wanted a migrant stream composed primarily of Scots, but in the interest of quickly settling the conquered province, he declared that he would welcome English and Irish colonists as well, if they were Protestant.[62] The petitions failed to elicit a positive response, in part because the British government was distracted by other wartime efforts (including the abortive expedition to Canada in 1711), but also because the comprehensive resettlement of Nova Scotia with Scottish, English, and Irish Protestants did not accord with the new Tory ministry's long-term plans. Vetch was also unsuccessful in his efforts to recruit unsubsidized, voluntary colonists. Scottish emigration to North America accelerated in the decades after 1710, but, contrary to Vetch's expectations, most Scots gravitated to warmer climes.[63] Nova Scotia's climate was not a positive draw, and for the next thirty years the province would not attract any significant body of civilian immigrants from anywhere in the British Empire.

The cumulative effect of Vetch's misfortunes was to leave him presiding over a tiny garrison of fractious troops, surrounded and outnumbered by a population composed almost entirely of French-speaking Catholic Acadians and Mi'kmaq. He received almost no support, financial or otherwise, from London, and depended for survival on a group of New England merchants who charged him interest for their help. Vetch began to hate all his former political allies. He accused Nicholson of Jacobitism, and according to one report he derided all New Englanders as liars and haters of the monarchy who operated under the influence of witchcraft beliefs.[64] The situation seemed almost intolerable, but instead of abandoning Nova Scotia, Vetch modified his plans.

By the spring of 1712 Vetch had moved closer to the arguments that had earlier been advanced by Tories, and concluded that his garrison would have to depend on the Acadians' labor and trade.[65] He had learned this lesson from hard experience, but in his petitions and other formal writings he pretended that he had reached his conclusion through a process of abstract reasoning. Using the language of political economy, he asserted that "the strength of all countries" consisted in being "populous."[66] As laborers, farmers, merchants, taxpayers and potential soldiers, the Acadians could strengthen the government in any region they inhabited. Since most of them would probably go to New France if they were deported, such a move would only benefit the French Empire. This argument for retaining the Acadian population would gain currency over the next generation, and by the 1750s it was an unspoken premise in most policy debates concerning the Acadians.

The retention of the Acadian population remained controversial among policymakers, however, in part because of their continuing allegiance to the Catholic Church. Most Britons in the early eighteenth century viewed Rome as a hostile foreign power, and they claimed that Catholic priests exercised a dangerous degree of control over their parishioners. Anti-Catholicism was a stance that united Whigs and Tories wherever they were—in England, Wales, Scotland, or the colonies.[67]

Adopting a position typical of the Tories, Nicholson favored drawing the Acadians away from their Catholic pastors through a concerted campaign of Protestant missionary work. In keeping with his own party position, Vetch was more forceful. He thought that if the Acadians were to remain in Nova Scotia it would be necessary to capture and expel the Catholic clergy.[68] In January 1711 he sent fifty armed men to seize the resident pastor at Annapolis Royal, but he was unable to apprehend the other priests in the province.[69]

Vetch's campaign against the Catholic clergy brought him into direct conflict with many of the Mi'kmaq as well as some Acadians. Mi'kmaq and other Algonkian warriors, acting in part on the advice of their missionaries and French military officials, took up arms against the British in the winter of 1710. In their most successful single engagement, in the spring of 1711, they killed thirty British soldiers.[70] Algonkian war parties also intimidated the Acadians, driving many villagers away from Annapolis Royal and enforcing a boycott on trade with the British that nearly starved the garrison of food and firewood. Vetch was near despair in the spring of 1711, but after a few difficult weeks the Acadian boycott failed as a consequence of divisions within the French-speaking community of Annapolis Royal.[71]

The departure of the French military had disrupted the local social order. Some ambitious Acadian men saw the arrival of the British garrison as a business opportunity and a chance to rise further socially than they could have under the French regime.[72] In the summer of 1711 Prudent Robichaud and others signaled their willingness to cooperate with the British, and they broke the boycott by offering farm products, firewood, and other provisions to the garrison in trade.[73]

Vetch had traded with Acadians in the past, and indeed many colonists in New England continued to suspect his loyalties because of his earlier illicit activities as a smuggler in the French colony.[74] But his role as a military governor in a violent region transformed his relationship with the Acadians into one of debilitating distrust. On one occasion in 1711, Vetch ordered his subordinate officers to force eighteen Acadian men into service digging coal.[75] If any of the Acadians objected to the order, the soldiers were to seize hostages to guarantee their cooperation. Such heavy-handed tactics occasionally worked, but they tended to make the Acadians resent Vetch personally. One British observer claimed that the governor treated the Acadians "more like slaves than anything else."[76] Some Acadians used similar language and complained to the French in Canada that he treated them "comme des négres."[77] Preferring to deal with someone other than Vetch, Acadians who wanted to trade with the garrison in the first year following the conquest sought out Hobby.[78]

The Acadians would have been in a worse position if Vetch had been able to direct British policy without dissension. Divisions within the garrison ameliorated the Acadians' condition by providing them political allies in their opposition to Vetch and by making it difficult for British officials to take concerted action. The British missionary project, for example, foundered in part because of disagreements within the garrison.

Francis Nicholson was a loyal member of the Church of England. In his capacity as commander of the troops during the siege, he appointed a permanent military chaplain for Fort Anne before handing over authority to Vetch. The pastor he chose, John Harrison, was Anglican, and Vetch, a devoted Scottish Presbyterian, never attended the chaplain's services. Vetch and Harrison argued frequently, and as their disagreements escalated Vetch began to place obstacles in the way of the chaplain's performance of his duties. At the climax of their conflict, in 1713, Vetch confiscated Harrison's chapel and turned it into a barracks.[79] Humiliated and angry, the chaplain left the province, and as a result the Acadians were free to remain Catholic without interference from Protestant missionaries.[80]

Vetch was dismissed as governor of Nova Scotia immediately after the ratification of the Treaty of Utrecht in 1713. The terms of that treaty represented in many ways the final rejection of Vetch's original vision of imperial expansion. The Acadians were given a year to decide whether they wanted to remain in their homes, and those who chose to stay as subjects of the British crown were assured the right to continue to practice the Catholic faith. The decision to guarantee religious toleration for Catholics in Nova Scotia came in the final days of the negotiations at Utrecht as a gesture of goodwill toward the French, but the concession, such as it was, was also consistent with Tory policy, and Tories dominated the British negotiating team when the terms of the treaty were concluded.

It fell to Nicholson, Vetch's onetime political partner and present enemy, to make the Tory vision of empire a reality in Nova Scotia. But he was ill-equipped for such an assignment. In 1710 Nicholson had left Annapolis Royal within days of the French surrender, and outside the context of that brief encounter, he had had no direct contact with the colony since the 1680s.

By the terms of the treaty the Acadians had the option of ignoring Nicholson's orders, because (at least for an interim period) they could retain their allegiance to France, gather their belongings, and leave. The new French colonial government on Ile Royale was encouraging the Acadians to emigrate, and the local villagers tried to exploit the leverage their position gave them in their dealings with Nicholson. They threatened to abandon the province en masse if they were unhappy with the new governor's orders. Nicholson was strong-willed and quick-tempered, and he was not prepared for negotiations. Surprised by the independent spirit of the Acadians, he declared that they were "all rebels" and ordered his soldiers not to leave the fort at Annapolis Royal because, he claimed, the villagers "would certainly cut their throats."[81] Nicholson's anger and fear left him totally ineffective. He departed from Nova Scotia within weeks, and for the next three years most of the political initiative in the region came from the Mi'kmaq, the Acadians, and the imperial authorities of France.

The French focused their attention on Ile Royale, a large expanse of land separated from the peninsula of Nova Scotia by a narrow channel. Most seventeenth-century mapmakers had assumed that the island was part of Acadia, but when the negotiators at Utrecht transferred Acadia to Britain they drew a new border around the peninsula by assigning Ile Royale and all the other islands in the region to France. In 1714 the French founded Louisbourg, and over subsequent years the authorities at Versailles allocated large sums of money to fortify it and to promote immigration and economic development there (see figure 9).

From the beginning of their colonization project in North America in the seventeenth century, the French had almost always had difficulty recruiting colonists.[82] Mindful of the value of settlers and fearful of losing colonial subjects to the British Empire, French officials on Ile Royale vigorously recruited immigrants from the colonies France had recently ceded to Britain, especially Newfoundland and Acadia. The first French governor on Ile Royale, Philippe de Pastour de Costabelle, had previously been governor on Newfoundland, and he succeeded in bringing most of that island's French colonial population with him to his new colony. Within weeks of arriving on Ile Royale in 1713, Costabelle sent missionaries to the Acadian villages of Minas and Beaubassin in an effort to recruit settlers, and a few families followed the advice of the clergymen and relocated.[83] But he encountered resistance from the Acadians when he asked them to move, and many of those who went to Ile Royale eventually returned.[84]

By 1720 Louisbourg had a population of 950, including 317 soldiers, and as a colonial capital it was a very different place from what Port Royal had been under its French regime.[85] Louisbourg's fortifications dwarfed anything the Acadians had seen before, and the French military dominated life on Ile Royale in a way it had never done in seventeenth-century Acadia. Furthermore, the economy of the island differed greatly from that of the older colony. Louisbourg was a center for France's North Atlantic fishery and a major transshipment point for goods crossing the Atlantic on their way to Canada, the French West Indies, New England, and France. The town was marked by large disparities in wealth and social status, and among the wealthy and powerful fashions were constantly changing, as merchants, officers, and other government officials imported new styles from France.[86] Most important from the Acadians' perspective, there was very little work for farmers on the island because it had rocky soil.

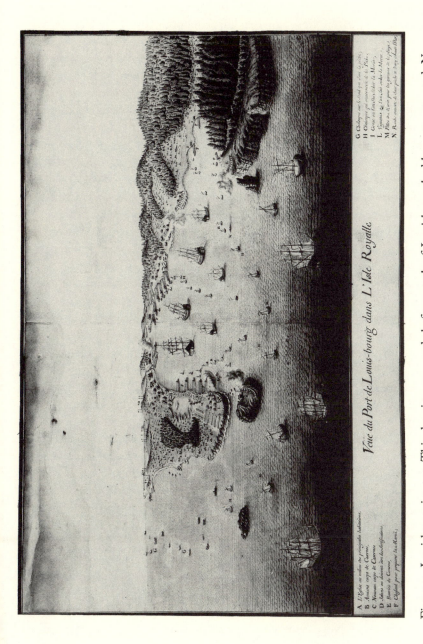

Figure 9. Louisbourg in 1717. This drawing was made before much of Louisbourg had been constructed. Nonetheless, by crowding the harbor with ships the draftsman has conveyed the ambitions of Louisbourg's founders, to
create a large, important Atlantic-oriented port. Photo courtesy of the Edward E. Ayer Collection, the Newberry
Library, Chicago.

Many of the issues associated with Acadian migration in this period can be illustrated by events in the life of the family of Jacques Maurice Vigneau. In 1715, after Nicholson had left Annapolis Royal, the men temporarily in charge of the British garrison adopted a more moderate stance toward the Acadians. Instead of antagonizing them and vilifying them as rebels, the commanding officers sought primarily to get the local colonists to declare themselves and state whether they would become British or French subjects. Most of the Acadians, however, took an ambiguous stance. They frustrated the British, who wanted them to swear an oath of allegiance, but they also frustrated the French because they refused to move permanently to Ile Royale.[87] Maurice Vigneau, the father of Jacques, initially behaved like his neighbors. He would not vow loyalty to the British monarchs, but neither would he move and give up his home. Fishermen like the elder Vigneau were in a distinctive position, however, because the British could patrol the sea effectively, at least within the confines of the Bay of Fundy. In 1717 the officers of the garrison at Annapolis Royal threatened to prevent the village's fishermen from leaving port if they continued to resist taking an oath of allegiance. Faced with the loss of their livelihoods, Vigneau and a group of others swore unconditional loyalty to Britain's King George.[88] Then, having obtained official permission to raise anchor, Vigneau boarded his family and sailed off, pretending to go on a fishing trip. The family disembarked on Ile Royale. Choosing to avoid Louisbourg, they made their new home on the shores of the Gulf of St. Lawrence close to the peninsula of Nova Scotia.[89]

Hundreds of Acadians left peninsular Nova Scotia in the decade after the British seizure of Port Royal, but most of them avoided the principal French colonial settlements. A significant number went to Ile-Saint-Jean (present-day Prince Edward Island), where the French military presence was weak.[90] Others went to present-day New Brunswick, a border region where they could live beyond the supervision of any imperial authority, British or French. The Acadian population was growing quickly, and demographic pressure as well as politics contributed to the impulse to move.

In similar ways, the British conquest of Port Royal altered the geographical orientation of the Mi'kmaq. After the Treaty of Utrecht was signed, the French imperial authorities in Paris directed the governors of Canada and Ile Royale to engage in a coordinated effort to encourage the Mi'kmaq to leave Nova Scotia and go to Ile Royale. Catholic missionaries were enlisted to inform the native people that they should move.[91] When directed to undertake this task, however, the churchmen dismissed the project as totally impractical. Félix Pain, who had provided pastoral care to the Mi'kmaq since 1694, reported that the Mi'kmaq had told him that "the woods [in Nova Scotia] were theirs, and no one would ever be able to move them."[92] Similarly, Pierre La Chasse, another cleric who had worked for many years among the Mi'kmaq, complained that the French ministry "must be ignorant of the extreme attachment these Indians bear to their country to make such a proposition." Instead, La Chasse suggested, the French should encourage the Mi'kmaq to seek a set of geographical demarcations within the province of Nova Scotia to "establish the boundaries between the two nations [the British and the Mi'kmaq]."[93] If the Mi'kmaq could negotiate such an arrangement, French missionaries and traders could continue to work among them without directly confronting the British. Responding to the missionary's recommendations, the secular authorities at Ile Royale instructed Antoine Gaulin to establish a mission at Antigonish, at the easternmost edge of peninsular Nova Scotia, as far from Annapolis Royal as possible. The establishment of the mission in 1715 served to encourage, and perhaps accelerate, a pattern of eastward migrations across the peninsula that may have already been underway.[94] The evidence is fragmentary, but it appears that Jean-Baptiste Cope, for example, moved away from the vicinity of Annapolis Royal after the British conquest.[95] Later in life he affiliated himself with the Shubenacadie band, in the center of the peninsula of Nova Scotia.

Almost all the Britons who had supported the conquest of Acadia, whether they were English or Scottish, Tory or Whig, had said the same things when they mentioned native peoples. The New Englanders were more divided in their objectives, but the British in general avowed two goals: engaging the native people in commerce and converting them to Protestantism. Vetch never wavered from endorsing these objectives, which were also consistently espoused by Nicholson and his successors. Nonetheless, after acquiring experience in Nova Scotia, almost every British administrator lost hope that the goals could be achieved.

Vetch's initial plan had been to conquer all of New France and oust the French from North America. He had originally hoped that the force of circumstances would drive the native peoples to trade with British merchants because they would have no other choice if they wanted to acquire European goods. The situation after the conquest of Nova Scotia differed from Vetch's imagined future because the French remained in the area; indeed, after 1714 they used Louisbourg as a base for their fur trade in the maritime region and relied primarily on Mi'kmaq trading partners.[96] In order to maintain ties with the Mi'kmaq and garner their trade, the

French exchanged gifts with Mi'kmaq leaders, conducted ceremonies that incorporated local native customs, and sent Catholic missionaries to villages and missions located in Mi'kmaq territories.

Vetch and his immediate successors failed, or refused, to adopt any of the strategies that worked for the French, and though some British officials were more effective in dealing with the Mi'kmaq than others, none of Vetch's successors wholeheartedly and effectively adopted the practices that would have been necessary to recapture the fur trade from Louisbourg, change the Mi'kmaq's political allegiances, or convert them to Protestantism. There were several impediments to such a policy. First, especially after engaging the Mi'kmaq in combat, most of the officers and soldiers in Annapolis Royal adopted a negative assessment of Mi'kmaq practices and refused to alter their own behavior for the sake of complying with native customs. Even before 1710 Vetch had referred to gift exchange as the "bribing of the natives for their friendships, or indeed, more properly speaking being tributaries to those inhumane savages for their favour and assistance."[97] After he became governor he never offered gifts to the Mi'kmaq, and never intended to. His opposition to gift-giving undermined his ability to establish a profitable relationship with the native peoples of Nova Scotia and impeded any effort he might have made to convert them.

As far as missionary work was concerned, within days of the French surrender Vetch joined in a petition to the British government and the Society for the Propagation of the Gospel (SPG) for missionaries to work among the Mi'kmaq.[98] But the SPG was slow to respond and lost interest in Vetch's project following the failure of the 1711 Canada expedition. Vetch's inability to acquire missionaries affected many aspects of his policy toward the Mi'kmaq beyond the immediate problem of religious conversion. Protestant missionaries, if they had arrived, might have become conversant in the Mi'kmaq language, and even if they had not, they would have learned more than Vetch did about how to communicate with the native people. They could have been used, for example, as interpreters and intermediaries between the Mi'kmaq and the British government. Without the help of Protestant missionaries Vetch and his successors had to communicate with the Mi'kmaq either in French or with the aid of French-speaking interpreters. Over time the officers of the British garrison came to depend on French Catholic missionaries and cooperative Acadians such as Prudent Robichaud to transmit messages to the native people, and this practice reinforced their suspicion that the French, the Acadians, and the Mi'kmaq were allied, and that in times of crisis they would join forces and fight for Catholic France.

The greatest problem Vetch faced in trying to work with the Mi'k-maq was that very few of them wanted to cooperate with him. The legacy of New England's wars with the Mi'kmaq almost certainly affected the Mi'kmaq view of all English-speakers and made them resistant to over-tures that came from Annapolis Royal. By the 1750s, after the British had maintained their outpost in Nova Scotia for decades, the Mi'kmaq had started to differentiate between groups of English-speakers, using "an-glois" as a general term and calling New Englanders "bostonais."[99] But there is no evidence that they drew such distinctions in the early years following the British conquest. All English-speakers answered for the former behavior of the New Englanders. Furthermore, the Mi'kmaq were deeply devoted to their own customs and to the network of alliances and trading relations they had established in the region, a network that in-cluded the French.[100]

In the fourteen years following the New England raid on Acadia in 1704, the politics of the region fundamentally changed. New players ar-rived on the scene—Scottish and English policymakers who broke away from the pattern of relations that had been established over the past cen-tury. Previously, intercolonial relations had been based on the maintenance of a wary distance between the peoples of the French and English Em-pires. The British officials who became involved in the affairs of the Bay of Fundy region after 1704, by contrast, espoused an interest in incorporating inhabitants of Acadia into the life of the "British" empire. A combination of factors undermined their plans. They failed to cooperate after the con-quest of Acadia, and their disagreements, combined with local resistance and the ongoing presence of the French in the region, made it impossible for them to take effective action. Uncertainty about the governorship also weakened British authority. After 1715 the Whigs returned to power in the British ministry, and they formally reappointed Samuel Vetch as gov-ernor of Nova Scotia, but he was already disillusioned and failed to return to the colony whose conquest he had arranged. By 1718 Nova Scotia had not had a resident governor for four years, no supplies had arrived from Britain in that time, and the dwindling British garrison survived only at the deference of the local Acadians.

So long as they used their threats judiciously, the officers of the garri-son could gain the respect of the region's inhabitants by reminding them that in a crisis they could draw on the military resources of New England and Britain. But most of the real power in the colony lay within the local communities, among the ostensibly conquered peoples, with three centers of authority—the Acadian villages, the Mi'kmaq bands, and the parishes and missions of the Catholic Church.

Chapter Three

Anglo-Mi'kmaq Relations, the French, and the Acadians, 1718–1743

RICHARD Philipps, a fifty-seven-year old military officer, was appointed governor of Nova Scotia in 1718 and served through the War of the Austrian Succession.[1] Born into an English-speaking aristocratic family in Wales, Philipps joined the military and distinguished himself early in his career as one of the first, most active supporters of William of Orange within the regular English army. Like Samuel Vetch, he had benefited from his early support of the Glorious Revolution, and from that time forward his prospects rose and fell with the fortunes of the Whig party. But he was unlike his immediate predecessor in at least two important respects. In contrast to Vetch, who had spent a good part of his life promoting the cause of Scottish imperialism, Philipps had paid very little attention to imperial affairs before his appointment as governor, and though he came from Wales, his participation in the British imperial administration was never complicated by any specific loyalty to his native principality.

Philipps became governor as the result of a complex political and monetary transaction. In 1712 he spent 7,000 guineas to purchase the command of a regiment; six years later he swapped that commission for one in the newly formed Fortieth Regiment, assigned to Newfoundland and Nova Scotia.[2] The colonial governorship came with the command. Though Philipps had indirectly purchased his commission, his status as a lifelong Whig and his close association with Whig political leaders facilitated his appointment and kept him securely in office for the next twenty-nine years.[3] Philipps arrived in the colony in 1720. He visited Nova Scotia only twice during his tenure in office and never stayed longer than two years, but nonetheless he was a central figure in many of the colonial administration's policy debates, especially in the 1720s.

Because of his lengthy tenure in office, the political support he received from London, and the long terms served by the men working under him in the colonial administration, Philipps had an opportunity denied previous British administrators, to bring order and stability to Nova Scotia. To some extent he and his associates succeeded; by 1743 the province had enjoyed eighteen years of relative peace. A long process of trial and error, involving negotiation, compromise, and a recognition of the limits of British power, had created an environment in which the peoples of the province could coexist under nominal British rule. But unsettling difficulties remained, stemming in part from the competing ambitions of different groups of English-speakers and from the inability of Philipps and the officials working with him in the region to justify or explain the ad hoc policies they had adopted.

From the time of the conquest onward, none of the officials involved in formulating British policy in Nova Scotia considered treating the Acadians and the Mi'kmaq alike. Some policymakers proposed expelling the Acadians and absorbing the Mi'kmaq into British colonial society. Others advocated driving the Mi'kmaq away and reserving a place for Acadians in colonial life. Less draconian approaches, such as the development of distinctive laws for the Mi'kmaq and Acadian communities within Nova Scotia, were also debated almost constantly. A few officials shifted positions, but their proposals remained consistent in at least one regard: they always assumed that the Mi'kmaq and the Acadians were fundamentally different, and that the approach they adopted toward one of the groups could not be applied to the other.

With regard to the Mi'kmaq, Philipps arrived in Nova Scotia with contradictory instructions that reflected a dichotomy in the way the British, and Europeans generally, thought about America's native peoples. Since the early sixteenth century, many Europeans had argued that American "Indians" were peoples at an early stage of historical development, innocent of the corruptions of "civilization," but ready for advancement with the help of European missionaries, educators, governors, and protectors.[4] But a rival image of "Indians" also gained currency, especially after the colonization of eastern North America began, one that depicted them as dangerous savages, unrestrained by the dictates of culture or Christianity. By the mid-eighteenth century this second way of thinking about native peoples assumed a racial component, as British colonial commentators, in particular, began to argue that the distinctive characteristics of the "Indians" were innate.[5]

In 1719 the Board of Trade directed Philipps to adopt measures designed to lead, in the long run, to the full incorporation of the Mi'kmaq into British colonial society. But the new governor was also encouraged to deal with the Mi'kmaq according to the protocols of Algonkian diplomacy, negotiating and trading with Mi'kmaq bands as groups, thereby respecting Mi'kmaq autonomy. In his initial efforts Philipps failed to adopt either approach successfully, in large part because of the influence of a group of New England fishermen who convinced him to support them in their effort to establish permanent colonial settlements along Nova Scotia's Atlantic coast. The Mi'kmaq resisted the governor's efforts to build towns on their territory, and in 1722 they went to war. The fighting ended in 1725, and the two treaties that the Mi'kmaq and the British concluded at the end of the conflict acknowledged that the Mi'kmaq could govern their own affairs.

The written treaties contained no territorial provisions, however, and their failure to establish physical boundaries between Mi'kmaq and colonial territories would lead to conflict in the 1740s and the 1750s. Nonetheless, in the short run after the agreements were ratified, the British restricted their movements and avoided entering lands the Mi'kmaq claimed for themselves, at least in the Atlantic region. More difficulties arose on the shores of the Bay of Fundy because the treaties failed to address another issue: they made no reference to Mi'kmaq-Acadian relations. By granting Mi'kmaq bands internal self-governance, the British agreed that the activities of the Mi'kmaq would be judged according to different legal standards from those that applied within Acadian communities. But the treaties provided no guidance concerning the criteria for determining whether an individual was Mi'kmaq, or the rules that would apply in situations where Mi'kmaq and Acadians acted in concert. Separating the Mi'kmaq from their neighbors for administrative purposes proved almost impossible. As a result, two patterns of relations developed in Nova Scotia. On the Atlantic coast the Mi'kmaq and the British successfully kept their distance from one another, but conflict was much more frequent in the region of the Bay of Fundy.

Both the legal and actual status of the Mi'kmaq remained uncertain following the ratification of the Treaty of Utrecht, as British colonial authorities struggled to assert their sovereignty over the Mi'kmaq and their lands. An analysis of the war of 1722–25, the treaties that ended it, and a courtroom trial conducted in Boston immediately after the peace agreements were signed will shed some light on the situation. The case, which involved both Mi'kmaq and Acadian defendants, highlights the difficulties the British faced in trying to maintain separate legal regimes for the

Mi'kmaq and the Acadians. Racial and national categories lay at the foundation of British colonial thought in Nova Scotia. But such categories were almost unusable in practice, particularly in the Bay of Fundy region where Acadians constituted a majority of the population.

The sections of the Treaty of Utrecht assigning Britain sovereignty over Nova Scotia in 1713 contained complex provisions defining the future status of the peoples of the region. Acadians were formally granted the power as individuals to determine their own legal status. Any among them "willing to remain" in Nova Scotia could become "subject to the Kingdom of Great Britain," so long as they made their intentions known within a specified period of time. By contrast, the treaty denied the "natives of America" the power of individual choice. Instead, the diplomats at Utrecht agreed to convene a conference of "Commissarys" who would determine whether the Mi'kmaq and the other nearby Algonkian peoples "ought to be accounted the Subjects and Friends of Britain or of France."[6] They based this provision on the assumption that the Mi'kmaq and other "natives" were wanderers. To facilitate the movements of the native peoples, the diplomats decided that regardless of the natives' status as subjects and "friends" of one empire or the other, they would be allowed to cross the boundary between the British and French Empires and everywhere enjoy the privilege of trade.

The terms of the treaty made it inevitable that the Mi'kmaq would occupy an indeterminate legal status in the short run. Until the commissaries met, even if Mi'kmaq individuals resided in territory assigned to the British, no one would know to which empire they belonged. As it turned out, the ambiguity lasted decades because the commissaries never met. But even if a meeting had been held and the delegates had assigned each native group to one empire or the other, it is clear that individuals identified as "natives" would have still held a status different from that of other French and British subjects. Regardless of their imperial affiliation they would have had access to resources and trade on both sides of the imperial border.

Some of the premises underlying the treaty makers' classification of peoples—for example their assumption that all "natives" traveled frequently—worked to the disadvantage of the Mi'kmaq when they negotiated a place for themselves within the territory of the British Empire, because when the British referred to the "inhabitants" of Nova Scotia, they often implicitly left the Mi'kmaq out of the category. But the diplomats' fundamental assumption that the Mi'kmaq were a separate people who should be dealt with collectively served the interests of Mi'kmaq leaders, who retained a measure of autonomy so long as the Mi'kmaq negotiated with the colonial authorities collectively as bands.

The classification process in Nova Scotia was complicated by the presence of a significant number of people of mixed ancestry. No one had developed a formula for classifying persons of mixed descent. None of the inhabitants of Nova Scotia adopted the label "métis" to describe themselves, and except in extraordinary circumstances comparable English words such as "half-breed" or "mulatto" were never used.[7] Nonetheless, descendents of mixed marriages were common in Nova Scotia, and French-speaking people with Mi'kmaq ancestors were accepted as members of the Acadian community.[8] There were as yet no similar mixed-race individuals living among Protestants and English-speakers, but some policymakers, particularly within the Whig ministry in London after 1715, hoped that intermarriage would facilitate the absorption of the Mi'kmaq into a Protestant colonial population. Therefore, though the Treaty of Utrecht denied individuals identified as "natives" the ability to choose individually to become British subjects, people of mixed ancestry could make the choice, so long as they convincingly identified themselves as colonists. In theory, at least, intermarriage and assimilation could have rendered the treaty's provisions governing "natives" a nullity, as individuals of mixed ancestry defined themselves as "British" or "French" and the Mi'kmaq nation gradually disappeared.

Philipps became governor with the assimilation of the Mi'kmaq as an official, long-term aim. His instructions directed him to offer subsidies to any colonists who married Mi'kmaq partners. Under the terms of the program he was told to implement, the European partner in any interracial marriage—the wife, if the husband were identified as Mi'kmaq—would receive prizes in the form of cash and land.[9] The proposed program served dual purposes: introducing "civility" and Protestantism to Mi'kmaq individuals who entered into bicultural marriages, and forging social links in the form of family ties between the unassimilated Mi'kmaq and the English-speaking community. As it happened, Philipps never paid any prizes. Few English-speaking colonists came to Nova Scotia, and it was not clear whether Acadians were meant to be covered by the program. In any event, with the exception of some Acadians, if any colonists formed partnerships with Mi'kmaq men and women they left British colonial society behind.[10] Especially in the early 1720s, the Mi'kmaq had no interest in embracing the British—sexually, politically, or in any other way—unless the British joined the Mi'kmaq community. The governor's policy had no practical effect.

To the extent that the intermarriage program was intended to create a unified society in which racial and cultural categories blurred, even its most optimistic proponents did not expect to reach that goal before the passage of a few generations. In the meantime the governor and his council concentrated on other objectives that seemed easier to achieve quickly; their first priority was to engage the Mi'kmaq in trade.[11] Philipps and his associates overestimated the profits that were available from the fur trade, but their interest in commerce with the native people stemmed from more than economic concerns. The governor thought that if the Mi'kmaq stopped taking furs to Louisbourg they would cut their ties with the French and redefine their position in the imperial rivalry. He knew that the exchange of goods played an important symbolic role in native diplomacy, and he hoped that regular trade with the Mi'kmaq would mark the creation of a Mi'kmaq-British alliance.

To facilitate good relations with the Mi'kmaq, in 1719 the Board of Trade authorized Philipps to offer gifts to the leaders of Mi'kmaq bands, and in 1721 the governor received a shipment of goods to present to the Mi'kmaq as presents.[12] According to his own account, Philipps "took care to advertise" the arrival of the goods "to the Indians throughout the whole province," though it is not clear how he spread the message. He directed the Mi'kmaq to meet him at the newly fortified British fishing settlement on Canso Island, off the Atlantic coast.

Only one Mi'kmaq leader, with a small retinue, accepted the invitation. Philipps tried to entertain the men and engage them in conversation, but the visitors seemed impatient and demanded that the governor hurry with the gifts. They took the presents and left, and a few days later a larger group of Mi'kmaq warriors arrived and attacked.[13]

There are several ways to interpret this turn of events. The governor suspected a trick, but it is possible that his advertisement failed to reach as many of the Mi'kmaq as he had wished. The Mi'kmaq delegation that visited Canso may have genuinely sought good relations but left in a hurry because they feared hostility from others among the Mi'kmaq (and the French) who disagreed with their decision to accept the British overture. Justifying their behavior to the French authorities on Ile Royale, the Mi'kmaq who received Philipps's gifts indicated that they had never sought an ongoing trading relationship with the British. They had only wanted to see what Philipps had to offer, in case the French ever neglected them.[14] Regardless of the accuracy of that explanation for their actions (when speaking to the French it served the Mi'kmaq's purposes to describe their behavior in this way), it is clear that Philipps did not know

how to communicate with the Mi'kmaq effectively. He could not identify their important leaders, and he could not easily interpret their words,
gestures, or actions.

Communication problems undermined Philipps's efforts at gift-
giving and alliance formation, but a more fundamental issue disturbed
Anglo-Mi'kmaq relations in 1721, which was associated with the island
Philipps chose as the venue for his efforts at trade and diplomacy. The
island of Canso lay close to shore at the mouth of the strait that separated
Nova Scotia from Ile Royale (see figure 10). Prior to 1720, when Philipps
directed the construction of a fort on the island, the British had maintained no permanent settlements on the Atlantic coast. Many Mi'kmaq
violently opposed the construction of the British fortifications, and although Philipps was aware of their opposition, he failed to understand
their reasons for objecting to his fort.

Canso had been used intermittently as a base for European fishing
operations since early in the seventeenth century. French-speakers and
Basques had dried fish on the island for more than one hundred years, and
at least since the 1680s English-speakers had often joined them there.[15]
The local Mi'kmaq tolerated the fishermen's presence, as long as they
did not establish permanent residence there and refrained from fighting
among themselves. Relations between the fishermen and the Mi'kmaq
became less predictable in wartime, and they gradually turned violent following the formal cession of Acadia to the British in 1713. Hostilities had
continued in large part because a small group of New Englanders hoped
to use the British fishery as a base for establishing year-round settlements
on lands that had been occupied only by the Mi'kmaq.

A central figure in the controversy was Cyprian Southack, an
English-born ship captain who had moved to Massachusetts in 1685 and
become a privateer.[16] Southack had been involved in the affairs of the region for decades. In 1690 he had commanded a vessel in the Massachusetts
attack on Acadia; he had served in a similar capacity on several successive
New England raids, in 1696, 1704, and 1707, and in the final, successful attack on Port Royal in 1710. By the early eighteenth century he had
also invested in fishing vessels, some of which operated off the coasts of
Acadia. In 1713, operating on instructions from the Massachusetts government, he had surveyed the Atlantic coast of Nova Scotia to determine
whether it was safe for the New England fishing fleet.[17] Southack brought
three fishing ships with him when he conducted the survey and lost two of
them to French privateers. He was upset by the loss, but he saw enough of
the coast to convince him that, once peace had been fully restored, Nova

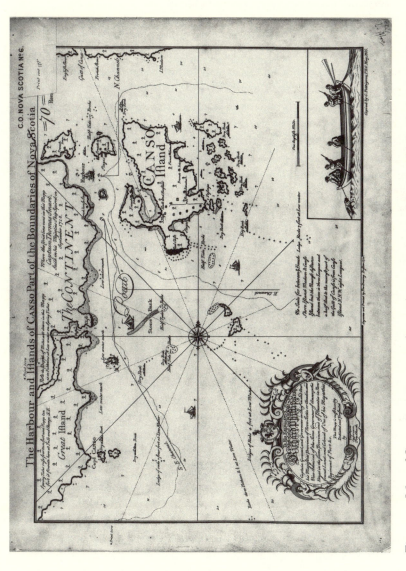

Figure 10. Map of Canso in 1718, prepared as evidence in support of Richard Philipp's decision to fortify the island and secure it for British–Empire fishermen. The map indicates that French fishermen have occupied Canso Island itself and the two smaller islands to the north, in order to dry their catches. 1915 copy by C. Petigrew, in the collections of the National Archives of Canada, Ottawa.

Scotia would be a good base for the fishery. He sent his conclusions to the Board of Trade and Samuel Vetch. Vetch responded to Southack's findings by petitioning the ministry to support his proposal to establish a string of settlements along Nova Scotia's Atlantic coast.[18]

In the summer of 1715 Southack returned to Nova Scotia and attempted to create a permanent fishing station at a place he named "Cape Roseway," near the southern tip of the peninsula. He and his crew built two houses and attracted other fishermen to join them from Massachusetts and present-day Maine. But before the fishing season was over the fishermen were approached by two visitors: a French-speaking Mi'kmaq man named "Jo. Muse" (or "Ja. Muse") and an Acadian man named François Tourangeau whom Southack identified as French.[19] The visitors told the New Englanders to leave and warned them that "one hundred Indians" were on their way to destroy their camp. Southack fled along with the other fishermen and Mi'kmaq warriors subsequently burned his outpost down.[20]

Muse and Tourangeau may have done Southack a favor by telling him that the Mi'kmaq warriors were coming. Other fishermen in the area that summer who had not been forewarned were taken captive.[21] But Southack was hardly grateful for the warning he had received. He interpreted the two men's behavior as evidence of a conspiracy, and he concluded that Tourangeau was acting on behalf of the French, who, aiming to reduce New England's fishing activities, had directed the Mi'kmaq to destroy his camp.

Tourangeau and some of the other local Acadians may have supported the Mi'kmaq resistance to the intrusions of the New Englanders, but Southack's suspicions were based on a misunderstanding of the official position of France. At the time of the confrontation at Cape Roseway the French remained committed to the terms of the Treaty of Utrecht and the partition of the maritime region into clear-cut British and French spheres. The Mi'kmaq had their own reasons for fighting the New Englanders and the British, and indeed in 1715 they resented France's political stance. At Utrecht the French had ceded sovereignty over the Atlantic coastline to Britain, but according to two fishermen who escaped capture in 1715, "the Indians say the lands were theirs and they can make war and peace as they please."[22] The Mi'kmaq stressed that they had not ratified the Treaty of Utrecht, nor were they bound by any promises made by French diplomats in Europe.

Nonetheless, when Southack confronted the Mi'kmaq he viewed them as agents of France. He adopted a view similar to that of many of

his New England-born neighbors in assuming that all his potential enemies were acting in concert against him. Southack was also typical of
English-speaking colonists in general, in failing to appreciate the peninsular Mi'kmaq bands' claims to their lands.

North of the Bay of Fundy in present-day New Brunswick, where
Mi'kmaq-speakers lived side by side with members of other Algonkian
nations, the Mi'kmaq and their associates in the Wabanaki Confederacy
may have interacted like many other Algonkian peoples, allocating specific, seasonal resources among members of different groups and thereby
sharing access to land.[23] But on the peninsula of Nova Scotia the Mi'kmaq
asserted that territorial boundaries were inviolable. They maintained that
their bands held exclusive authority over most of the peninsula of Nova
Scotia, particularly along the Atlantic coast. Southack misunderstood this
because he, like the negotiators at Utrecht, assumed that the Mi'kmaq
were a transient people. He believed that they wandered the entire region and that they had recently received a directive to oppose the New
Englanders from the French governor on Ile Royale.

Hoping to strike a blow against the Mi'kmaq and the French, Southack and his supporters decided to seek a confrontation with both groups
at Canso. In 1718 he convinced the government of Massachusetts to seize
two French fishing vessels that had anchored near the island.[24] And in
the winter of 1719, Southack and other New England fishermen met with
Philipps in Boston and convinced him to fortify Canso and station a permanent garrison there to keep the French and Mi'kmaq away.[25] They
persuaded the new governor that the fortification of Canso would bring
security to the entire coastline and encourage widespread year-round
English-speaking settlement, which would lead in turn to economic diversification across a large section of Nova Scotia. After listening extensively to the fishermen, Philipps informed the Board of Trade that the
island was a "lure." With a garrison in place, once the fishery at Canso
was fully established, "people will by degrees extend themselves along the
[Atlantic] coast."[26]

In 1720 Mi'kmaq warriors attacked the fortifications on the island as
they were being built, killed three men, and caused significant damage.[27]
According to one account, they also celebrated the action by boisterously
chanting "Vive le Roy!"[28] The words may have reflected a genuine belief on the part of the warriors that the French supported them in their
action, or the slogan may have been a tease, intended in part to intimidate
the British by suggesting that the full power of France was behind the
Mi'kmaq cause. That message may have backfired on the Mi'kmaq, how-

ever, because the idea that France's colonial authorities and the Mi'kmaq were coordinating their actions may have given Philipps reason for hope. Though the French had a plausible claim to Canso themselves and had pursued it diplomatically, by 1721 the French ministry had tacitly acquiesced in the British fortification of the island, and Philipps guessed that the Mi'kmaq would similarly reconcile themselves to the presence of the troops.[29]

When the governor invited the Mi'kmaq to visit him on Canso he thought that the construction of the fort had established peace in the region. His gift-giving ceremony conveyed the message that he hoped his new fort could serve as a congenial and convenient meeting place between the Mi'kmaq and English-speaking colonists. But the establishment of permanent facilities on the island violated long-standing agreements between the Mi'kmaq and the fishermen, and instead of improving relations it helped precipitate a war.[30]

From 1720 through 1724 New England fishermen helped soldiers defend the island against Mi'kmaq warriors, and when the New Englanders were involved the fighting could be brutal. On one occasion two vessels manned by New Englanders engaged in a two-hour naval battle with a group of Mi'kmaq warriors who were sailing in captured ships. The fishermen tossed bombs and set fire to the Mi'kmaq vessels. The warriors tried to swim to land, but the New England men fired on them in the water. They reported killing twenty-two, though only five bodies washed ashore. As a warning to the survivors the New Englanders decapitated the corpses and set the severed heads on pikes surrounding Canso's new fort.[31]

The actions of the New Englanders encouraged an escalation of violence. New England's participation in the fighting also reinforced a perception among the Mi'kmaq that the seizure of Canso was part of a larger pattern of New England expansionism extending from the island to the interior of present-day Maine. At the same time that the fishermen, soldiers, and Mi'kmaq warriors were fighting at Canso, tensions between New England settlers and the Algonkian peoples of Maine turned violent. The coincidence of warfare in the two locales helped inspire the Mi'kmaq and the native peoples to their west to revive and strengthen their alliance. The Mi'kmaq joined forces with their Wabanaki allies in Maine, while native peoples from the vicinity of northern New England traveled to peninsular Nova Scotia to assist the Mi'kmaq in their struggles there.[32] As the conflict spread, fighting broke out not only at Canso but also at the eastern end of the Bay of Fundy, and eventually further west in peninsular Nova Scotia near Annapolis Royal.

The French colonists at Ile Royale and in Canada avoided direct participation in the conflict, but as the fighting escalated French colonial officials in North America increasingly came to hope that the Mi'kmaq would evict the British from Annapolis Royal and Canso.[33] They provided discreet assistance to the Mi'kmaq in the war, for example by providing food and shelter to the wives and children of the warriors and by sending advice to war parties through the agency of French missionaries.[34] They insisted publicly, however, that they were never involved; as the governor of Canada declared in 1725, "this war did not concern the French."[35]

The fighting was sporadic. Approximately one hundred soldiers manned each of the two British garrisons, at Annapolis Royal and Canso, and they were able to defend their forts. But even with the help of the New Englanders they could not pursue the Mi'kmaq over any distances, and they had no hope at all of patrolling the woods. The soldiers and officers of the two garrisons were terrified of the Mi'kmaq warriors, and it did not take long before they began to generalize and condemn the Mi'kmaq people as a whole. In an official proclamation in 1722, Lieutenant Governor John Doucette declared that the Mi'kmaq were "a people of no faith, nor honour, but common enemies to all mankind."[36] Such sentiments were reflected in the way the soldiers fought. They adopted tactics designed to terrify and intimidate the Mi'kmaq as a group, including taking hostages (killing at least one), mutilating corpses, and reviving the scalp-bounty policy that Massachusetts had pioneered in the region in 1696.[37] By the time the fighting ended in 1725, no one in the provincial administration harbored hopes of assimilating the Mi'kmaq into British colonial society. The peace agreements both implicitly and explicitly directed the Mi'kmaq and the British to stay apart.

The formal treaties ending the war—one was concluded in Maine in 1725 and another, similar document was signed and ratified at Annapolis Royal in 1726—provided that the Mi'kmaq would govern their internal affairs.[38] Furthermore, the treaties specified that if any Mi'kmaq individual committed an offense against a colonist, the Mi'kmaq as a group would give compensation. These arrangements were similar to those the Mi'kmaq had established with the French colonial regimes at Port Royal before 1710 and at Louisbourg after 1713.[39] They also fit with the categorization scheme contained in the Treaty of Utrecht, which distinguished the "natives of America" from other peoples and suggested that the imperial governments should interact with "natives" as groups rather than as individuals. But given the complexity of community life in British Nova Scotia, the scheme seemed clearer on parchment than in practice.

Jean-Baptiste Cope attended the ratification ceremonies in 1726 as a representative of the band inhabiting the valley of the Shubenacadie River, an area that had grown in importance over the previous five years. In 1722 Antoine Gaulin, the founder of the Catholic mission at Antigonish, chose a site on the Shubenacadie as a base of operations for missionary work in central Nova Scotia. The location served his purposes well. Between fifty and one hundred fifty Mi'kmaq families lived near the mission site along the Shubenacadie, and many more Mi'kmaq groups and individuals traveled through the valley every year. The river cut a north-south path across the peninsula and served as a trade route connecting the eastern Bay of Fundy region with the Atlantic coast. Acadians as well as Mi'kmaq plied the river and a few Acadian families lived near the Mi'kmaq on the riverbanks. Acadian settlers established five or six farms within a few miles of the mission itself.[40]

The new mission, like the one Gaulin had established a few years earlier at Antigonish and another he helped found at Maligoueche on Ile Royale in 1724, served as a venue for religious events that brought together members of several Mi'kmaq bands.[41] These gatherings carried political significance, as they helped unite the Mi'kmaq by instilling in them a sense that they belonged to a single religious community. Acadians, French travelers from Ile Royale, and representatives of Algonkian nations from the region north of the Bay of Fundy also attended religious ceremonies at Gaulin's chapel on the Shubenacadie, and so the mission helped to strengthen the links that tied the various Catholic peoples of the maritime region together. The mission served as a communication center, where Mi'kmaq leaders, missionaries, and others shared news and messages that had come to them from peninsular Nova Scotia, Louisbourg, and the islands and mainland coasts of the Gulf of St. Lawrence. Indeed, during the recent conflict the mission had been used as a meeting place where leaders of the Wabanaki Confederacy had coordinated their attacks.[42]

Among the demands made by the Mi'kmaq and their allies at the treaty negotiations in 1725 and 1726 was the right to the services of their religious pastors. The British had been suspicious of almost all contacts between the French and the Mi'kmaq during the war, and they had tried to expel several French missionaries before the fighting ended.[43] Nonetheless they acceded to the demand, and the peace treaties guaranteed that the missions would survive. This concession reflected the strong position of the Wabanaki Confederacy in the negotiations, and a dilemma that the British faced when they contemplated their future in Nova Scotia. Their security and economic prospects depended on the maintenance of orderly relations with the Mi'kmaq, which required the British to identify leaders with whom they could communicate effectively to mediate disputes. Direct negotiations with Mi'kmaq leaders had often proved difficult, however, and so for pragmatic reasons the British decided to seek the cooperation of Catholic missionaries. Gaulin, for example, advised the Mi'kmaq closely during the peace talks. Though neither the French authorities nor the British were sure what advice he had given to the Mi'kmaq bands, Gaulin soon became a favorite of the British colonial administration.[44]

The treaties of 1725 and 1726 formalized the practice of treating the Mi'kmaq as a separate people, but the British could not find a way to disassociate their relations with them from their dealings with the French and the Acadians. The administrative difficulties involved in distinguishing the Acadians from the Mi'kmaq were revealed within weeks of the ratification of the 1726 treaty, in two well-publicized criminal trials conducted in an admiralty court in Boston.[45]

The two defendants at the first trial were men from the Atlantic coast of Nova Scotia, a father and his son, both named Jean-Baptiste Jedre, who were charged with piracy after an attack in the spring of 1726 on a Massachusetts fishing ship.[46] The second trial involved the same alleged crime, but it centered on the actions of three co-defendants who were identified as "Indians": James Mews, Phillip Mews, and John Missel. James Mews may have been the man who visited Southack at Cape Roseway in 1715, though ambiguities in the documents make it impossible to know for sure. The two trials were very similar. Both sets of defendants were convicted and sentenced to die. All five men were publicly hanged shortly after the conclusion of the court proceedings.[47]

Jedre and his son were implicitly classified as Acadian though they were related by marriage to two of the defendants at the second trial who were labeled "Indian." Furthermore, the younger Jedre may have spent part of his childhood living in the Mi'kmaq community. Two of the defendants identified as "Indian" were of mixed ancestry; indeed, they were probably direct descendants of a high official in the old French colonial government of Acadia.[48] But their legal status was very different from that of the Jedres, which necessitated the convening of separate trials.

An important issue in the cases tried in Boston was whether the government of Massachusetts was still in a state of war when the five men allegedly attacked the New England fishing ship. At the trial of the three defendants identified as "Indian," the prosecution offered proof that the war was over in its initial presentation of its case, because if a state of war had existed the alleged offense would not have been appropriate for criminal prosecution. The issue was cloudier in the trial of the two Acadian defendants, because the Acadians had never officially taken sides in the conflict. Nonetheless, the elder Jedre tried to raise a war-related defense when he spoke to the court.

Jedre claimed that during their war with the Mi'kmaq the New Englanders had captured his son Paul and held him as a prisoner of war. Paul had remained in captivity after the fighting ended, and Jedre had decided to take action in an effort to secure the young man's release. He and the son who stood trial with him had sought the assistance of two of their relatives, Mi'kmaq men who helped them recruit a body of warriors and seize the fishing ship. Together they hoped to hold the ship and its crew hostage, to give them bargaining power in negotiations for Paul's return.[49]

In making this defense Jedre invoked principles of justice based on communal responsibility. He implicitly argued that any New Englanders who visited Nova Scotia would be liable for capture and could be held hostage if the Acadians or the Mi'kmaq had a sufficiently important grievance against New England. One way to interpret this stance would be to see it as a claim that the war with New England continued, and that warlike tactics continued to be justified, at least in cases involving the release of former war captives. Another interpretation would center on long-standing Algonkian understandings of intertribal relations. Algonkian communities in the early eighteenth century commonly operated on the assumption that groups could be held responsible for the actions of their members. When one group had a grievance against another, the aggrieved community would often seek retribution or compensation against the other as a whole, sometimes by taking a member of the other group captive.[50] During the trials in Boston the prosecuting attorney warned against allowing the Acadians or the Mi'kmaq to continue to employ hostage-taking. He argued that if the five defendants went unpunished for their actions, violence would escalate, and the ensuing chaos would "almost certainly terminate in the breaking up of our Fishery, the most valuable Branch of our *New England* Trade."[51]

Some of the New Englanders involved in the trials of the five alleged pirates thought that the proceedings represented an important watershed for Nova Scotia, because the prosecutions served as a rejection of local norms of conduct and demonstrated the applicability of English law. The officers of the court worked self-consciously to demonstrate the fairness of the English legal system. The defendants received all of the formal protections that they would have been granted had they been New Englanders, from arraignment through sentencing. Indeed, a greater effort was made to guarantee procedural regularity at their trials than was usually the case. Though indigent defendants in New England had been assigned court-appointed lawyers before, there was no legal requirement that this be done, and only a minority of the accused in New England received the assistance of counsel. In these two cases, not only were the defendants provided attorneys, but the court also hired French- and Mi'kmaq-speaking translators to assist them.[52]

In an effort to convince the Acadians of the merits of English law and prepare them for the establishment of English-style courts, the authorities in Massachusetts sent copies of the trial records to Nova Scotia, and in the spring of 1727 the records were read aloud to the Acadian inhabitants of the eastern village of Beaubassin.[53] No English-style institutions of governance had yet been established in Beaubassin, and the records were read to the villagers in an effort to inform them about what to expect after regular courts were established.[54]

At the second trial in Boston the defense attorney had boasted that the Mi'kmaq in Nova Scotia would be positively impressed by English criminal procedure. He told the court that its "Candour and Indulgence" toward his clients would "convince even the barbarous and Salvage Tribes to which they belong" (the Mi'kmaq) of the "great Justice and Impartiality" of English law.[55] But despite the lawyer's naïve expectation of a positive Mi'kmaq response, no effort was made to read the trial records in Mi'kmaq communities, because the provincial authorities in Nova Scotia had no interest in regulating the behavior of the Mi'kmaq through the application of English law. Given the weakness of their policing power, it would have been difficult for them to apprehend or try alleged wrongdoers from among the Mi'kmaq. When allegations of theft, assault, or other offenses were made against members of Mi'kmaq bands, it was easier for the authorities to seek compensation from the leaders of the bands. Furthermore, the bands were willing to cooperate with such a system, because they were better able to retain their traditions and sovereignty if they kept the English legal system out.[56] The treaties of 1725 and 1726 had codified this arrangement and guaranteed the Mi'kmaq's separate status and exemption from the daily application of English law.

Nonetheless there were difficulties inherent in maintaining separate legal regimes for peoples who lived side by side. It would never be easy to classify individuals, and as the piracy trials in Boston suggested, it was also difficult to place incidents in categories to determine the appropriate legal response. For these reasons, among others, the Mi'kmaq saw the expansion of British authority and English-style institutions into Acadian communities as a threat to Mi'kmaq autonomy, even though the treaties of 1725 and 1726 guaranteed the Mi'kmaq internal self-governance.

In 1727, when officials in Nova Scotia's provincial council developed their long-term plan for establishing an English-style court of justice in Beaubassin, it was part of a larger project. The councilmen hoped to promote Protestant immigration throughout the eastern Bay of Fundy region, and in addition to courthouses they planned to build roads, military posts, churches, mines, and schools.[57] In 1732, in an effort to facilitate further economic development in the region, the council commissioned the first of these proposed buildings, a storehouse in Minas, the largest village between Beaubassin and Annapolis Royal.[58] The councilmen hired an Acadian carpenter to erect the building, but three members of the regional Mi'kmaq band paid him a visit and told him to quit.[59] The men, whom he identified as Jacques Winaguadesh, Antoin, and Andres, declared that "King George had Conquered Annapolis, But not Menis [Minas]." The Mi'kmaq still ruled the eastern end of the Bay of Fundy and they would not allow the construction to proceed. Either intimidated by the Mi'kmaq or persuaded, the carpenter refused the commission. Similar incidents derailed the provincial government's other plans for the region.[60] Despite the councilmen's hopes, the people of Beaubassin would never witness an English-style courtroom trial.[61]

The declaration of the three Mi'kmaq men highlights an ambiguity surrounding the peace agreements of the 1720s. The written treaties contained no territorial provisions, but in the aftermath of the conflict the British had refrained from expanding their settlements beyond their two outposts at Annapolis Royal and Canso.

In the Bay of Fundy region the close association of the Mi'kmaq and Acadian communities led to frequent low-level conflicts. On the Atlantic coast, by contrast, the Acadian population was smaller and more intimately involved in Mi'kmaq life. Agriculture was impossible in most of the area, and after 1725 the prospect of establishing new English-speaking settlements seemed dim. As a result, the Mi'kmaq and the English-speaking settlers at Canso found it possible to live side by side almost without interacting. As late as 1723 some British imperial promoters had still harbored hopes of establishing a string of coastal communities along Nova Scotia's Atlantic coast.[62] After the war, however, the British kept themselves to the island of Canso, with only a few huts and outbuildings on the adjacent shore.

Within those confines the New Englanders and the British established a thriving seasonal fishing community. During a visit to Canso in 1729 Philipps saw 250 fishing vessels and between fifteen hundred and two thousand men.[63] For a variety of reasons the fishery began to decline after 1739, but until that time the masters of the fishery and the Mi'kmaq abided by an implicit agreement that protected the interests of both. The Mi'kmaq discovered that they could tolerate the settlement at Canso because it had a minimal impact on the land. The fishermen spent most of their time aboard ship, and virtually none of them stayed in the region year-round.[64] The garrison Philipps had placed on the island stayed over the winters, as did approximately fifty civilian relatives of the soldiers, artisans, and merchants, but the Mi'kmaq assiduously avoided contact with them.[65]

For their part, the owners of fishing vessels did not need access to any more territory in order to prosper. Indeed, more extensive British settlement in the region might have undermined the vessel owners' economic interests by making it more difficult for them to control and retain labor. There were few economic opportunities for fishermen at Canso, but even there the owners of fishing ships at times had difficulty keeping hold of their workforce. Spokesmen for the fishery claimed that the local garrison recruited men off fishing vessels, enticing them away from their contractual obligations. Labor retention would have become more difficult if there had been extensive British settlement and economic diversification in the area.[66]

The Mi'kmaq and the settlers at Canso found a way to coexist, but underlying animosities remained. In 1732 an adventurous group of Mi'kmaq men visited the fort at Canso and received presents from the garrison commander. This may have been an effort to establish better relations and perhaps initiate a new pattern of trade. But the Mi'kmaq men were reprimanded by their elders and never returned.[67] According to a French Catholic missionary, a prominent merchant at Canso named Edward How once visited an assembly of Catholic Mi'kmaq on Ile Royale and castigated them for their devotion to their church.[68] His comments could hardly be called cordial—he ridiculed the Mi'kmaq as superstitious Catholics—but they suggest at a minimum that conversation was possible without violence.

After 1726 the Mi'kmaq and the English-speakers on the Atlantic coast avoided trouble by keeping their distance from one another. The accommodation worked, but it was not a stable one, because the provincial government and the leaders of the Mi'kmaq bands did not share a common understanding of the extent of British authority in Nova Scotia. Many Mi'kmaq continued to believe that a territorial settlement had been reached in which the British tacitly agreed to restrict their presence to Canso and Annapolis Royal, but no one in the provincial government acknowledged such a commitment. By formal treaty they had agreed to respect Mi'kmaq autonomy, but they did not believe their agreement with the Mi'kmaq restricted them in the policies they could adopt toward the Acadians, or toward the land. Lingering uncertainties surrounding the meaning of the treaties of 1725 and 1726 left the Mi'kmaq and the colonial government facing a strong potential for conflict. That potential was more apparent in the Bay of Fundy region than along the Atlantic coast, because the British and the French-speaking Acadians interacted on a daily basis. Nonetheless, when warfare resumed in 1744 the first combat occurred at Canso, and the Mi'kmaq turned violently against the British presence in the Atlantic region. The resumption of armed hostilities (which will be discussed in Chapter 5) proved that the Mi'kmaq and the English-speaking settlers had never reached an agreement on the meaning of British sovereignty in Nova Scotia, but it also owed much to the continuing involvement of the French in Anglo-Mi'kmaq affairs.

Chapter Four

Anglo-Acadian Relations, the French, and the Mi'kmaq, 1718–1743

RICHARD Philipps came to Nova Scotia without specific instructions as to the policies he should adopt toward the Acadians. While still in London after his appointment, he had advanced a set of tentative proposals to the Board of Trade, including one that foreshadowed the projects that were attempted in mid-century—to introduce English-speaking, Protestant settlers into the Acadian villages in the expectation that the language, religion, and customs of the newcomers would soon be adopted by all the local villagers.[1] But the board did not endorse this proposal, and there is no record indicating that anyone on the governor's council in Nova Scotia (which was composed almost entirely of military officers who had served in the garrison at Annapolis Royal over the previous decade) gave any support to the idea of surrounding and assimilating the Acadians. After Philipps arrived in the colony in 1720 and listened to the advice of the councilmen, he began to contemplate other measures, and in 1721 he proposed deporting the Acadian population and replacing it with subsidized British immigrants.

Initially the deportation proposal received a sympathetic hearing in London, but in 1722 the financial crisis precipitated by the collapse in the stock price of the South Sea Company cooled the Whig ministry's enthusiasm for imperial expenditures. Sir Robert Walpole, the man who dominated the ministry after the South Sea Company crisis, abandoned many of the Whigs' old priorities and pursued a foreign policy similar to that of the Tories during Queen Anne's reign. His main objectives were to expand Britain's commercial presence overseas and avoid unnecessary confrontations with the French.[2] After 1722 the project of deporting the Acadians lost any prospect of ministerial support.

This shift in the British political climate coincided in Nova Scotia with the formal start of the war between the Mi'kmaq and the colonial government, which in turn inspired a rethinking of British policy toward the Acadians. Though few if any Acadians participated directly in combat during the Anglo-Mi'kmaq war, some Acadian villagers provided food, shelter, and intelligence to Mi'kmaq warriors opposed to British rule. At the same time, other Acadian families offered logistical support to the men of the British garrisons. These events convinced some members of the provincial council that they needed to build a stronger base of support among the Acadians, and before the war ended the councilmen had begun to promote the interests of those within the Acadian villages who were willing to cooperate with the British authorities. After the fighting ceased the colonial government appointed Acadians to newly created administrative posts, and entered into negotiations with Acadian leaders in an effort to get all the adult male villagers to swear allegiance to the British crown.

By 1730, almost every Acadian male who had reached adulthood had taken an oath of fidelity to the British monarchy, but most of them made their oaths conditional by insisting on an exemption from compulsory military service. In the coming decades some British officials would question the validity of such conditional oaths and ask whether the Acadians had effectively declared themselves British subjects. Philipps and others would eventually raise similar questions concerning the legal implications of the Acadians' continuing adherence to Catholicism, since the rights of Catholics were restricted almost everywhere in the British Empire. Nevertheless, in the 1730s pragmatic considerations took precedence over legal niceties. Without advancing a coherent legal or political theory to justify their policies, the colonial authorities treated the Acadians as British subjects in some contexts—for example by appointing them to administrative posts—but refrained from allowing them suffrage or representation in a colonial assembly.

Economically the years from 1726 through 1743 were good for the Acadians. They reclaimed new lands from the sea, expanded their settlements in the eastern Bay of Fundy region, and put additional acreage under cultivation near Annapolis Royal and on a smaller scale further afield, in present-day New Brunswick. The expansion of Louisbourg provided them with a large new market, and Acadian merchants brought livestock and produce to Ile Royale as well as Boston. Their population boomed in these years, reaching 10,000 by 1744.[3] (By contrast, there were approximately 3,000 Mi'kmaq-speakers in the region and in the wintertime fewer than 500 English-speakers divided between Annapolis Royal and Canso.[4])

Though the Acadians were becoming more numerous and prosperous, they could not dominate the region economically, politically, or in any other respect. They were dependent on the trade of their neighbors, the New Englanders, the French on Ile Royale, and the British in the garrison in the provincial capital. Both the British and the French maintained a sufficient military presence in the region to pose an abstract threat, but in the eastern region of the Bay of Fundy and to the north in present-day New Brunswick it was the Mi'kmaq and their Algonkian allies who provided the most visible and active force policing the Acadians' behavior. When they were eventually called on to explain why they would not fight for Britain, some Acadians declared that they felt too closely tied to the French to contemplate taking up arms against them. But others asserted, with justification, that they had no choice but to refuse military service. They could not bear arms for Britain, or even serve in administrative posts for the colonial government, because they feared reprisals from native warriors, French trading partners, Catholic priests, and Acadian neighbors who remained loyal to France.

At Annapolis Royal the British were able to overcome the reticence of many Acadians, and by the 1730s a vibrant bilingual community had emerged. The soldiers' families interacted with the Acadians on a daily basis, and indeed the British occasionally submitted themselves to the judgment of Acadians serving in the administration. Anglo-Acadian relations were more strained, however, outside the capital. In the most distant Acadian villages, in the disputed border region that is now New Brunswick, many villagers disavowed any obligation to respect the wishes of the British colonial authorities. A geographical pattern emerged in which the Acadians' political stance seemed to depend in large part on the village in which they resided. Those who lived close to Mi'kmaq-dominated regions or the French imperial boundary were less likely to cooperate with the government. These circumstances reinforced among the British a set of ideas that would work dramatically to the disadvantage of the Acadians in the years ahead: a belief that the Acadians could be characterized in groups, and that their physical and cultural surroundings had a determinative effect on their political behavior.

Like Chapter 3, this chapter begins with the Treaty of Utrecht, which contained a set of guidelines for determining the legal status of the Acadians as subjects of Britain or France. The treaty's provisions proved unworkable, however, and no coherent set of rules was devised to replace them. The Mi'kmaq, the British, and the Acadians all held power at various times in different places within the putative borders of Nova Scotia, and an ever-changing array of economic, military, and diplomatic considerations affected how each person behaved. Nonetheless, the period from 1726 through 1743 was one of relative peace, because none of the peoples involved in the life of the province had the military power or political will necessary to impose answers to the questions that remained unresolved, including whether the Acadians could always be held accountable to the colonial government, and whether they could be called upon to resist competing demands made upon them by the Mi'kmaq and the French.

By its explicit terms, the Treaty of Utrecht granted the Acadians an unconditional right to remain in Nova Scotia for only one year. Those who chose to leave during the year would be allowed to take their property with them or to dispose of it before leaving. Those who chose to stay could do so only if they agreed to become "subject to the Kingdom of Great Britain." After the terms of the peace agreement were announced in 1713, dozens of Acadian families boarded ships for the French colony at Ile Royale, and hundreds of others declared their intention to go.[5] Assuming that the Acadians had reached a decision as a group, Samuel Vetch predicted in 1714 that only two French-speaking residents would remain.[6] But, as it happened, no wholesale exodus occurred. Recognizing the weakness of the provincial government, the Acadians concluded that they could risk staying in Nova Scotia without obeying the government's demand that they take an oath of allegiance to the British monarch.[7]

Most Acadians—at least those who publicly expressed their opinions—declared that they would obey British law so long as they remained in the province, but they would not give the colonial government their active support.[8] By 1717 this position had been refined into a declaration of principle that Acadians would reiterate for years to come: they vowed to respect the authority of the British in Nova Scotia, but they would not fight for them, nor would they take up arms in support of France.[9] To be sure, not all Acadians adopted this position. As early as 1711, some villagers in Annapolis Royal had sworn unconditional allegiance to Queen Anne, and in 1717 Maurice Vigneau and some other fishermen, whose livelihoods were threatened by a fish-licensing system recently announced by the colonial government, took an unconditional oath of allegiance to King George.[10] But the vast majority of Acadian men refused to take such an oath unless they were guaranteed an exemption from military service. Looking back on the oath-taking controversy in 1756, an exiled Acadian writer provided a simple explanation for their stance. The Acadians had "relations and friends amongst the French, which they might have destroyed with their own hands had they consented to bear arms against them."[11]

The Acadians' refusal to take an unconditional oath of allegiance infuriated almost all the colonial government's officials. Many argued that placing a condition on one's allegiance was the same as disavowing it, and they suspected that the Acadians remained, both legally and in terms of their personal loyalties, subjects of France. Therefore, it seemed, under the terms of the Treaty of Utrecht they should not have remained in Nova Scotia. During his brief tenure as governor, Francis Nicholson had responded to this situation by declaring that the Acadians were "all rebels."[12] Other administrators were more restrained in their assessment of the state of affairs, but none thought the Acadians should be allowed to stay without declaring their allegiance unconditionally. The Acadians' stance toward oath-taking left them in a position that most British officials considered untenable. Until they took a valid oath of allegiance they were, as Philipps described them in 1718, "neutral subjects of another prince" living within the formal boundaries of the British Empire.[13]

The legal status of the Acadians was further complicated by their continuing fidelity to the Catholic church. The Treaty of Utrecht guaranteed that they could "enjoy the free exercise of their Religion, according to the Usage of the Church of Rome, as far as the Laws of *Great Britain* do allow the same."[14] It was never clear, however, which "Laws of *Great Britain*" would apply to them. The rights of Catholics were restricted almost everywhere in the realm in the first half of the eighteenth century, but the nature of the restrictions varied according to locale. Catholics were barred from voting, holding office, or serving in the military in Britain and Ireland, and in Ireland Catholics' economic rights were restricted.[15] Catholics were prevented from voting or holding office in several of the British North American colonies as well, but on Minorca, a British possession with an overwhelming majority of Catholics, fidelity to Rome was not a bar to government service.[16] The variability of the rights of Catholics in different parts of the empire served to heighten the confusion surrounding the policies Nova Scotia's government would adopt on questions concerning religion and the political rights of Acadian Catholics, and the resulting uncertainty caused apprehension among the Acadians themselves.[17]

In Nova Scotia, the British authorities' concerns were exacerbated by the fact that the Acadians and the Mi'kmaq often shared the same pastors. Most British officials believed that the missionaries and other clerics exerted a powerful influence over their charges by withholding the sacraments from those who displeased them and by granting absolution to those who followed their commands.[18] As tensions escalated between the Mi'kmaq and the colonial government, many British officials suspected that the missionaries were using their influence to forge an anti-British alliance between the Mi'kmaq and the Acadians. These fears focused particularly on Minas and Beaubassin, which lay far from Annapolis Royal and relatively close to the missions at Antigonish and on the Shubenacadie River. Even before he arrived in Nova Scotia, Philipps had heard reports that Antoine Gaulin and his associates at the Antigonish mission "precide in the quallity of Governors over Minas and Chignecto [Beaubassin]."[19]

For their part, the British had no effective institutions of governance in the eastern Bay of Fundy region. During the previous decade they had devised an ad hoc system to regulate their affairs with the villagers, but it fell far short of effective administration. Throughout the province, each Acadian settlement sent spokesmen to Fort Anne to relay the consensus of their communities to the provincial council and to send reports of the council's decisions to the Acadian villages.[20] These delegates, whom the British called "deputies," did not hold positions of authority. They were not official agents of the provincial government, nor were they anything like legislators, judges, or constables in the communities they served. Their only function was to maintain a line of communication between the villages and the British.[21] This system accorded with the way the Acadians had customarily governed themselves; the deputies were usually village elders, wealthy men, and traditional leaders within the community.[22] But no British law or precedent justified the existence of such an office. Furthermore, the provincial council's recognition of the office of deputy reinforced a sense of village autonomy. The deputy system was a pragmatic solution to the immediate problem of maintaining orderly relations with the Acadian villages, but neither Philipps nor any of the colonial officials with longer experience in Nova Scotia considered it a solution to the problem of governance.

Soon after Philipps arrived he summoned the deputies. Neither he nor anyone else knew what the British ministry wanted him to do, and so with remarkable candor, and probably recognizing the political value of instilling fear, he told the deputies about his uncertainties. He assured them that he would do nothing on his own, but warned them he would deport the Acadians to France if he received specific instructions to do so from London.[23] Then he issued a series of orders that reflected the ambivalent nature of his position. He declared that any Acadian who refused to take an oath of allegiance within four months would be compelled to leave.[24] But not wishing to encourage an immediate mass exodus to

Ile Royale or Canada (which would have weakened the military position of his own colony), he began placing obstacles in the way of those who wanted to depart. He announced that emigrants would not be permitted to take anything with them beyond an allowance of two sheep per family.[25] He convinced the provincial council to prohibit any vessels on the Annapolis River from carrying passengers or cargo.[26] And he announced that anyone intending to leave the province would have to notify the provincial secretary at least ten days in advance. Those with outstanding debts would be required to post a bond covering their obligations.[27]

While he was issuing these directives Philipps was also lobbying the Board of Trade and the king to deport the Acadians from North America.[28] The effort achieved modest political success—in 1720 and again in 1721 the Board of Trade endorsed the proposed expulsion—but Philipps received no money, no troops, and in the end no official permission to carry out the plan.[29] In 1722 the rise to power of the fiscally conservative Walpole regime made it very unlikely that the ministry would authorize the expenditure necessary to expel the Acadians. Earlier Whig ministries, such as those that oversaw the French evacuation from St. Kitts in 1702 and the coerced departure of French colonists from Newfoundland in 1715, might have given full support for a mass deportation.[30] But despite his Whig credentials, Walpole pursued a cautious and conciliatory foreign policy. He wanted to nurture and maintain Britain's new alliance with France and avoid provocative actions.[31]

In the meantime conditions within Nova Scotia took a turn for the worse, as the colonial government and the Mi'kmaq entered into a full-scale war. The conflict exposed the garrison's vulnerabilities. The Acadians, in general, did not fight, but had they joined forces with the Mi'kmaq the soldiers at Annapolis Royal would have been outnumbered and surrounded. Furthermore, even though the Acadians did not take up arms, the war served as an object lesson on the role the local population could play in the provision of logistical support and intelligence. Although very few Acadians actively participated in combat, some Acadian opponents of the government gave Mi'kmaq warriors refuge during the conflict and offered news, advice, moral support, and supplies.[32]

In 1722 the council made it a crime for any Acadian to offer food, shelter, or assistance to any Mi'kmaq.[33] But the directive proved difficult to enforce because the government did not have the manpower necessary to police the daily lives of the inhabitants. Consequently the council occasionally resorted to communal justice and exemplary punishment. In one notorious incident the homes of three Acadian families were burned because someone who lived nearby (the authorities never determined who) gave refuge to Mi'kmaq warriors who were preparing to attack British soldiers.[34]

The councilmen knew that such scattershot retaliatory actions were risky. They did not want to alienate the entire Acadian community or drive them into open resistance. Therefore, at the same time that the councilmen endorsed regulating the activities of the Acadians as a group and punishing them communally or in an exemplary manner, they also sought to nurture good relations with various leaders of the Acadian community, including village elders, merchants, and priests, who cooperated with them. These two policy tracks—holding the Acadian villagers communally responsible for the actions of their neighbors while at the same time attempting to identify helpful individuals—were not easily reconciled, as can be illustrated in the case of Prudent Robichaud.

Robichaud had signaled his willingness to cooperate with the British as early as 1711.[35] In 1715 his signature appeared first in a declaration signed by thirty-six Acadian men which stated that they were willing to respect the orders of the British government.[36] In 1718 he carried a message from the provincial council to a French missionary working with the Mi'kmaq in the eastern part of the province, and in 1720 he offered to serve the council as a deputy.[37] In the summer of that year his son (also named Prudent) testified helpfully to the council concerning the activities of Mi'kmaq warriors around Canso.[38] The Robichauds were merchants who spoke both French and Mi'kmaq, and they were useful to the council in part because of their ties to the Mi'kmaq community.[39] But those ties also brought them trouble. In 1723 the elder Robichaud was accused of trading with the Mi'kmaq. Testimony before the council revealed that he had been observed sitting with some Mi'kmaq men drinking rum. Robichaud admitted to sitting with the men but denied that they were drinking. The councilmen warned him not to fraternize with the Mi'kmaq, but because of the weakness of the evidence decided not to charge him with a crime.[40] In 1725 Robichaud was again brought before the council on charges of having "entertained" a Mi'kmaq visitor in his house. This time he was placed in irons and displayed as an example to his Acadian neighbors.[41] Robichaud was punished as an exemplary Acadian, but soon after this incident the government turned to him again for help. In 1726 he served as a translator during peace negotiations with the Mi'kmaq, and in subsequent years the government frequently called on his services to smooth relations with both the Mi'kmaq and the local Acadians.[42]

Of all the leaders of the Acadian community, the French Catholic priests (who were all foreign-born and not, strictly speaking, Acadians, but held great influence within the Acadian villages) attracted the greatest attention of the colonial administrators. The council issued orders banning particular priests who were deemed overly sympathetic to the Mi'kmaq war effort, but they simultaneously gave encouragement to Catholic clergymen who supported the authority of the provincial government.[43] Outside the vicinity of Annapolis Royal (where the local priest was apprehended and expelled) the orders banning priests often proved ineffective. But the effort to establish close ties with cooperative clergymen bore fruit. In 1724 three new priests arrived in Nova Scotia, reported their presence to the provincial council, and formally requested permission to work in the province.[44] The councilmen granted their requests, and when jurisdictional conflicts arose between competing pastors, the council supported the claims of the cooperative ones (sometimes by issuing fines against parishioners who attended the services of the favored priest's rivals).[45] By the time the war ended, several of the Catholic priests serving in Nova Scotia owed their positions to the support they received from the provincial council, and after 1725 the new arrangement was made official. Lieutenant Governor Lawrence Armstrong concluded an agreement with the bishop of Québec that the church would not station missionaries or other clergymen in Nova Scotia without the government's consent.[46]

Just as the government sought order in its relations with the Catholic church, so, after its war with Mi'kmaq ended, it tried to stabilize its relationship with the Acadian villagers. The colonial administrators hoped to exploit the ties they had established with leaders of the Acadian community in order to reform the Acadians and redefine their status within the colony and the empire. With the assistance of Prudent Robichaud and others, in 1726 the provincial council entered into negotiations to get the Acadians to swear allegiance to the British crown.

The negotiations were torturous in every village. When the Acadians were willing to swear allegiance at all, they insisted that their oaths be conditioned on a promise that they would not be summoned into military service. At times various colonial officials acceded to their requests and promised that they would be exempted, and some Acadian villagers took conditional oaths of allegiance in 1726 and 1727.[47] But in 1727 the councilmen ruled that conditional oaths were void and thus cast doubt once again on the Acadians' legal status.[48] So things stood until 1729, when Philipps, who had been away from his post, returned for the last time to Nova Scotia. The governor refused to put his promise in writing, but told the Acadians that they would be exempted from conscription.[49] Upon hearing his promise almost every Acadian male over the age of fifteen swore allegiance to King George II.[50]

In the immediate aftermath of the oath-taking ceremonies, despite some possible misgivings about the conditional nature of the Acadians' allegiance, most provincial officials believed they had inaugurated a new era for the political development of Nova Scotia. After the Acadians began taking the oath of allegiance in 1726, the colony's officials implicitly modified their opinions concerning the eligibility of Catholics for government service. Officially the councilmen continued to maintain that persons "of the Romish persuasion" were "unqualified to bear any Civil Office by Commission in the Government."[51] But in 1727 they began appointing Catholic Acadians to a constabulary and named Prudent Robichaud a justice of the peace.[52] A few years later two Acadians accepted invitations to serve as inspectors of the flocks.[53] Around the same time the provincial authorities assigned two Acadian men the job of collecting quitrents for the government, and created a night watch with Acadian members.[54] In perhaps the most dramatic example of empowering Acadians as government officials, in 1734 the provincial council appointed a group of Acadian men from Annapolis Royal to investigate frauds committed by British merchants. In their commission the Acadians were given the authority to compel testimony from British civilians and soldiers.[55]

These appointments placed Acadians in positions of authority, but not at the highest levels of government. The provincial authorities continued to maintain that Catholics could not serve in legislative positions, and this prevented them from establishing a representative assembly in Nova Scotia.[56] Furthermore, in the 1720s the provincial council began to sit as a court of quarter sessions, and in that capacity, if its jurisdiction was invoked, it had the final word on all civil and criminal matters.[57] Nonetheless, the councilmen believed that the Acadians as a group, throughout the province, had joined a new political community, and they hoped to reform the political structure of the Acadian villages everywhere in Nova Scotia. Outside Annapolis Royal, however, many Acadians resisted British-inspired reforms. The Acadians' stance was greatly affected by where they lived.

Approximately one dozen outlying Acadian families lived along the St. John River in present-day New Brunswick.[58] They shared the valley with a large number of Algonkian inhabitants, including Mi'kmaq- and Wuastukwiuk-speakers.[59] The Algonkians outnumbered the Acadians, and in the absence of any effective colonial administration, French or British, they exerted a strong influence over the life of the region. In their statements to colonial officials, the local native peoples proudly defended their political autonomy, but for the most part in the competition between the empires they favored the French.[60]

In general the Acadians who lived alongside the Algonkians in the St. John region denied that the British had any authority over them. The Treaty of Utrecht had been vague about the location of the imperial border, and though France had not established any governmental institutions in the area, those Acadians who moved to the St. John valley after 1710 believed they had returned to the French Empire. In 1732 an Acadian merchant from Annapolis Royal went to the mouth of the St. John to collect on a bill of exchange. After payment was refused, he threatened the maker of the bill with "la justice d'Annapolis Royalle." All those present laughed at him. Furious, he went to the council in Annapolis Royal and petitioned for help. After hearing his story the councilmen ordered the inhabitants of the St. John valley to swear allegiance to the British king. They agreed to do so but pointedly refused to guarantee the safety of British officials who came into their area, and they made no promises concerning the money allegedly owed to the merchant.[61] The British authorities were dissatisfied with this turn of events, but they did not have the logistical capacity to impose their will in the area.

Shortly after this incident Lawrence Armstrong, the acting governor of Nova Scotia, wrote to the governor of Massachusetts asking for his help in fortifying the St. John River. Not only did he hope to establish authority over the Acadians, but he also thought that the establishment of a trading post would draw the Wuastukwiuk- and Mi'kmaq-speaking peoples of the area away from their supposed allegiance to the French.[62] But the Massachusetts government was not prepared to undertake the expense, and despite petitions to London, the authorities in Nova Scotia could not acquire the manpower or financial resources necessary to establish an outpost of their own on the river.[63] Four years later, the Acadian settlers in the St. John River valley again denied that the British could exercise authority in their region. Echoing some of their Algonkian neighbors, they declared "the said land &c belonged to them." [64]

Halfway between the St. John River and Annapolis Royal, in Beaubassin, Minas, and in other villages at the eastern end of the Bay of Fundy, Acadians often signaled their willingness to cooperate with the government, but their circumstances made cooperation difficult. British officials seldom visited them, and the Acadians in the area had better communication with the French on Ile Royale than they did with the British at Annapolis Royal or Canso. Regardless of the villagers' personal inclinations, it was often impractical or impossible for them to do what the British wanted. For example, Philipps ordered the Acadians in the eastern region to conduct trade at the provincial capital, but many preferred to sell to merchants who came to them. Arranging transportation was difficult and many of the local people could have redirected their trade to Annapolis Royal only at a substantial monetary cost.[65]

Similarly, the provincial council would have liked the eastern Acadian villagers to do more to resist the demands of Mi'kmaq warriors, but the government could offer no troops to protect them. As we saw in Chapter 3, when the government tried to change this situation by proposing that a road be built linking Minas to Annapolis Royal and that a storehouse be built for British travelers at Minas, Mi'kmaq warriors intervened and intimidated those Acadians who wanted to cooperate. That episode, and a similar confrontation on the isthmus of Chignecto in the following year, lessened the apparent authority of the British and diminished the attractiveness of government office for Acadians living in the region. Most of the residents of Minas and Beaubassin were willing to pay nominal quitrents to the provincial government, implicitly acknowledging its authority over them. Some also accepted government posts, but when they did so they often faced ostracism and threats from their neighbors.[66]

From the late 1720s onward, chapels in the eastern Acadian villages increasingly became centers of low-level resistance to the colonial government. Despite the structures the colonial authorities had put in place to regulate the government's affairs with the Catholic clergy, controversies occurred frequently when the pastors appeared to assume too much authority over the lives of their parishioners, or when colonial officials seemed to make excessive demands on the priests. The government held the upper hand when these disputes arose in Annapolis Royal, but elsewhere in the province the clergymen, with support from their Mi'kmaq and Acadian communicants, enjoyed greater autonomy. The Mi'kmaq, in particular, often stood ready to aid Catholic pastors who ran afoul of the provincial authorities. In 1729 and again in 1736, pastors evicted from their posts in Annapolis Royal simply moved away from the capital and found refuge with Mi'kmaq bands.[67] In the eastern Bay of Fundy region, where the government's policing powers and military capabilities were particularly weak, the British lacked the ability to discipline disobedient pastors or keep them away from their congregations.

An episode from the early 1730s illustrates the autonomy of the church in the eastern region; one of the parishioners involved was Jacques Maurice Vigneau.

After coming of age on the western coast of Ile Royale, Vigneau returned to the peninsula of Nova Scotia in the 1720s and settled in the village of Beaubassin, where he married and began raising a family. He also acquired a ship and became a successful merchant, probably carrying goods (as he would later in life) between the Acadian villages of Nova Scotia and Ile Royale.[68] In 1732 Vigneau learned that an English boy named George had left his family at Canso, declaring that he was a Catholic; he sought refuge from the Protestant English and religious instruction with the Acadians' priests. He made his way across peninsular Nova Scotia uncertain of his destination, hoping to reach Louisbourg, Canada, or some other "Catholic country." As he made his way he found sanctuary in chapels and the homes of discreet Acadians. When George reached Beaubassin, Vigneau offered him work so that he could acquire the necessary provisions to continue his journey. The British authorities heard rumors of the boy's progress and sent warnings of reprisals if he were not returned. But Vigneau and his accomplices spirited George away, secure in the knowledge that their pastors and neighbors would protect them. The British could not assert their authority in Beaubassin.[69]

In the late 1730s and early 1740s there was a shortage of pastors for the eastern Bay of Fundy region. Jean-Louis Le Loutre, a missionary serving the Mi'kmaq at the Shubenacadie mission, visited the Acadian villages regularly and assumed partial responsibility for their pastoral care.[70] It was a time of rising tension between the British and French Empires, and by the early 1740s Le Loutre and several other French priests serving in the eastern region of Nova Scotia had become openly antagonistic toward the British colonial government. On occasion they threatened to excommunicate men who accepted positions in the provincial administration, and in at least one instance they denied a man from Minas who had accepted a government commission access to the sacraments. The pastors admonished their parishioners not to interact with the man.[71]

The deputy system, which remained the principal means of communication between the Acadian villages and the government, contributed to a growing sense among government officials that the Acadians of the eastern region were temperamentally and morally different from the villagers who lived near Annapolis Royal. Because the deputies from Minas and Beaubassin claimed to speak for their entire communities, if anyone in the villages behaved in a way that seemed to contradict the sentiments expressed by the deputies, government officials were likely to interpret the event as a violation of trust. It is likely that there were divisions of sentiment within every Acadian village in Nova Scotia, but colonial officials began to categorize the Acadians according to where they lived. The worst, from the British authorities' perspective, resided in the St. John valley. The best by far were those who lived in the vicinity of Annapolis Royal, where by the 1730s a sense of community had developed embracing both English-speakers and Acadians.

In contrast to the soldiers who participated in the conquest of Acadia, those who came to Annapolis Royal in peacetime were often likely to stay beyond their minimum terms of enlistment and develop productive relationships with the Acadians. Some of the soldiers lived in Nova Scotia for many years and others stayed only for short periods, but it was common even for the soldiers who resided in the province only briefly to commit time, emotional energy, financial resources, and physical effort into making the place their home. A combination of factors, including hunger, loneliness, boredom, sexual desire, and the perception of economic opportunity, drew the men out of the garrison and into the complex community life of the French-speaking village.

According to a survey of the garrison in 1720, at least sixty-eight soldiers, approximately one-quarter of the men, were "artificers" with special skills that could be useful in the civilian economy.[72] The garrison included weavers and tailors, tanners and shoemakers, carpenters and blacksmiths. Among the rest there were many who were willing to do manual labor for extra pay. The soldiers had time, skills, and ample opportunity to hire themselves out. When the soldiers accepted private commissions, they were sometimes able to make themselves rich. For example, by 1744 bombardier Samuel Douglas had an estate worth £540.[73]

Over time, owing in large part to private economic activity, rival hierarchies developed among the troops at Annapolis Royal. The soldiers continued to defer to men of higher military rank, but if they could find employment on private commissions, especially if they worked for powerful clients, they could remove themselves from the direct supervision of their commanding officers.[74] Enlisted men who did freelance work could gain power and status through the acquisition of material wealth. By the early 1740s the most important status hierarchy among the military men at Annapolis Royal may not have been one distinguishing officers from soldiers, but one dividing men who lived in barracks from those who had acquired their own houses.

Within the army in the early years of the British occupation, privacy was a luxury reserved for officers. Most of the troops slept in barracks, with dozens of men sharing a room. The governor, by contrast, enjoyed a house almost as large as the barracks for one hundred soldiers.[75] The governor's residence was situated prominently inside the fort next to the parade grounds. The other officers acquired or rented houses outside the fortifications. An officer gained prestige and authority by living in a private house, even if he lived outside the fortress walls. It was considered a prerogative of rank to meet with soldiers and subordinate officers in one's own home.[76] And if the officer or soldier had a house and family, he was less likely to be given assignments that would take him away from the provincial capital.[77]

As soldiers earned extra money by hiring themselves out, plying their crafts, and engaging in trade with each other and with the Acadians, living in a private house ceased to be an exclusive prerogative of officers. During the 1720s and 1730s several prominent landowners in Annapolis Royal, including the governor and a few Acadian merchants, financed the construction of houses that were rented to soldiers.[78] By 1744 there were at least twenty officers and soldiers living in private houses in Annapolis Royal, and there may have been many more.[79] In addition to privacy, prestige, and physical comfort, houses gave the men a much better opportunity to marry and raise families.

Marriage often tied the soldiers and officers to the Acadian community. A few of the men who acquired homes married Acadian women and found themselves absorbed directly into a local kinship network.[80] Most of the married soldiers had English-speaking spouses who had come with them to Annapolis Royal or joined them there; nonetheless, despite their foreign upbringing, the soldiers' wives were easily absorbed into the daily life of the village. The case of Mary Davis illustrates this well. In 1734, Davis brought a complaint before the provincial council alleging that an Acadian woman named Jeanne Picot had slandered her. The council ordered Picot ducked, but Davis intervened and asked instead for an apology, and specified that Picot make her statement on the steps of the local Catholic chapel. The council records do not indicate whether Picot spoke English or Davis spoke French, but the accusation of slander and the demand for an apology, especially in the forum Davis chose, strongly suggest that the soldiers' wives had begun to speak the language of the Acadians.[81]

If the soldiers' wives became bilingual, it is even more likely that their offspring could speak both English and French. The sons and daughters of the soldiers in Annapolis Royal grew up in a place where French was the language of daily life. By 1727 the soldiers, as a group, had at least fifty children living with them, and the upbringing of these children was a matter of official concern. Richard Philipps and others within the administration spent considerable energy trying to recruit a resident Protestant chaplain for the garrison, in part so that he could establish a school for these children. He recruited a chaplain who opened a school, but controversies surrounding the chaplain's salary and supplies forced the school to close after a few years.[82]

Though some soldiers and officials of the provincial government had misgivings about the Acadians' close ties to the garrison, the growing perception that the Acadians living near the fort were loyal to the government reinforced the belief current among the province's officials that the Acadians in general could be transformed if they lived in communities dominated by politically loyal Protestant settlers.[83] One of the earliest advocates of this view was Philipps, who had proposed surrounding the Acadians with Protestants in 1718. But in the later years of the Philipps administration the most insistent advocate of this view was a French-born Protestant officer of the garrison named Paul Mascarene.

Mascarene's own life suggested the possibilities of cultural assimilation. Born in France to Protestant parents, he traveled extensively in Europe following the revocation of the Edict of Nantes. In 1708 he enlisted in the British army, and he came to America two years later to serve as an officer in the regiment that took Port Royal. His knowledge of French made him useful to the commanders, and he stayed in Nova Scotia after the fighting ended. He did not live year-round in the province, however, but chose to spend his winters in Boston. Mascarene socialized ambitiously in the Massachusetts capital and eventually became a leading personality. He married the daughter of a prominent Boston family in 1714, constructed a large brick house, and eventually raised four children in the city.[84] In 1715 he was elected to the vestry of King's Chapel, Boston's principal Anglican Church.[85] Few Bostonians were mentioned favorably in the newspapers more frequently than Mascarene. When he fell ill a local newspaper published a poem dedicated to his recovery.[86] When he had his portrait painted by the noted local artist John Smibert, the newspaper published a poem praising the likeness.[87] Mascarene's life suggested that French ancestry by itself was no barrier to entry into British colonial society.

In the early 1730s Mascarene joined forces with several other members of Nova Scotia's provincial council and Andrew Le Mercier, the pastor of the French Protestant church in Boston, and tried to recruit at least one hundred French Protestant families to settle in Nova Scotia.[88] They argued that their project would help bring security and prosperity to the province. As it happened, Boston's Huguenots did not come, but Mascarene continued to believe that French-speaking Protestant immigrants could change the religious and cultural life of the Acadians, and if he could not find other immigrants to do the job, he would do it himself. In the late 1730s and early 1740s, to promote the conversion of the Acadians, Mascarene engaged in an extended correspondence with Claude de la Vernede de St. Poncy, one of the Acadians' most strong-willed and defiant priests.

St. Poncy had arrived in Nova Scotia in 1732 to officiate among the villagers of Annapolis Royal. Upon his arrival he was assigned a chapel built by the provincial government within cannon shot of the fort. He indicated that he would have preferred a chapel farther away from the cannons, but the council refused to allow him to move, saying the church under the guns should stand as a "memorial" to the intransigence of some of his predecessors.[89] St. Poncy defied the government by saying mass in private homes farther away from the fortress, and for this and other offenses he was ordered out of the province in 1736.[90]

St. Poncy went to Louisbourg in the late summer of 1736 in compliance with his deportation order, but in October he returned and asked the council to permit him to resume his duties.[91] Over one hundred Acadian men from Annapolis Royal signed a petition in support of his request. The parishioners complained that they would be in spiritual danger if the government blocked their access to a priest.[92] By a margin of one vote, the council relented and agreed to allow St. Poncy to conduct services, but only in the chapel next to the fort and only until a new priest arrived to take his place.[93] St. Poncy served the local villagers that winter, but when his replacement arrived he refused to leave the province. He went to Beaubassin, resumed his clerical functions, and thereby implicated his new parishioners, including Jacques Maurice Vigneau, in his disobedience of the state.[94]

In 1738, despite the ongoing controversy over St. Poncy's defiance of the government, Mascarene sent him a letter encouraging him to convert to Protestantism. He enclosed a copy of the Thirty-nine Articles of the Church of England. The priest responded enthusiastically, but not in the way that Mascarene had intended—St. Poncy tried to recruit Mascarene into the Catholic Church. The two men traded letters for the next three years, arguing over the merits of the Reformation and, citing precedents from early church history, debating the relationship between civil and ecclesiastical authority, hierarchy among the bishops, and papal infallibility.[95]

In 1740 Mascarene became acting governor of the British garrison and president of the provincial council. He used his new authority to make a friendly gesture to St. Poncy by granting him permission to spend four months at Minas.[96] The priest accepted the invitation, spent his allotted time at Minas, and obediently moved out of Nova Scotia when the time expired. But the attempt at official reconciliation went sour a few months later when St. Poncy notified Mascarene that he was back at Beaubassin.[97] He remained there for two years in defiance of government orders.[98] In 1742, St. Poncy tried to renew his correspondence with Mascarene over the merits of Protestantism, but the councilman put the priest's letter away unopened. In his last message to St. Poncy, Mascarene indicated that he would have liked to continue the correspondence but he could not do so without compromising his authority as president of the council.[99] The wholesale conversion of the Acadians would never be discussed so amicably again.

Looking back on his career from retirement in the 1750s, Mascarene took pride in what he called his "mildness."[100] When he headed the council he referred most matters of controversy to the deputies and the local Catholic priests, and he tried to maintain nominal British authority with the help of cooperative Acadian leaders. Mascarene's strategy worked best in Annapolis Royal, where his overtures to the Acadians almost certainly helped secure the support, or at least the obedience, of many of them during the War of the Austrian Succession. But Mascarene's ultimate failure to get St. Poncy to comply with government orders revealed a contradiction within his tactics. While he wanted the Acadians' loyalty and voluntary cooperation, he was unwilling, as a matter of abstract principle, to compromise his government's authority over the Acadians' lives. Thus the Acadians could not rely on "mildness" as a permanent policy, and no kind words or gestures could resolve the uncertainties surrounding their legal status as inhabitants of a nominally British-ruled land.

After the oath-taking ceremonies in 1729 and 1730 the Acadians were officially deemed subjects of the British crown, but questions persisted concerning the extent to which they had become "British" or fully acquired the rights normally associated with that status. The lingering uncertainty surrounding their position within the empire was reflected in the vocabulary that was commonly used to refer to them. Almost every English-speaker in the region still called the Acadians "French." The more specific word "Acadian" had barely entered into the English language. After the start of the War of the Austrian Succession in 1744, many English-speakers began calling the Acadians "French neutrals," and that label would remain in common use through the 1750s. Its meaning, however, was complicated. The Acadians were called "neutral" because they had forsworn participation in armed conflict. But by the 1740s many English-speakers doubted the sincerity of the Acadians' oaths, and for them "French neutral" became a term of derision, frequently used in print alongside dismissive parenthetical qualifiers such as "(as they are improperly called)" or "(falsely so-called)."[101] These phrases served to emphasize that many English-speakers had no label they could apply comfortably to the Acadians.

Such labeling issues were particularly important in the regions beyond the vicinity of Annapolis Royal. In the provincial capital, British colonial officials were able to assess the loyalty and service of the local villagers as individuals. But in their dealings with Acadians in other communities they judged them in groups. The deputy system exacerbated the problem. While it facilitated peaceful relations between the Acadians and the provincial government until 1744, it also established a pattern of interaction in which the authorities issued orders to entire villages, and no statutes or legal precedents defined the circumstances under which the Acadians could be punished collectively. This was an issue that would be confronted repeatedly during the mid-century wars.

Chapter Five

Ile Royale, New England, Scotland, and Nova Scotia, 1744–1748

IN 1739, after a series of disputes arising out of Spanish efforts to regulate trade in the Caribbean, Britain went to war with Spain. Sir Robert Walpole had tried to settle his government's differences with Spain peacefully, but domestic opposition to his foreign policy forced his hand. The Walpole ministry's opponents rallied a significant portion of the British public in support of war with Spain in part by associating the interests of British merchants abroad with the political liberties of Britons at home. They cited the government's willingness to negotiate with the Spanish as evidence of Walpole's corruption and an indication that he was willing to sacrifice British liberty and subordinate himself to the Catholic powers to advance his own political ends. At public rallies and in the press, the supporters of war called themselves "patriots," and by linking domestic liberty with power overseas, they created a new, broader base of political support for British imperial expansion.[1]

The inhabitants of North America's eastern maritime region followed these events with great interest, assuming that the Anglo-Spanish conflict would broaden into a larger conflagration and that Britain and France would soon be at war. One result was a precipitous decline in the number of New England fishermen visiting Canso. The New Englanders feared a French attack on the island, and many abandoned it after 1739. It turned out that the fishermen were right, though Europe's diplomats staved off war between the British and the French longer than the colonists anticipated. The War of the Austrian Succession, Britain's war with France, began only in 1744, after Walpole had been driven from power. It started far from the coasts of Nova Scotia, but the French on Ile Royale exploited the outbreak of hostilities almost immediately by joining forces with Mi'kmaq allies and attacking the British settlement on Canso after the word arrived from Europe that war had been declared.

In response to the attack on Canso, Massachusetts entered the conflict, first by sending reinforcements to defend the garrison at Annapolis Royal, and then in 1745 (acting alongside forces from elsewhere in New England) by seizing Louisbourg. The New Englanders sent most of the French colonial population of Ile Royale to France, but the French military remained active in the region nonetheless, particularly in the eastern part of peninsular Nova Scotia.

The fighting disrupted the conditions that had allowed for relative peace in Nova Scotia over the previous eighteen years by forcing almost all the inhabitants to answer questions that many of them had previously been able to avoid. The Mi'kmaq and the English-speaking colonists, especially on the Atlantic coast, had to define in clearer terms the meaning of Mi'kmaq claims to the land. The Acadians throughout the province had to determine under what circumstances they were obliged to support the British colonial government or resist demands made on them by the government's French and Mi'kmaq opponents. Persons of mixed ancestry, and others whose way of life defied simple categorization as "French," "British," or "Indian," had to decide for official purposes in which community they belonged.

Almost every facet of daily life became politically significant. Growing crops and raising livestock in certain areas served the war efforts of the Mi'kmaq and the French and left the Acadians vulnerable to British reprisals. Other activities such as worshipping alongside native warriors or French soldiers, dancing with the men or helping Mi'kmaq women care for their children, acquired new importance in the context of the war. And even those who avoided contact with the fighting men or their families had reason to monitor and reevaluate their habits because the British used behavioral cues to determine whether a person was Mi'kmaq. From 1744 onward the Massachusetts government offered prizes for the scalps of the native people.

The New England colonists who participated in military action in and around Nova Scotia in some respects closely resembled those of earlier generations who had fought in the maritime region, and the War of the Austrian Succession only served to intensify existing patterns of interracial violence. But in other respects the mid-eighteenth-century New Englanders were very different from their predecessors. Partly under the influence of the new brand of imperial patriotism, which had spread across the Atlantic since the start of the war with Spain, many New England colonists saw their actions as part of a larger imperial project, one they embraced without the misgivings of the old Puritans. Following their victory at Louisbourg the colonists celebrated in a way they had never done before.[2]

After 1745 political developments in Britain helped recast the terms of the debate surrounding the Acadians. In 1746, in the aftermath of an uprising in Scotland on behalf of the Stuart claimant to the throne, the British government debated a series of measures designed to pacify broad stretches of the Scottish Highlands and culturally assimilate the High-landers. Ideas originally developed as a solution for perceived problems in Scotland were considered as policy options for the Acadians. Perhaps the most important idea that reached America in this way was a proposal to move suspect populations within the British Empire. Before the pacifi-cation of the Highlands, those who had proposed moving the Acadians imagined that they would be expelled altogether from the British colo-nies (as the New Englanders sent the French colonists from Ile Royale to France in 1745). But from 1746 forward, under the influence of propos-als developed in the Scottish context, the debate shifted as policymakers considered forced migrations designed to incorporate the Acadians into the communal life of British North America.

In the years following the outbreak of the War of the Austrian Suc-cession, events far from Nova Scotia had profound effects on the lives of the peoples of the province. This chapter highlights the influence of groups who came to the colony from elsewhere in the British and French Empires. It begins with the decision of the French colonial administrators on Ile Royale to attack the British fishery at Canso, and proceeds with an analysis of the military response of the New Englanders and the impact of the imperial war on the lives of the Mi'kmaq and the Acadians.

When the French colonial authorities began the large-scale settle-ment of Ile Royale in 1714, they had hoped that the island colony would attract most, if not all, of the Mi'kmaq and the Acadians. The French suc-ceeded in convincing some Acadian families to move, though fewer than they expected. Similarly, Ile Royale attracted fewer Mi'kmaq than the French would have preferred, and many of those who went only visited. Nonetheless, even without a wholesale migration of Mi'kmaq and Aca-dians from Nova Scotia, the French colony on Ile Royale prospered. By the early 1740s, Louisbourg alone had nearly two thousand inhabitants; three-quarters were civilians, including the families of soldiers, fishermen, colonial officials, merchants, artisans, and laborers. The island as a whole had a population approaching five thousand.[3]

Though the French could not entice all the Mi'kmaq or Acadians to move to Ile Royale, various French missionaries and colonial officials remained interested in the affairs of the peoples of Nova Scotia. They continued to think of the Acadians as compatriots, and they thought of the Mi'kmaq as a client people, dependent on the French for pastoral care, trade, and a measure of political direction. As early as 1734, Joseph Saint-Ovide de Brouillan, the governor of Ile Royale, made tentative plans to retake Nova Scotia in the event of a war.[4] His advisors assured him that all of the Acadians and most of the Mi'kmaq would greet the French forces as liberators. Subsequent administrators continued to hold similar views.[5] The outbreak of the War of the Austrian Succession presented the colony's officials with an apparent opportunity to bring the Mi'kmaq and the Acadians back within the borders of the French Empire. Instead of asking them to move, the French would try to shift the boundary and drive Britain's colonial administration away.

The French attack on Canso was intended as a first step toward recapturing all of Nova Scotia. There were several reasons for striking the fishing settlement first. Driving the British from Canso foreclosed any possibility that the island could be used as a base for privateers. The French also hoped to cripple the British fishery in the North Atlantic and thereby acquire a larger share of the world market in fish. Canso seemed vulnerable, and since some of the British settlers there had well-furnished homes, the possibility of plunder made it easier for the French to recruit volunteer troops in Louisbourg. Furthermore, many of the Mi'kmaq continued to resent the British presence on the Atlantic coast, and thus the attack on Canso helped secure a wartime Franco-Mi'kmaq alliance.[6]

The decision to start with an attack on the fishing settlement appears in retrospect to have been a strategic mistake, however, because it had the effect of bringing New Englanders into the conflict from the moment the fighting began.[7] Though they had lost Canso, New England's fishermen and privateers could reach the waters off Nova Scotia from other bases, and the Atlantic fishing banks soon became a battle zone, as New Englanders sought retaliation against the French, and the French responded in kind. In a matter of months hundreds of fishing vessels were taken or destroyed.[8] Within Massachusetts, fishermen supported Governor William Shirley's decision to reinforce the garrison of Annapolis Royal, and fishermen were among the earliest proponents of his project to seize Ile Royale.[9]

More than anyone else it was Shirley who defined and directed New England's response to the renewal of conflict in the maritime region. In many ways he personified an increasingly dominant, cosmopolitan outlook among active members of New England's political elite.[10] He was an

English-born lawyer who had trained in London; he had lived in Massachusetts only since 1731, and remained equally at ease on both sides of the Atlantic Ocean. Shirley secured the Massachusetts governorship in 1741 with the help of his patron, Secretary of State Thomas Hollis-Pelham, the duke of Newcastle, and he entered office at a time when Massachusetts was badly divided. Economic disruptions associated with the war with Spain, political struggles over the emission of paper money, and religious upheavals associated with revivalism had combined to divide the colonial population into a complex set of mutually antagonistic groups.[11] Shirley never gained the support of all the colonists, but, as several historians have shown, his military ventures gave him the patronage power he needed to secure political support from the competing factions and govern Massachusetts effectively.[12] Self-interested merchants and office-seekers supported Shirley and his campaign against the French, as did a broad cross-section of the colonial public, including evangelical preachers, conservative Congregationalists and Anglicans, fishermen, and young men eager to advance their prospects through military service and the acquisition of land. The New England churches abandoned their earlier reticence and endorsed Shirley's actions.[13] It helped that the French and the Mi'kmaq appeared to be the aggressors.

The early reports of combat appearing in the Massachusetts newspapers emphasized the participation of Mi'kmaq warriors and presented them in the worst possible light. In June 1744 a correspondent to the *Boston Gazette* indicated that the Mi'kmaq who took part in the attack on Canso had pleaded with the French for permission to slaughter the English-speaking residents of the town and that the French had struggled to restrain them.[14] Similar stories were repeated often during the war and served to convince many New Englanders that the Mi'kmaq were innately irrational and violent.[15]

Such beliefs had long circulated in Massachusetts, and they inspired the New England colonists during the War of the Austrian Succession to adopt a stance toward the Mi'kmaq similar to the one they had adopted in their previous wars. But in 1744 and 1745 the colonists were mobilized for war in the maritime region on an unprecedented scale.

On October 20, 1744 the government of Massachusetts officially declared war on the Mi'kmaq.[16] Five days later the Massachusetts General Court offered a bounty of £100 (provincial currency) for the scalp of any adult male member of the Mi'kmaq nation. For the scalps of women and children, the legislature offered £50.[17] Similar rewards were available for Mi'kmaq prisoners taken alive. Recognizing that it would be difficult to identify scalps by tribe, on November 2 Shirley announced that he would grant a reward for any "Indian" killed or captured east of the St. Croix River, regardless of his or her language group. By necessity he made an exception for native warriors serving under the Anglo-American military command.[18]

There is no record of Jean-Baptiste Cope's activities during the war, but the mission near his home on the Shubenacadie River became a center of Mi'kmaq resistance. The resident missionary at the Shubenacadie mission, Jean-Louis Le Loutre, served as the principal intermediary between the French forces and the Mi'kmaq on peninsular Nova Scotia. It was Le Loutre who informed the Mi'kmaq in the interior of Nova Scotia of the plan to strike at Canso, and, acting on the advice of the governor of Louisbourg, he also sent them directions to lay siege to Annapolis Royal in the weeks immediately after that attack. Le Loutre accompanied Mi'kmaq warriors to the British colonial capital and played an active role as an advisor to the Mi'kmaq in the first three years of the war.[19] Pierre Maillard, another missionary working among the Mi'kmaq, also traveled with the bands on the peninsula of Nova Scotia and at Ile Royale. He provided advice and delivered speeches aimed at strengthening the warriors' discipline and resolve.[20] After disease struck the Mi'kmaq in 1746, the missionaries told them that the British had deliberately infected them by distributing contaminated cloth.[21]

Le Loutre and Maillard may have argued more strenuously than necessary, because the scalp-bounty policy, by itself, was enough to foreclose easy reconciliation between the Mi'kmaq bands and the British. At least among those living within the traditional bands, almost all of the Mi'kmaq supported the war effort. They were fighting not just for land but for survival, and men, women, and children overcame severe hardships to keep the warriors afield. The choices facing the Mi'kmaq bands seemed simple; Mi'kmaq-speakers who lived away from their ancestral bands among the Acadians, and the descendents of such individuals, had more complicated decisions to make.

On January 4, 1745 a group of Acadian deputies from eastern Nova Scotia brought a petition to the provincial council. They had heard about the new scalp-bounty policy and feared for the safety of some of their neighbors. The Acadians, they said, had "a great number of mulattoes amongst them who had taken the oath and who were allied to the greatest families."[22] The delegates asked the council to rule whether people of mixed ancestry were liable to be scalped. The council deliberated on the matter and decided that persons with Mi'kmaq ancestry who lived

in the Acadian villages would not be subject to the bounty policy. Paul
Mascarene, the acting governor at the time, explained the decision.

In regard to the notion the inhabitants had amongst them that all who had any
Indian blood in them would be treated as enemies, it was a very great mistake,
since if that had been the design of the New England armed vessels it might very
well be supposed that the inhabitants of this river, many of whom have Indian
blood in them, and some even who live within the reach of the cannon, would
not be suffered to live peaceably as they do.[23]

The petitions from the Acadian deputies revealed the difficulty of
applying a racially based policy in Nova Scotia. Ancestry did not always
determine how a person lived, or what community he or she belonged to.
Nor did biology necessarily dictate anyone's political stance. The council's
statement to the Acadian deputies was intended to reassure them, though
it did not contain any clear standards for determining a person's vulnerability under the scalp-bounty program. At best, the councilmen had suggested that ancestry by itself did not define the risk. Farmers, herders,
merchants, and fishermen who spoke French, lived in Acadian villages,
and conformed to European customs would be exempted from the bounty
policy. But the ruling left an important question unanswered concerning
how thorough a person's integration into the Acadian community would
have to be to gain an exemption. The vagueness of the ruling promoted the
government's interest in an important respect: the ambiguity of national
categories made it imperative for many Acadians, particularly those with
family ties to the Mi'kmaq, to stay away from their Algonkian neighbors if
they wanted to avoid reclassification. But the question raised by the deputies would not go away. Officials in Nova Scotia struggled to define the
boundaries between the Mi'kmaq and the Acadian communities for the
next eleven years.

After their seizure of Louisbourg, the New Englanders transported
the French-speaking population of Ile Royale to France.[24] That decision inspired a brief debate within the provincial council of Nova Scotia
over the possibility of similarly expelling the Acadians, though the option
was ultimately rejected as impractical.[25] Proponents of deportation argued
that the Acadians had not taken valid oaths of allegiance and that their
refusal to contemplate military service undermined the credibility of their
professed loyalty to Britain. The councilmen also cited the Acadians' recent behavior. Those who favored removing them argued that they had
helped supply the French army and Mi'kmaq warriors and refused to sell
provisions to the British except at exorbitant prices. The Acadians had

seemed slow to inform the British about French and Mi'kmaq military preparations, and the councilmen assumed that they provided the French and the Mi'kmaq useful intelligence. Along with providing information and logistical support, the Acadians behaved in ways that boosted enemy morale. According to a report of the provincial council, when Mi'kmaq warriors and French soldiers first laid siege to Annapolis Royal, Acadian "men, women and children frequented the enemy's quarters at their mass, prayers, dancing and all other ordinary occasions."[26]

As the debate over expelling the Acadians made clear, the outbreak of armed hostilities increased the political ramifications of many aspects of the Acadians' lives. When Acadian merchants and farmers raised the price of food, the men in the garrison interpreted the action as a show of support for the king of France. When Acadian women danced with French soldiers, provincial councilmen took it as evidence of sedition. In part because their daily behavior came under scrutiny, many Acadians who had formerly worked closely with the provincial government fled Annapolis Royal when the fighting began.[27] Prudent Robichaud, for example, disappeared.[28]

Acadian men and women reacted to the pressures of living in wartime in various ways, and it is difficult to generalize about their behavior. A few young men left their homes and went to fight alongside Mi'kmaq warriors.[29] Others hired themselves out as civilian workers for the British army.[30] At least one merchant who had formerly traded with the British garrisons offered his services to the French military and spent the war ferrying men and equipment to French-controlled regions at the eastern end of the Bay of Fundy.[31] At the other extreme, Jacques Maurice Vigneau responded to the news of New England's capture of Louisbourg by volunteering his services to the council at Annapolis Royal. In 1746 he began carrying men, provisions, orders, and intelligence from the provincial capital across the isthmus of Chignecto and on by sea to British-controlled Louisbourg.[32]

If there was anything "typical" about the Acadians' pattern of behavior, it was that almost none of them could hold a consistent political stance. Vigneau, for example, had earlier played host to a commander of the French army. French soldiers had occupied his village, and he had little choice but to allow the officer to stay in his family's home. But according to French accounts Vigneau had been more than accommodating. He gave the commander information and advice, and made his ship available when the French decided to attack Annapolis Royal.[33] The British may not have known about Vigneau's earlier behavior when they gave him their business in 1746, but they would have had difficulty finding any merchant in Beaubassin who had refused to offer services to the French during the military occupation. Later in the war, when the French military returned, Vigneau and his family would again offer the commanding officer assistance.[34]

By 1746 the policy debates surrounding the Acadians had changed. Early in the conflict, Shirley and various members of Nova Scotia's provincial council had contemplated mass deportations or large-scale retributive raids, especially against the Acadian villagers at the eastern end of the Bay of Fundy, who seemed to have given the most assistance to the French and their native allies.[35] In 1745, writing to his commander on Ile Royale, Shirley had wistfully complained, "It grieves me much that I have it not in my power to send a part of 500 men forthwith to Menis [Minas] and burn Grand Pré, their chief town, and open all their sluices, and lay their country waste."[36] But by the winter of 1746 Shirley had shifted his efforts and began to seek ways to gain the Acadians' cooperation and ultimately win their hearts.

Several factors contributed to this change in thinking. In the previous summer a French fleet sent to recapture Louisbourg foundered on the Atlantic coast of Nova Scotia, and from that time forward the British military position seemed more secure, particularly at Annapolis Royal. Disease had swept through the Mi'kmaq community, killing hundreds and weakening the military power of the survivors.[37] Equally important, the New Englanders within the garrison at Annapolis Royal gradually changed their outlook toward the Acadians. Given more time to interact with the villagers outside the context of an immediate military crisis, they began to believe that they could gain the Acadians' friendship. The soldiers depended on Acadian farmers and merchants for food and firewood, and the social environment encouraged the men to seek the company of Acadians outside the context of trade.

In the first year of the war relations between the garrison and the community had deteriorated. Most of the Acadians in Annapolis Royal had shunned the English-speakers in their village when French or Mi'kmaq forces were in the area. In any event there were fewer English-speakers in the French-speaking village; most of the married officers and soldiers at Annapolis Royal had sent their wives and children to Boston for protection, and the departure of their families helped cut the men off from the Acadian community, at least temporarily.[38] Over time new bonds were formed, however, and by the last two years of the war, official British discussions of the Acadians returned repeatedly to the issue of intermarriage between the soldiers and Acadian women.[39]

Overcoming significant cultural obstacles, by 1747 a few New England soldiers managed to court and marry Acadian women in Annapolis Royal.[40] According to reports that reached Shirley, the women who married the New England men were punished with excommunication from the Catholic Church. Shirley complained bitterly about the church's reaction. Though he hoped that the women would leave the church eventually, he knew that church-imposed sanctions would humiliate them and isolate them from their neighbors; excommunication was a strong deterrent to intermarriage. Shirley objected not only for the sake of the soldiers and their spouses, but also because he believed that the church's policy deterred British settlement in Nova Scotia. Almost certainly exaggerating the influence of the policy, he claimed that it "has had so general an effect as to prevent the settlement of any one English family within the province."[41]

When Shirley referred to "English" families, he meant families in which the husband spoke English. This is evident, not only in the context of his concern over the marital fortunes of the soldiers, but also in light of long-term proposals he was developing to promote marriages between Acadian women and English-speaking settlers in Nova Scotia. Intermarriage became a central feature of Shirley's project to transform the Acadians culturally. He wanted to convert them to Protestantism, teach them English, and make them loyal British subjects. As part of that program, he wanted to change the composition of the Acadians' families by encouraging soldiers to settle permanently in Nova Scotia and providing Acadian women with incentives to marry English-speakers and Protestants. He also wanted to force the Acadian women to send their children to English-language schools so that their descendants would become, as he succinctly put it, "English Protestants."[42]

Shirley advanced this plan in response to the experiences of the soldiers at Annapolis Royal. Though only a few marriages had taken place between the men of the garrison and Acadian women, he saw those unions as a model for social development in the entire colony. In 1747 Shirley began designing a project to intermingle soldiers and Acadians throughout the eastern Bay of Fundy region, to facilitate integration and gradual assimilation. Annapolis Royal gave him inspiration, but he was also responding to contemporary events in Britain, where the ministry was engaged in a similarly forceful effort at cultural assimilation.

During the winter of 1745, Charles Stuart led an uprising in Scotland in an effort to place his father on the British throne. Though he was ultimately defeated, he received considerable support in certain parts of the Scottish Highlands. Charles was a Catholic and he had counted among his supporters a disproportionate number of Catholics and "nonjurant" Anglicans, communicants in a conservative wing of British Protestantism. It also seemed from the perspective of British policymakers that his support had been strongest among impoverished Highlanders who came from remote pastoral regions where the clans maintained their own juridical traditions and where a considerable amount of economic activity depended on barter and other forms of nonmonetary exchange. After defeating the Stuart forces, the British government adopted a set of measures designed to "pacify" the Scottish Highlands by destroying the economic and cultural conditions that they believed underlay support for Charles.[43]

Beginning in 1746, Parliament outlawed Highland dress, made it illegal for the Highlanders to carry weapons, abolished the local court system, and confiscated the property of all those who had fought for the Stuart cause. Missionaries were sent to the Highlands along with land speculators and other investors with the aim of establishing model towns where, through a combination of educational work, economic coercion, and government regulation, the Highlanders could be converted to authorized forms of Protestantism and taught to participate in the market economy. One individual involved in the pacification program summed up the theory as follows: "Make then the Highlanders as rich and industrious as the people of Manchester and they will be as little apt to rebel."[44]

In 1746 Admiral Charles Knowles, who had helped guard the sea lanes to Britain during the Stuart uprising, became governor of British-occupied Ile Royale.[45] After he moved to America he continued to participate in the policy debates surrounding the pacification of Scotland, and he brought William Shirley into the debates. Knowles endorsed an idea advanced by William Augustus, duke of Cumberland, that entire Highland clans should be sent to America, and he suggested that space should be cleared for them in Nova Scotia. The Acadians, he argued, could be moved to make room.[46]

When he first learned of this proposal Shirley opposed it, but after a raid against New England troops stationed in Minas in the winter of 1746–47, he entered into an extensive correspondence with Knowles, and the two men worked out a plan to relocate at least part of the Acadian population.[47] They agreed to abandon the idea of replacing the villagers with Highlanders, but endorsed the general theory behind that plan, that shifting peoples within the empire would be an effective way to control them. In a joint letter to the secretary of state they recommended using military force to expel the most "obnoxious" Acadians and replace them with Protestant immigrants. In time the Protestants would come to dominate their

new communities, and under their influence "the present generation of the
French [Acadians] might be made at least contented, peaceable subjects,
and the next generation good Protestant ones." [48] The governors predicted
that the introduction of immigrants, and the creation of a cosmopolitan
society, would transform the Acadians and turn them into loyal subjects.
They did not believe that all of the newcomers had to come from Great
Britain. Citing the history of Pennsylvania, they claimed that Swiss and
German settlers could serve effectively as promoters of British imperial
culture.

In spite of his original misgivings, Shirley soon discovered that he
liked the idea of directing the process of migration with the purpose of
transforming Acadian society, and he began developing more elaborate
plans. In the summer of 1747 he proposed sending two thousand New England troops to the isthmus of Chignecto, to clear the region of its inhabitants and settle on the vacated land. The dispossessed Acadians would be
taken to New England and placed in scattered towns in Rhode Island,
Connecticut, Massachusetts, and New Hampshire.[49] If everything proceeded as Shirley anticipated, the New England settlers in Nova Scotia
would intermingle and intermarry with the Acadians. Similarly, the relocated Acadian families would get absorbed into New England.[50] Shirley
was ready to proceed with this experiment, but his superiors in London
stopped him. As long as the war with France continued, the ministers opposed the relocation program on the grounds that it would divert scarce
resources from other projects, and when the war ended in 1748 the military
justification for moving the Acadians lost its force.[51]

The Treaty of Aix-la-Chapelle ending the War of the Austrian Succession ceded Ile Royale back to France.[52] The cession was controversial
in Britain and even more so in Massachusetts, where hundreds of families had lost husbands, sons, and fathers in military service on the island.[53]
The Massachusetts government had also nearly bankrupted itself and destroyed the value of the provincial currency financing the Louisbourg expedition, an aborted 1746 expedition to Canada, and the reinforcement of
Nova Scotia.[54] After the terms of the treaty were announced Shirley tried
to soften the blow by getting the ministry to reimburse the Massachusetts government for its expenses. He also asked the imperial authorities
to sponsor an effort to resettle and fortify Nova Scotia so that it could
be prosperous, secure, and self-sufficient. A central element of Shirley's
project was to assimilate the Acadians into a new, cosmopolitan, British
colonial society, and he hoped to accomplish this feat by directing a series
of large-scale migrations.

In the winter of 1748 Shirley commissioned a survey of the eastern
end of the Bay of Fundy. He wanted to identify hills and islands appropriate for forts, and farmland that could be confiscated to support new
immigrants (see figure 11).[55] Shirley sent his surveyor's report to London in February 1749, along with a proposal to resettle Nova Scotia with
farmers from England, Germany, Switzerland, and other parts of Europe.
He did not intend to send any of the Acadians out of Nova Scotia to make
room for the new settlers. He suggested instead that some of the Acadians should be moved within the colony. Shirley considered short-distance
moves necessary, because he wanted to intermingle European immigrants
with Acadians. If all the current inhabitants of Nova Scotia were allowed
to stay where they were, the province would remain divided, with a geo-
graphically separate French-speaking Catholic community.[56]

The proposal to settle Nova Scotia with Protestants from continental
Europe helped Shirley politically in Massachusetts. At least since 1747, in
serialized publications and newspapers, the governor's opponents in Boston had complained that the Louisbourg expedition and the reinforcement of Annapolis Royal had drained New England's labor supply.[57] Citing treatises on political economy, they had generalized from recent experience and argued that population density was the source of economic
and military strength. By scattering the population, any effort to expand
the territories of the British Empire in North America risked leaving the
existing colonies underpopulated, poor, and vulnerable.[58]

The most prominent writer advancing these arguments was William
Douglass, a wealthy, Scottish-born medical doctor who had lived in New
England since the 1720s.[59] In the early 1740s Douglass served as a commercial agent for Nova Scotia's acting governor, Paul Mascarene.[60] Because of his association with Mascarene, Douglass was well informed on
the history of Nova Scotia and conditions within in the eastern province.
Especially in the late 1740s he was angry that the Massachusetts governor
seemed to disregard his advice.[61] But in 1749, in the aftermath of the Treaty
of Aix-la-Chapelle, Shirley's political position seemed precarious, and he
and his supporters went out of their way to demonstrate that they were
willing to listen. In support of their argument that Nova Scotia should be
settled by Britons and continental European Protestants, they cited principles of political economy that had been popularized in New England
by Douglass. Pleased to see the theories he had advanced paraphrased,
Douglass applauded Shirley's efforts to get the ministry to fund Protestant
settlement in Nova Scotia. He agreed with the governor that a regulated
program of immigration, carefully scattered placement, education, mis-

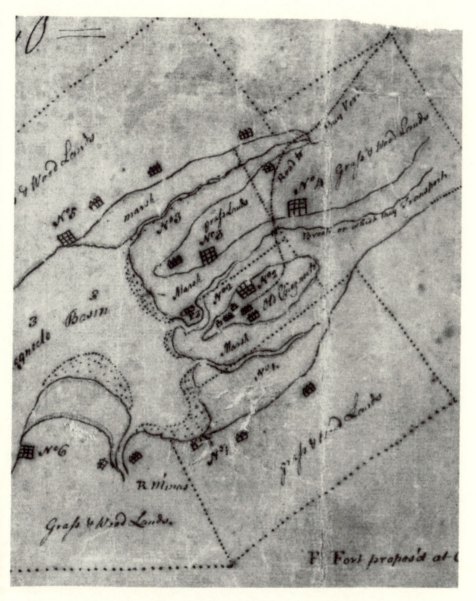

Figure 11. Map prepared by Charles Morris identifying proposed locations for the settlement of Protestant colonists in and around the Acadian village of Beaubassin, or "Old Chignecto." The nine-square grids represent sites for the placement of Protestant settlers; the small cottage-shapes with roofs represent Acadian villagers. Map in the collections of the British Public Record Office, Kew, England, CO 700, Nova Scotia 13.

sionary work, and intermarriage could transform both the Acadians and the European immigrants into loyal, industrious British subjects, and that New England would not lose population in the process.[62]

British political elites as well as New Englanders had taken an interest in Ile Royale in the long months of negotiation leading up to the conclusion of the Treaty of Aix-la-Chappelle.[63] It was a measure of the new importance of imperial issues in British politics that the government's opponents in Parliament and in the press hoped to exploit the cession of the island back to France as an embarrassment to the ministry. In an effort to limit political damage at home, alleviate the social ills associated with demobilization, and placate restive New Englanders, in 1749 the Board of Trade appointed Edward Cornwallis, a veteran of the pacification of the Scottish Highlands, as governor of Nova Scotia, and Parliament allocated a large sum of money to encourage Protestant settlement in the colony.[64] The British government offered veterans free transportation, land, tools, and a year's worth of provisions, and asked nothing in return except that they take the trip to Nova Scotia. It offered the same terms to carpenters, bricklayers, and other laborers with economically valuable skills.[65] In 1749 the ministry spent over £40,000 to encourage the settlement of the province.[66] In addition to recruiting in England, agents of the government traveled to France, the valley of the Rhine, and Switzerland in search of Protestants willing to move.[67]

The Board of Trade directed Cornwallis to establish a Protestant town at Chebucto Harbor (present-day Halifax) and then disperse some of the new colonists in Acadian-dominated regions around the Bay of Fundy.[68] The board also instructed him to make sure that the new townships included both Protestants and "French Inhabitants" (Acadians), "to the End that the said French Inhabitants may be subjected to such Rules and Orders as may hereafter be made for the better ordering and governing the said Townships."[69] The governor was also told to establish "Protestant schools," "to the end that the said French inhabitants may be converted to the Protestant religion and their children brought up in the principles of it."[70] Following Shirley's advice, the Board of Trade directed Cornwallis to encourage intermarriage between Acadians and Protestants, and to apprehend, try, and punish any Catholic priest who censured his parishioners for marrying out of the faith.[71] If everything had gone as the ministers wished, within a few generations the Acadians would have converted to Protestantism and joined the new colonists as equals in a single society.

The project of resettling Nova Scotia with a diverse Protestant population, and the articulation of the plan to absorb Acadians into the cultural mix, reflected political developments beyond the shores of the colony. In many parts of the British Empire, public officials were rethinking what it meant to be a British subject and trying to devise new ways to incorporate persons of varying cultural backgrounds into a single political community. The eighteenth-century "British" nation had always been an aggregation of peoples with distinctive histories and traditions. As Linda Colley has argued, the promoters of British nationalism accommodated themselves to the existence of cultural differences in part by concentrating on a few ideals that Britons were presumed to share, such as opposition to Catholicism and loyalty to the Crown.[72] The opening of the British colonies to Protestant immigrants from continental Europe reflected a growing confidence that such settlers would adopt these minimal necessary attributes of "Britishness." Nonetheless, the recent events in the Scottish Highlands served as an object lesson on the dangers that could arise when culturally distinct communities within the realm refused to adhere to the necessary ideals.

Cornwallis was chosen for the post of governor of Nova Scotia in part because of the experience and reputation he had gained serving in the pacification of the Scottish Highlands. He knew almost nothing about Nova Scotia, and neither did many of his assistants. After they arrived on the Atlantic coast of the peninsula the conditions of life there surprised them. Like Samuel Vetch a generation earlier, they would have to modify their plans.

Chapter Six

The French, the Mi'kmaq, and the Collapse of the Provincial Government's Plans, 1749–1754

JUST as the British responded to the Treaty of Aix-la-Chapelle by establishing a new fortified settlement at Halifax and attempting to expand their presence in the Bay of Fundy region, the French attempted a similar set of projects. They repaired and expanded Louisbourg, built forts on lands claimed by the British on the St. John River and at the northern end of the isthmus of Chignecto, and attempted again to draw the Mi'kmaq and the Acadians out of peninsular Nova Scotia. Neither the Mi'kmaq nor the Acadians were willing to leave the peninsula en masse, however, and the combined effect of the founding of Halifax and the resurgence of French imperialism in the region was to divide both the Mi'kmaq and the Acadian communities and plunge Nova Scotia into an era of endemic violence. Mi'kmaq warriors took up arms to defend their lands on the Atlantic coast of Nova Scotia from further British intrusions. Nova Scotia's provincial government renewed the policy of offering bounties for the scalps of Mi'kmaq men, women, and children; and after the fighting started the French authorities on Ile Royale gave the warriors encouragement by offering prizes for the scalps of British soldiers. In the Bay of Fundy region, Acadian villagers who refused to move to French-controlled territory faced threats of physical violence from three sources: the British, the Mi'kmaq, and the French military.

In 1749 and 1750 the issues dividing the peoples of the region seemed to resolve themselves into a pair of stark oppositions. The territorial dispute between the empires resulted in a military standoff on the isthmus of Chignecto, where the opposing sides built two forts, one French and the other British, to mark a de facto imperial border. Similarly, the conflict between the Mi'kmaq and the British colonial government resulted in the drawing of a boundary line, only slightly more abstract, classifying and separating peoples. Cornwallis declared his intention to reserve the peninsula for persons of European descent and exclude anyone identified as "Indian." In response, various leaders of the Mi'kmaq articulated what appeared to be exactly the opposite position, that the peninsula belonged exclusively to *les sauvages*. But the apparent simplicity of both of these oppositions, dividing lands and peoples, proved illusory. Even after the construction of the forts on the isthmus of Chignecto the territorial border between the empires was permeable, and events on the peninsula quickly shattered any notion that the inhabitants of Nova Scotia could be categorized simply into two groups. Every community was divided internally and a web of interrelationships linked members of all the peoples of the region—Acadians, Mi'kmaq, "foreign Protestants," British, and French.

By 1751, in the context of ongoing warfare between the British and the Mi'kmaq, various officials in London and Halifax began to doubt the wisdom of Cornwallis's original instructions. Instead they advanced alternative proposals designed to keep the "foreign Protestants," in particular, away from the Mi'kmaq and the Acadians. They were concerned for the safety of the new settlers, but they also feared that the Acadians, Mi'kmaq, or French might exert a subversive influence on the immigrants. Simultaneously, Cornwallis and his successors sought peace (on their own terms) with the Mi'kmaq. But the one treaty they managed to negotiate, with Jean-Baptiste Cope as leader of the Shubenacadie Mi'kmaq band, collapsed within months of its ratification. Thereafter, none of the policies that the government pursued could bring order to the province.

The administrative difficulties an earlier generation of colonial officials had encountered in the 1720s, when they tried to establish distinct legal regimes for the Mi'kmaq and the Acadians, were compounded in the more complex environment of the early 1750s. The introduction of new settlers from Britain and a variety of European nations, coupled with the assertiveness of the nearby French imperial regime and the Mi'kmaq bands, undermined the confidence of the men charged with governing Nova Scotia. In these circumstances they no longer trusted their own ability to assess, track, and predict the political allegiances of the region's diverse communities. Furthermore, at crucial moments the colonial officials' practice of characterizing entire villages, bands, and nations as groups prevented them from working amicably with individual men and women among the Mi'kmaq or the Acadians who might have offered them assistance.

The narrative of this chapter emphasizes the role Jean-Baptiste Cope and Jacques Maurice Vigneau played in the conflicts of the early 1750s. Their experiences demonstrate how difficult it was for contemporaries—

and remains to be for historians—to evaluate the loyalties of the region's inhabitants or interpret their behavior. Almost all the players active in Nova Scotia during this tumultuous decade were forced to shift their political stance in response to specific events. Furthermore, given the pressures placed upon individuals such as Cope and Vigneau, almost everything they said and did was subject to conflicting interpretations. One immediate result of these circumstances was a breakdown of trust. Many British colonial officials, in particular, began to doubt whether they could settle Nova Scotia peacefully alongside either the Mi'kmaq or the Acadians.

After France recovered Ile Royale in 1748, French colonists came back to the island with renewed ambition. A large number of the former settlers who had been evicted by the New Englanders in 1745 returned, and they brought along with them a significant body of new colonists and the largest contingent of resident troops the island had seen in peacetime. The French fishery on Ile Royale was soon operating at pre-1744 levels, and Louisbourg resumed its place as a prominent port in the North Atlantic.[1]

Prior to 1744 the settlers and soldiers at Louisbourg had depended on Acadian-grown food. But with the strengthening of Britain's military position in the region after 1749, it seemed unlikely that the Acadians would be able to travel so freely to Ile Royale in the future to engage the French in trade.[2] Therefore the French had a strong pragmatic incentive for luring the Acadians out of British-ruled Nova Scotia. They planned to establish new settlements along the coasts of the Gulf of St. Lawrence and on the northern shores of the Bay of Fundy. They also intended to establish a military presence among the Acadians in present-day New Brunswick, on lands that the British claimed lay within the boundaries of the British-ruled colony.[3] The territorial dispute led to a military standoff between the French and the British on the isthmus of Chignecto in 1750.

The scope of France's imperial projects, coming at the same time that the British were establishing their settlement at Halifax, guaranteed that there would be tension in the maritime region. But despite the dramatic simplicity of the confrontation on the isthmus of Chignecto, where the French and British built forts within a few hundred yards of each other, the controversies of the early 1750s involved more than the location of the imperial boundary. The French and the British were also engaged in a struggle over the status of the Acadians, and the Mi'kmaq were simultaneously arguing, with each other and with the British, over the extent of their autonomy and the nature of their claims to land. Everyone in the region, whether they spoke English, French, Mi'kmaq, or German, had particular interests to defend, and rather than simply pitting the British against the French, the conflicts of the 1750s divided every community in Nova Scotia.

Jean-Baptiste Cope was one of the first inhabitants of the region to see his community divided. Cope's band was based along the Shubenacadie River near the mission that since 1738 had served as the base of operations for Jean-Louis Le Loutre, a missionary passionately engaged in promoting the imperial interests of France.[4] In 1749 Le Loutre announced that he was moving his mission to the isthmus of Chignecto, where he, along with a body of French soldiers, military officers, and sympathetic settlers, hoped to establish a new community loyal to the French crown.[5] Le Loutre encouraged the Mi'kmaq living along the Shubenacadie to join him.

Conscious of the Mi'kmaq's devotion to their homes, the missionary did not issue any ultimatums. He did not threaten to abandon those who refused to leave their ancestral villages, nor did he (despite British predictions of missionary behavior) ever suggest that he might deny those who stayed access to the sacraments. Nonetheless, regardless of Le Loutre's intentions, the effect of his announcement was to divide the Shubenacadie Mi'kmaq band. By moving his mission, Le Loutre placed a physical distance between those who stayed on the river and the religious institutions that had long helped maintain links between the band and the other Algonkian—and French-speaking Catholic communities in the region.

Dozens of Mi'kmaq accepted Le Loutre's offer and followed him to the isthmus of Chignecto. In the fall of 1749, several of them accompanied him on tours of Acadian villages, where they tried to convince the Acadians to join them in leaving the peninsula.[6] But at least ninety of the Mi'kmaq refused to abandon their homes on the Shubenacadie. Cope was among them, and he soon became their principal elder and leader.[7] Cope's stance may have brought him temporarily into conflict with Le Loutre, but he would face a longer-term challenge from Nova Scotia's colonial government because Cornwallis had arrived with territorial ambitions of his own (see figure 12).

Cornwallis's instructions directed him to establish settlements of Protestants at several locations on the peninsula of Nova Scotia. The Board of Trade concentrated its attention on the Bay of Fundy region, where the Protestants were to be intermingled among the Acadians, but Cornwallis was directed to colonize other areas as well. The Shubenacadie region was not specifically targeted in the governor's initial instructions, but it was situated between two places that were: Chebucto Harbor, the

Figure 12. Edward Cornwallis. Portrait painted in 1755 by Sir George Chalmers. In the collection of the Public Archives of Nova Scotia, Halifax.

site of Halifax, and the eastern end of the Bay of Fundy. Cope and his followers had reason to feel threatened by the expansion of British settlement in both places, and furthermore they supported the Mi'kmaq on the Atlantic coast who eventually took up arms to defend their land.

Chebucto Harbor lay in an area that the British had refrained from entering since the end of their war with the Mi'kmaq in 1725. As early as 1746 William Shirley had identified it as a good place to begin the resettlement of Nova Scotia, but establishing a new town there violated implicit agreements between the British and the Mi'kmaq that had been in place for more than two decades.[8] Cornwallis anticipated that the Mi'kmaq might resist his efforts to place a settlement there, but he thought he could overwhelm them. He had thousands of settlers-in-waiting, and after they arrived they built Halifax at a furious pace. The stockades went up first, followed by barracks and houses, and within two months Halifax boasted more than 2,500 inhabitants (see figure 13).[9] In his optimistic moments the governor expected that the Mi'kmaq would be so intimidated by the scale of his project that they would accept it without a fight.

In the summer of 1749, as a preliminary step to facilitate the introduction of settlers across the peninsula, Cornwallis negotiated a peace agreement with Algonkian leaders from the northern side of the Bay of Fundy.[10] Then he directed the British commander at Fort George (on Casco Bay, in present-day Maine) to distribute food, blankets, and other provisions to the native peoples who came to his post.[11] The governor hoped that he might be able to convince the Mi'kmaq to make room for his settlers voluntarily.

But given the long history of armed hostilities between the English-speakers and the Mi'kmaq in the eighteenth century, such a peaceful outcome was hardly likely. The first shots were fired by English-speakers, probably New Englanders, who assumed that the Mi'kmaq would resist their efforts to occupy land. In the summer of 1749 a group of men whom the Mi'kmaq and the French identified as "English" arrived at Canso with the apparent intention of reviving the local fishery. The newcomers discovered a community of Mi'kmaq women and children whose fathers and husbands had gone away to hunt and fish. According to the Mi'kmaq, the "English" killed twenty women and children.[12] In September, when a second ship arrived at Canso from Boston, Mi'kmaq warriors seized the vessel and took twenty of the crew captive. Perhaps hoping to avert a full-scale war, they released the prisoners, but soon thereafter the fighting spread, first to the isthmus of Chignecto and finally to the vicinity of Halifax itself.[13]

Cornwallis was ready for this news; even before it arrived he had begun making tentative plans for a campaign against the peninsula's Mi'kmaq bands. He vowed that this would be the last Anglo-Mi'kmaq war and that there would be no peace agreement at the end of the fighting. Instead, he declared, he would "root" the Mi'kmaq out, forever.[14] The

Figure 13. Halifax in 1750. Detail from a map by Thomas Jefferys, "A Map of the Southern Part of Nova Scotia and Fishing Banks . . ." in the collections of the National Archives of Canada, Ottawa.

governor and his advisors predicted that expelling the Mi'kmaq would be "very practicable," and "no very difficult matter."[15]

When Cornwallis learned of the seizure of the ship at Canso he adopted a two-pronged strategy. First, he ordered the construction of new fortifications at the eastern end of the Bay of Fundy in an effort to cut the Mi'kmaq off from the Acadians and protect the Protestants whom he hoped to settle there.[16] Second, he reenacted the orders issued by the government of Massachusetts in 1744 and offered bounties for the scalps of Mi'kmaq men, women, and children. Following the advice of his council, on October 2 Cornwallis offered ten pounds sterling for each scalp and issued a proclamation directing the settlers at Halifax to "annoy distress take or destroy the savages commonly called Micmacs wherever they are found."[17] The councilmen refrained from formally declaring war on the Mi'kmaq because to do so would implicitly "own them a free people," and instead of organizing an expensive, large-scale military operation they chose to rely on the personal initiative of volunteers.[18]

The French on Ile Royale responded to these events by giving aid to the Mi'kmaq in their war.[19] In the closing years of the War of the Austrian Succession, the French had paid Mi'kmaq warriors for the scalps of British soldiers, and after 1749 they resumed the practice.[20] Assisting the Mi'kmaq in this way seemed to advance French imperial interests in the region, because warfare was likely to impede the growth of Halifax, which in turn would give a head start to the French at Louisbourg in the redevelopment of the fishery and in the competition for transatlantic trade. Equally important, Anglo-Mi'kmaq hostilities had the potential of preventing the British from spreading across the peninsula and surrounding the Acadians with Protestant settlers. The French wanted the Acadians for their own imperial projects.[21]

Though most of the Mi'kmaq were willing to accept French assistance, in their public pronouncements their spokesmen suggested that they were engaged in a war against all European intrusions into Nova Scotia. Declaring their opposition to the founding of Halifax in 1749, one group of Mi'kmaq leaders stated that the peninsula of Nova Scotia belonged to "les sauvages," a distinctive race literally born from the land. The translation of the statement that appeared in the British colonial newspapers read as follows: "I am sprung from the land as doth the grass. I that am savage, am born there, and my fathers before me. This land is mine inheritance, I swear it is, the land which God has given me to be my country forever."[22] Over the next few months Mi'kmaq resistance leaders repeatedly emphasized their status as "sauvages," and soon they began to claim that they represented all the native peoples of North America, "Micmacs, Mariches, Canbres, Hurons, Abenaquis et Esquimaux et le reste."[23]

By classifying persons by ancestry in their public pronouncements, the Mi'kmaq resistance leaders adopted a rhetorical stance in many ways similar to that of the British, who were offering prizes for the scalps of men, women, and children based on their classification as "Indians." The Mi'kmaq war leaders and the British were also pursuing military strategies that in some ways resembled each other. Both sides sought to segregate and isolate the other. Through intermittent raids the Mi'kmaq were able to confine the new settlers to the vicinity of Halifax. Similarly, the British intended to keep the Mi'kmaq away from the French and the Acadians.

These circumstances placed the Acadians in a difficult position. Economic interests, family ties, religious convictions, and friendships tied them variously to the Mi'kmaq, the British, and the French. Each Acadian village was divided in its loyalties, and physical coercion, in the form of threats of military action, forced many Acadians to behave in ways that may not have reflected their true convictions.

Some Acadians had greeted Cornwallis with apparent warmth when he first arrived at Chebucto Harbor in 1749. Teams of Acadian workmen helped build the walls around Halifax, while other Acadians cut a road linking the new provincial capital with Minas.[24] Acadian farmers and merchants helped feed the early settlers and declared that they wanted to cooperate with the new administration.[25] But within weeks reports began to reach Cornwallis from scattered parts of the Bay of Fundy region suggesting that the Acadians in that area were supporting the Mi'kmaq in their war. He heard from Jacques Maurice Vigneau's village of Beaubassin, for example, that in the winter of 1749 the villagers had cared for the wives and children of Mi'kmaq warriors who were engaged in hostilities against the British. The inhabitants of Beaubassin may or may not have considered such aid to their Mi'kmaq-speaking neighbors military assistance, but Cornwallis suspected that they were guilty of sedition.[26]

Cornwallis's doubts about Vigneau's village grew in the following spring, when a large body of native warriors joined forces with a contingent of French troops from Canada and entered Beaubassin. They asked the villagers to move to French-controlled land. Then someone stoked a fire and the village burned. One hundred forty houses were destroyed, and the warriors and soldiers escorted the newly homeless villagers to the northern side of the isthmus of Chignecto, where they established a new settlement called "Beauséjour." In the aftermath of the burning of Beaubassin the British engaged in a debate over the active role of the villagers in these events. Had they decided as a group to move to French-controlled territory and burned the houses they left behind? Or were they the victims of French aggression? Were they divided amongst themselves? The evidence seemed contradictory, and no satisfactory answer was found.[27]

During the following summer the French built a fort at Beauséjour (see figure 14). A community of Acadian émigrés, including dozens of migrants from Beaubassin, tended cattle in the lowlands surrounding the French battlements. They also worked on dikes, drained the salt marshes, and began preparing farms.[28]

Jacques Maurice Vigneau fared better than most in the new location. He had his ship with him, and he became a leading merchant in the area. But Vigneau blamed the French authorities for the sequence of events that had destroyed his old home. None of the Acadians were accustomed to encountering large-scale destruction from the actions of the French military or its agents, and Vigneau spoke for many when he voiced his resentment. In 1751 the military commander at Beauséjour asked the Acadians living in the area to swear allegiance to the king of France. Vigneau refused, and in a heated exchange with Le Loutre he declared that he wanted to "regain his independence" ("se rendre indépendant").[29] Overtly he spoke only for himself, but implicitly he made this declaration on behalf of all Acadians. Taking advantage of his stature in the local community, he became the chief spokesman for the refugees from Beaubassin who were displeased with the treatment they had received from the French authorities, and he delivered petitions on their behalf to the French colonial administration.[30]

In the autumn of 1750 the British sent an expeditionary force to the isthmus of Chignecto under the command of Charles Lawrence (the future governor of Nova Scotia). Lawrence's official mission was to dislodge the French from Beauséjour, but after he arrived and saw the French fortifications, he reassessed the situation and established an outpost of his own a few hundred yards to the east.[31] Shortly thereafter, an officer from Lawrence's camp was shot dead by an unidentified man in disguise.[32] Looking back on the incident years later, Cope claimed credit for killing the British officer.[33]

Several similar skirmishes occurred in the vicinity of Halifax, where civilian settlers as well as soldiers were subject to attack.[34] These actions did not result in large numbers of casualties, but they were sufficient to undermine the British government's plan to scatter Protestants across the peninsula. The cumulative effect of the intermittent attacks went beyond instilling terror. The provincial government's war with the Mi'kmaq divided the Protestant settlers and created an environment in which the

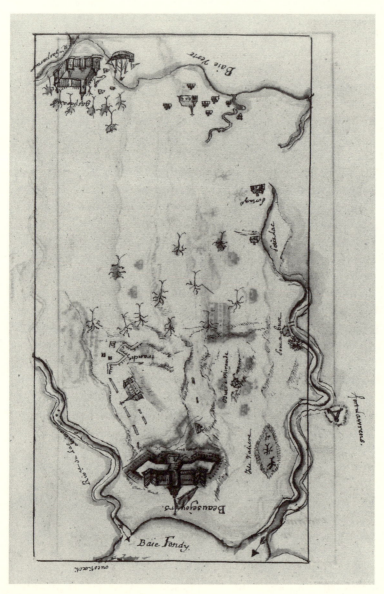

Figure 14. Unsigned drawing of the fort at Beauséjour on the isthmus of Chignecto, circa 1750. A smaller British encampment, known as "Fort Lawrence," stood a few hundred yards to the west. The prominent chapel behind fort Beauséjour was constructed under the direction of the missionary Jean-Louis Le Loutre. Reproduced courtesy of the McCord Museum of Canadian History, Montreal.

colonial authorities feared that "foreign Protestants" would be poor agents of British imperial expansion.

Cornwallis had been more optimistic at the outset. When he first disembarked at Chebucto Harbor in 1749, he brought with him a number of French-speaking Protestants, including the family of a man the governor identified as a "gentleman and schoolmaster," Jean-Baptiste Moreau. Moreau was a native of France and had formerly been a Catholic priest, but he had disavowed Catholicism and joined the Church of England. Some prominent figures involved in the founding of Halifax, including the pastor of its new Anglican church, wanted Moreau to move with his wife and children immediately to an Acadian village to start the work of Protestant evangelization.[35] Cornwallis himself favored placing French Protestants among the Acadians quickly, to "remove their prejudices in favor of a French government and the Romish faith."[36] But that autumn conditions in the Bay of Fundy region were far too dangerous to allow French Protestants to settle there, and by the spring of 1750 some members of the Board of Trade responded to the news of combat in Nova Scotia by questioning whether French Protestants should be placed among the Acadians. They worried that the new French-speaking settlers might discover that their common ancestry and cultural ties with the villagers were stronger than whatever kinship they felt with the British as Protestants. Fearful of a political alliance linking all the French in Nova Scotia, the board ordered the governor in 1750 not to place French Protestants in the Bay of Fundy region. Instead the board members hoped Germans and English-speakers would move to the Acadian villages, preferably in mixed groups.[37]

Over time other Protestant groups came under suspicion. Some of the "foreign Settlers" fled Halifax and ran inland during the war with the Mi'kmaq, and the colonial authorities suspected that they had gone to join Acadian émigrés in New France.[38] Others who remained in Halifax hired Acadian women to help them in their households, and officials in the provincial government worried that the immigrants' children were falling under the influence of Acadian nurses who were "breeding them up in the Romish persuasion."[39] Additionally, a significant number of the Germans among the new arrivals were suspected of being Catholic.[40]

When Lunenburg was established as a German-speaking town in 1753, Nova Scotia's colonial authorities consciously placed it far from the Acadians' villages.[41] The governor at that time feared that "the French" might infiltrate the town. Nonetheless, placing the Germans in an isolated location failed to ease his apprehensions. After a riot among the settlers in Lunenburg in the winter of 1753, he complained that the Germans "affected the same sort of independency that the French inhabitants have done. They [the Germans] have always insisted that the Indians would distinguish them from the English and never interrupt them, which notion I believe has been privately propagated among them by French emissaries."[42] Far from securing Nova Scotia as a British colony, the "foreign Protestants," and the Germans in particular, now appeared in the context of the Anglo-Mi'kmaq war as yet another distinct community whose political allegiance was difficult to assess.

Cope and the other Mi'kmaq who fought the British had failed to prevent the construction, fortification, and growth of Halifax, the establishment of other towns around Chebucto Harbor, or the founding of Lunenburg, but they had succeeded in derailing the original British plan of intermingling Protestant settlers and Acadians in the Bay of Fundy region, and as early as 1751 Cornwallis had decided to alter his original plans for Nova Scotia. Recognizing that he could not evict the Mi'kmaq entirely, he came to believe that the peoples of the province—British, "foreign Protestant," Mi'kmaq and Acadian—could find the basis for a begrudging truce.[43]

The governor and his advisors developed a strategy involving the construction of trading posts and forts in the interior of the peninsula designed to control the Mi'kmaq and exploit them economically.[44] This policy gained tacit support from the Board of Trade, which had mildly reprimanded Cornwallis in 1750 for his indiscriminate harshness toward the Mi'kmaq.[45] For more than a year, through the summer of 1752, Cornwallis sought out Mi'kmaq leaders willing to consent to the establishment of trading posts and negotiate a peace.[46] The fighting subsided for a while—an encouraging sign—but Cornwallis resigned his commission and left the province before any Mi'kmaq leaders on the peninsula accepted his invitation to talks. Then, shortly after Cornwallis left, Cope came to Halifax.[47]

On behalf of the small Shubenacadie band, Cope negotiated a treaty with the provincial government.[48] The pact contained no detailed territorial provisions, but during the negotiations the new governor, Peregrine Hopson, assured Cope and his band, "If you think fit to settle your wives and children upon the Shubenacadie no person shall hinder it."[49] The governor promised aid for the Mi'kmaq on the Shubenacadie, and in broad terms the treaty guaranteed Mi'kmaq hunting and fishing rights. Hopson was satisfied with the terms of the agreement, but he wanted more of the province's Mi'kmaq to ratify it, and so he asked Cope to recruit other leaders to join the peace.

During the fall of 1752 and spring of 1753 Cope helped arrange meetings between British emissaries and various Mi'kmaq leaders. The British delegations, composed primarily of soldiers, ventured far from Halifax to Mi'kmaq fishing villages carrying gifts and offers of friendship in an effort to persuade the leaders of other Mi'kmaq bands to come to the new provincial capital and ratify the treaty.[50] At least one leader accepted the invitation, but a much larger group opposed the peace agreement because the British had not recognized any specific Mi'kmaq claims to land.[51] Hopson was disappointed, and he became increasingly skeptical about Cope's influence among the Mi'kmaq.[52] Then he heard disturbing news.

In the spring of 1753 a delegation of soldiers left Halifax to meet with Cope and disappeared. Only one in the party, Anthony Casteel, returned.[53] Casteel's report on the incident darkened the prospects for an immediate peace.

Casteel testified before the provincial council that Cope and his followers had ambushed the British emissaries and killed all of them except himself. Casteel had been taken captive, and he had traveled with Cope and his followers across the peninsula of Nova Scotia. He indicated that Cope carried orders from the French military, and that the leader of the Shubenacadie had celebrated the humiliation and slaughter of the British soldiers. According to Casteel, Cope boasted of his deception and claimed that he had made friendly overtures to the government in order to instill false confidence and make the British vulnerable to surprise. He reported that Cope had left his copy of the peace treaty with an Acadian family over the previous winter and that in the spring of 1753 he had retrieved it. In Casteel's presence Cope had thrown the treaty into a fire, declaring "that was the way they made peace with the English."[54]

Casteel also told the council that Cope was familiar with Jacques Maurice Vigneau, and indeed it had been Vigneau and his wife Marguerite who had arranged for Casteel's release. Cope, or his followers, had taken Casteel to see Vigneau in Beauséjour to negotiate the payment of a ransom. Casteel had haggled over the price to be paid, and at the height of the controversy one of the Mi'kmaq men had threatened to kill him. Terrified, he fainted, only to awaken in the Vigneau family home. Marguerite was there when he regained consciousness, asked him if he was hurt, gave him some wine, and loaned him the money he needed to buy his freedom.

In microcosm, Casteel's testimony epitomized the difficulties the British were facing in trying to assess, predict, or direct the political loyalties of the peoples of Nova Scotia. Both Cope and Vigneau figured prominently in the story, and their behavior, as Casteel described it, raised similar questions about the political allegiances of both men.

Casteel testified that the Vigneau family had presented themselves to him as friends of the British. They had told him that they had arranged for the payment of similar ransoms before, and that if necessary they would do so again, because they hated to see British people suffer. But others cast the family's activities in a more sinister light. A French military officer told Casteel that Vigneau was the equivalent of a slave trader, because he made a profit offering war captives loans (at interest) to obtain ransoms. Vigneau had indeed negotiated similar deals before, and the behavior of the Mi'kmaq warriors in the Casteel episode suggests that they had worked well with him in the past and enjoyed his services.[55] Inadvertently or purposefully, the Vigneau family may have encouraged hostage-taking, but nothing they said indicated that that was their intention.

After this incident Vigneau established more direct contacts with the British military. In 1753 and 1754 he served as a spy carrying information between Beauséjour and Halifax and passing messages to officers in the British fort on the isthmus of Chignecto.[56] But various British officials remained doubtful of his loyalties and suspected him of opportunism. The officer who served as Vigneau's contact and received intelligence from him summed up his view of him and the other Acadians this way: "If these people see that indications are favourable to the English they will be pro-English, and *per contra*."[57]

Cope's political development over this period may be easier to interpret in retrospect, because at the time of the ambush he had reason to believe that the British had violated the terms of the treaty. A recent skirmish on the Atlantic coast had resulted in the deaths of three Mi'kmaq women and two children.[58] Cope and his followers responded to this event as a breach of the peace agreement, justifying their retaliatory action against Casteel's delegation. Nonetheless, from the British perspective, attacking a diplomatic team seemed duplicitous, and Casteel's report suggested that Cope had never intended to abide by the terms of his agreement. If the colonial authorities believed that that were true, they had little hope of negotiating another treaty, at least not with Cope.

After 1753 Cope resumed his militant opposition to the British colonial government, and he reestablished contact with Le Loutre. In 1754 he accompanied the missionary on a tour of Acadian villages, giving speeches in French encouraging the Acadians to move off the peninsula. He warned them that the Mi'kmaq would consider them enemies if they opted to stay in British-ruled Nova Scotia.[59]

Animosities arising out of the collapse of Cope's peace agreement made it more difficult for future British and Mi'kmaq negotiators to gain each other's trust. From 1753 through 1755 various Mi'kmaq leaders tried to resume negotiations with the British, but their proposals consistently involved an explicit territorial settlement, demarcating regions exclusively accessible to the Mi'kmaq.[60] The British rejected all such proposals because they assumed that the Mi'kmaq were a transient people allied with the French. Acknowledging Mi'kmaq claims to land seemed tantamount to ceding territory to France, and in November 1754 the acting governor of Nova Scotia declared the Mi'kmaq's territorial proposals "insolent and absurd."[61] The provincial authorities had grown frustrated in their relations with the Mi'kmaq and increasingly concentrated their efforts on building new communities on the Atlantic coast and patrolling the Bay of Fundy region to keep the Mi'kmaq and the French away from the Acadians.

For the first time since the seizure of Port Royal in 1710, the British had a permanent military force in the eastern Bay of Fundy region, with forts and garrisons on the isthmus of Chignecto and at Pisiquid and Minas. In the 1740s William Shirley had advocated the construction of these forts as a part of his program for cultural integration, but contrary to Shirley's earlier hopes, in the early 1750s there were no intercultural marriages between soldiers and Acadian women in the fortified eastern villages. Indeed, there was very little evidence even of friendship. Soldiers supervised the villagers' daily behavior, placed limits on their freedom of movement, and compelled them to work to support the garrisons.

After 1753 Acadians needed passes to travel from one part of Nova Scotia to another, as well as permits to transport crops or goods.[62] The soldiers refused to authorize the transportation of more grain than the minimum necessary to keep the inhabitants of any given district healthy and alive.[63] The purpose of these restrictions was to prevent the Acadians from moving to French-controlled territory and to cut them off from their Mi'kmaq neighbors and the French. As the British gained confidence in their ability to regulate the Acadians' lives they decided with increasing frequency to exploit their labor.[64] After 1752 the British garrisons in all the forts of the province required the farmers in their areas to provide them with wood.[65] At Minas, those living near the fort were also compelled to rent their houses to the army for use as barracks.[66] And throughout the east the local population was put to work repairing bridges and roads.[67]

In September 1754, under the leadership of their pastor, Henri Daudin, the inhabitants of Pisiquid refused to comply with an order that they gather wood for the local garrison. The garrison commander notified the authorities in Halifax, who told him to renew the order, and if the inhabitants disobeyed he was to begin burning houses, starting near the fort and working outward until the farmers relented or the local community was destroyed.[68] Before the proposed demolitions began, the provincial council summoned Daudin, who, pleading illness, failed to appear.[69] On October 3 the pastor was arrested and detained pending deportation from Nova Scotia.[70] Later that month a delegation from Pisiquid appeared before the council and apologized on behalf of the townspeople. The pastor also apologized and the council released him.[71]

This episode epitomized the evolution of British policy toward the Acadians during the first five years of the 1750s. Government officials stopped seeking voluntary cooperation from Acadian villagers and instead relied increasingly on coercion. In part, this change in tactics reflected the shift in power relations that had resulted from the founding of Halifax and the construction of new forts. But it also reflected many government officials' deepening distrust of all Acadians.

When Edward Cornwallis was appointed governor of Nova Scotia, his instructions reflected a relatively simple conception of Nova Scotia's future. An aggregation of Protestant settlers would spread across the peninsula, and together with the Acadians they would forge a common British colonial identity. After Cornwallis arrived at Chebucto Harbor and the Mi'kmaq took up arms against him, a darker aspect of this vision was revealed. Cornwallis suggested that the peninsula should be peopled exclusively by persons of European descent and offered prizes for the lives of persons identified as "Indian." The Mi'kmaq answered him with a similar declaration of their own, suggesting that the land belonged only to "les sauvages."

It did not take long, however, before the complexity of life in Nova Scotia reasserted itself. Despite their wartime rhetoric, many Mi'kmaq maintained close ties to the French and the Acadians. Furthermore, the Mi'kmaq and the Acadian communities in Nova Scotia were divided internally, and soon the governor discovered that the Protestant settlers he had brought with him were factionalized as well, and that some of the newcomers had managed to forge links with persons identified as Mi'kmaq and Acadian.

These circumstances were unsettling to the British in two ways. The stubborn presence of the Mi'kmaq and their close association with the other peoples of the region impeded British colonial efforts to plant settlers across the peninsula. Additionally, fears and suspicions stemming from the ongoing Anglo-Mi'kmaq war made life almost continuously un-comfortable for the colony's administrators. By 1753 officials within the colonial administration had revived the idea that order could be restored to Nova Scotia only if the French-speaking Catholic population was re-moved. As the events of 1755 would show, they had not abandoned the idea of culturally assimilating the Acadians, but they were thinking of performing the experiment in another place.

Chapter Seven

The Acadian Removal

THE Seven Years' War, which began in 1754, was the last Anglo-French imperial war on the mainland of North America. It was unlike the three earlier conflicts between the British and the French in that it started in the colonies. Two years passed between the first skirmishes near the Ohio River and the official declarations of war in Europe.

In Massachusetts and Nova Scotia, British colonial officials who were already contemplating the removal of the Acadians recognized the outbreak of hostilities as an opportunity to take action. In 1755 a combined force of New Englanders and regular British soldiers drove the French militarily from Beauséjour and the St. John River, and before the year had ended they had detained, removed, and resettled nearly seven thousand Acadian men, women, and children. Acadian villagers were taken from peninsular Nova Scotia, the isthmus of Chignecto, and the northern coasts of the Bay of Fundy and sent to nine of the thirteen English-speaking colonies to the south and west, where most of them were placed in scattered townships in the hope that they would gradually adopt the language, religion, and political loyalties of their new neighbors.

Many Acadians, however, escaped capture. Some went to Ile Royale, Ile-Saint-Jean, and the French-controlled mainland coasts of the Gulf of St. Lawrence, which turned out to be an unfortunate choice because the British seized those territories in 1758 and deported the settlers they found to France. Some more fortunate Acadians found refuge on the two islands that France recovered at the end of the conflict, St. Pierre and Miquelon; the largest community to survive in the region was north of the isthmus of Chignecto in present-day New Brunswick, which became a center of Acadian life after the war.

The Mi'kmaq and their Algonkian allies in the Wabanaki Confederacy assisted those Acadians who eluded the British authorities, and at least until 1758 Mi'kmaq warriors were able to harass the British and the New Englanders and slow their efforts to place new settlers on the lands vacated by the Acadian removal. But the ouster of the French from Ile Royale in 1758 deprived the Mi'kmaq of an important source of assistance, and by 1761, after sixteen years of almost continuous hostilities, the Mi'kmaq were impoverished and diminished in numbers, and ready to negotiate a peace.

The peace the Mi'kmaq negotiated, along with other long-term consequences of the events of the 1750s, will be discussed in the conclusion to the book. This chapter concentrates on the mid to late 1750s, beginning with the events that led to the government's decision to relocate the entire Acadian population. It proceeds with an examination of the details of the removal process and ends with the effects of these events on the lives of Jean-Baptiste Cope and Jacques Maurice Vigneau. In spite of his individual quirkiness, Vigneau in particular suffered and struggled in ways that speak to the experience of all his compatriots.

The Acadian removal represented the culmination of a long effort by the British to impose order in Nova Scotia and regulate the lives of the Acadians. The consequences of the action were not nearly as simple as the policymakers wished. Instead of encouraging the integration of Acadians into British colonial society, the experience of forced relocation served to reinforce, for many of the exiles, a sense of communal solidarity and distinctiveness.

The first combat in the Seven Years' War occurred in the upper Ohio River valley in the summer of 1754, but in the months preceding those famous first battles several colonial officials, including Massachusetts governor William Shirley, had begun making specific plans for a military confrontation with the French. Indeed in May, Shirley had written the secretary of state in London requesting authorization to drive the French from their outposts on the St. John River and at Fort Beauséjour.[1] In making this proposal he was working in close consultation with Charles Lawrence, who had become Nova Scotia's acting governor in the preceding year.

Lawrence was an English military officer who had arrived in North America's maritime region in 1747 to serve in the British garrison at Louisbourg.[2] After Ile Royale was restored to the French he traveled with his regiment to Nova Scotia, and once there he rose in the colonial administration, thanks in part to the influence of his patron, George Montagu Dunk, the earl of Halifax and president of the Board of Trade. Lawrence also distinguished himself through the active role he played in several critical events in the early 1750s, including the fortification of the isthmus of Chignecto and the placement of German settlers at Lunenburg.

By the time Lawrence became acting governor in the summer of 1753, the provincial council of Nova Scotia was already engaged in a debate on the propriety and feasibility of sending the Acadians out of the colony. Peregrine Hopson, Lawrence's predecessor in office, had ordered provincial secretary William Cotterell to survey the records of the provincial council to determine whether the Acadians had ever taken an unconditional oath of allegiance to the British crown. Cotterell reviewed the files and found evidence that some of the townspeople near the fort at Annapolis Royal had taken an unconditional oath in 1726, but he added that only one year later those same people had refused to repeat the oath without first obtaining an exemption from military service. The other inhabitants of the province had consistently refused to swear allegiance unconditionally.[3] At the same time that Cotterell was preparing his report, Charles Morris, who had surveyed the eastern end of the Bay of Fundy at William Shirley's behest in 1748, submitted a memorial to the council detailing pragmatic reasons for expelling the Acadians. Morris argued that the Acadians had aided the Mi'kmaq in their ongoing war with the British and that they still occupied the best farmland.[4] These reports were relayed to the Board of Trade, which responded in 1754 by warning Lawrence not to do anything that might imply official recognition of the Acadians' title to land unless they took a new, unconditional oath of allegiance.[5]

By the summer of 1754 Lawrence and Shirley had begun making detailed plans to "drive" the French from the isthmus of Chignecto and the northern side of the Bay of Fundy.[6] Shirley hoped to place Protestant settlers from Ulster or New England on the isthmus, particularly on the lands the Acadians had vacated around the destroyed village of Beaubassin. By moving to Beauséjour in 1750, the former residents of Beaubassin seemed to have demonstrated their disloyalty to Great Britain, and according to the Board of Trade they had forfeited whatever title they had had to land in Nova Scotia.[7] Shirley thought that placing Protestants in the abandoned village would seal the Acadians on the peninsula off from the French. He also repeated the predictions he had made in the 1740s, that "Traffick and all manner of Intercourse" between the new settlers and the Acadians on the peninsula would "gradually induce the English manners, customs and language among them."[8] Shirley revived his earlier proposals to send French Protestant missionaries among the Acadians, to expel the Catholic clergy, and to encourage Acadian parents to send their children to English-language schools. His plans centered on the vacated lands around Jacques Maurice Vigneau's old village of Beaubassin, but Shirley was silent concerning the status or future of the former residents who had been forced to move.

Lawrence did not want those villagers to remain in the region. He adopted this position as early as January 1755, but the provincial council of Nova Scotia continued to debate the issue through the following spring.[9] In a letter to Colonel Robert Monckton, who was raising an army in Massachusetts for the expedition against Fort Beauséjour, Lawrence described the deliberations of the council.

The point was much debated, and it seemed to be thought the most prudent method [of pacifying Beauséjour] to drive away the inhabitants and destroy the country, because that would render it very difficult for the French to reestablish themselves in case of a war. However the council have deferred coming to any determination upon this head until they have your opinion upon the matter, and by that time we may probably hear from England and be better able to judge of our own circumstances.[10]

In the summer of 1755, before the authorities in Nova Scotia received detailed instructions from London, a combined force of New England troops and British regulars laid siege to the French fort at Beauséjour. Unaware that the soldiers were planning to deport him, Vigneau welcomed them when they arrived. As one New England soldier put it, "Jockey Morris is very good and takes a fatherly care of us."[11] But other Acadian men took up arms against the British and New Englanders, and fought alongside French regular troops defending the fort.[12]

It was not a particularly long or bloody battle. Some local farmers and native warriors allied to the French shot a few of the attacking soldiers, but the main armies stayed out of each other's range. On June 16, after a British bomb killed three men in the fort, the French commanders agreed to enter into negotiations for a surrender.[13]

The status of the Acadian villagers in Beauséjour was a point of controversy in the negotiations, and the French commanders insisted that a clause be inserted into the capitulation agreement guaranteeing a pardon to those Acadians who had aided the French.[14] Monckton acquiesced in this demand, and in his journal Colonel John Winslow recorded his understanding of the pledge. There would be no legal action taken against the Acadians who had aided the French, but instead they would be allowed to remain in Beauséjour "in the same situation as they were when we arrived and not be punished for what they had done since our being in the country."[15]

On June 18, perhaps wishing to establish a legal basis for relocating the villagers in spite of their recent pardon, Monckton summoned the inhabitants of Beauséjour to appear before him and swear unconditional loyalty to George II.[16] He had been warned earlier not to do this because if the Acadians had sworn allegiance it might have complicated the legal case for removing them.[17] Lawrence repeated that admonition later in the week.[18] But no damage was done to the colonial government's legal position, because none of the Acadians, not even Vigneau, responded positively to Monckton's order. Maintaining their traditional stance, the Acadians refused to make any statements that might suggest that they were willing to bear arms against the French.

Many of the local inhabitants, anxious to placate Monckton, offered him help in other ways. Some brought eggs, chickens, milk, and strawberries to the new British garrison.[19] Others offered their services as messengers and guides.[20] When the commander ordered the inhabitants to give up their firearms, more than three hundred men immediately complied.[21] Nonetheless, on June 28, 1755, Lawrence wrote to London and reported his intention to relocate the "deserted French inhabitants," those who lived in the region behind the old French fort. But he had not yet decided on a general evacuation of Acadians from peninsular Nova Scotia.[22]

In July the men of the provincial council embarked upon a series of tumultuous negotiations with deputies from several Acadian communities in the Bay of Fundy region. The councilmen asked the Acadians on threat of deportation to take an unconditional oath of allegiance to the British crown. The deputies responded that they could not comply with the councilmen's demands because the Acadians would never swear allegiance to Britain unless they were exempted from military service. The councilmen would not extend them that exemption, and in the process stoked suspicions that they intended to enlist Acadian men in the British colonies' undeclared war against the French. The negotiations deteriorated. The first set of deputies went to jail. After a day in confinement they reconsidered their position and offered to take an unconditional oath of loyalty, but the councilmen declared that it was too late for them to change their minds—the individual deputies would be deported regardless of the statements they now made under duress.[23] The council ordered the Acadian communities to send new delegations and warned them to send more compliant representatives this time. On July 28 a new set of deputies came to Halifax, but, obeying their constituents' instructions, they told the councilmen they would not swear unconditional allegiance to the British crown. The councilmen immediately resolved to transport all the Acadians out of Nova Scotia, regardless of their place of residence or prior record of behavior.[24]

Recognizing that their order raised difficult legal issues (English law sanctioned collective punishment only in extraordinary circumstances), the councilmen enlisted the aid of Jonathan Belcher, Jr., the new chief justice of Nova Scotia and a protégé of William Shirley, to issue an advisory opinion justifying the deportation. Complying with the council's request, Belcher advanced several arguments.[25] First, he claimed that the Acadians were "rebels" and therefore liable to be punished as a group. Though he could not cite many instances in which Acadians took up arms against the provincial government, Belcher claimed that they had fought through proxies and that they were responsible for military attacks conducted by the Mi'kmaq and the French. He cited the Mi'kmaq's war in the early 1720s, incidents around Minas and Beaubassin in the early 1730s, and French and Mi'kmaq military operations in Nova Scotia in the decade after 1744. Belcher's second argument was that the Acadians had permanently forfeited their right to be considered British subjects when they failed to swear unconditional allegiance to the British crown. He acknowledged that Acadian men had sworn allegiance repeatedly, but their frequent insistence on an exemption from military service had negated the legal effect of the oaths. Finally, Belcher argued that the deportation of the Acadians was mandated by military necessity, that it would facilitate the resettlement of the province, and that a better moment for undertaking the removal would probably never arise. As he wrote at the outset of his opinion, "such a juncture as the present may never occur [again]."[26]

There is no evidence that the councilmen spent any time discussing the fate of the Acadians after their removal from Nova Scotia. The influential conversations on that issue had taken place earlier. Acting without open dissent within his administration, Lawrence implemented a modified version of the plan William Shirley had devised in 1747 and ordered that the Acadians be sent to New England and other English-speaking colonies to the south and west. In a letter to the governors of the colonies receiving deportees, Lawrence recommended dispersing the Acadians. He indicated that so long as they could not "easily collect themselves together again," it would be "out of their power to do any mischief, and they may become profitable and, it is possible in time, faithful subjects."[27]

Even as the provincial government endorsed the policy of scattering and assimilating the Acadians within the thirteen colonies, it took measures that had the practical effect of undermining the program. The government's method of capturing, detaining, and deporting the Acadians heightened their sense of injury and strengthened the communal bonds that allowed them to resist assimilation after they had been relocated. A central feature of the government's tactics was to exploit the familial loyalties of women and children in order to extract their cooperation in the relocation process.

At the time of the Acadian removal the British had a variety of justifications for their actions, with contrasting implications for men and women, adults and children. Women and children played a critical role in the plan to assimilate the Acadians into British colonial society, because intermarriage and a particular approach to child rearing were considered indispensable aspects of the process of cultural change. But when the British analyzed deportation as a punitive measure or in military terms, women occupied a more ambiguous position in British reasoning. In his formal opinion justifying the Acadian removal, Belcher made no explicit reference to women or children. Furthermore, at least two of the charges he laid against the Acadian people—that they had failed to take an unconditional oath of allegiance to the British crown and that they had occasionally taken up arms against the provincial government of Nova Scotia—did not implicate either group at all. If women were accused of any wrongdoing in the opinion it was only implicitly, in allegations that the Acadians had "supplied," "maintained," "supported," and "received" Mi'kmaq and French enemies of the provincial government.[28]

In part because the official British justifications for the Acadian removal had distinctive implications for women and children, the British soldiers and New Englanders who undertook the actual process of deportation treated women and children differently from men. Strictly speaking, most of them were never apprehended.[29] Instead the British commanders arrested and transported the adult males and told the women and children to follow their husbands, fathers, brothers and older sons voluntarily.

The best firsthand account of the physical removal of the Acadians comes from the pen of Colonel John Winslow.[30] Winslow was a New England soldier and a veteran of the War of the Austrian Succession. He participated in the campaign against the French at Beauséjour in 1755, and almost immediately thereafter was ordered to oversee the evacuation of the village of Minas.[31] Like many New England soldiers of his time, he kept a detailed diary, and though he never would have expected it, the language of his entries describing the Acadian removal would inspire novelists, poets and lyricists in subsequent generations.[32]

Winslow arrived at Minas with 315 soldiers on August 18, 1755. He instructed his troops to build a stockade around the churchyard and erect tents for themselves within the enclave.[33] On September 2 he ordered all the male inhabitants of the village over the age of nine to appear before him in three days' time. A total of 418 Acadian men and older boys responded to the order, perhaps expecting leniency in exchange for cooperation. Winslow placed them in confinement. For the next five weeks they spent their days in the fenced-in churchyard. At night they slept, under guard, crowded in the chapel.[34]

One problem Winslow faced was the fact that the villagers' wheat was still in the field in early September. Someone had to harvest it or everyone in the area, soldiers and Acadians alike, would go hungry. The farmers held in captivity asked Winslow to release them to harvest the crop. They offered twenty hostages who could suffer on behalf of the group if any of them misbehaved. Winslow declined the offer. He believed that the Acadian women and the children aged nine and under could do the work that needed to be done. In an effort to guarantee their obedience, he announced that the army would not feed any of the prisoners. Their wives, mothers, and children would have to bring them food to keep them alive. Winslow conceded that the women could not operate flour mills, and so he agreed to release a few male millers in shifts.

The colonel held four hundred men under the watch of three hundred troops. This should have been an adequate guard, but he wanted greater security. On the morning of September 10 he asked the prisoners to line up in the churchyard according to age, with the youngest men all on one side. Then he asked 141 of the youngest to board an awaiting ship which would stay in the harbor. This is how he described what happened next:

[I] order[ed] the Prisoners to March. they all answered they would No go without their Fathers. I Told them that was a word I did not understand for that the Kings Command was to me absolute & Should be absolutely obeyed & That I Did not Love to use Harsh Means but that the time Did not admit of Parlies or Delays and Then ordered the whole Troops to Fix their Bayonets and advance Towards the French [Acadians], and bid the 4 right hand Files of the Prisoners Consisting of 24 men wch I told of my Self to Divied from the rest, one of whome I Took hold on (who opposed the Marching) and bid March. He obeyed & the rest followed. Thoh Slowly, and went off praying, singing and crying, being met by the women and children all the way.[35]

Once the young men had boarded the vessels, Winslow asked for volunteers from among the remaining prisoners to join them. Eighty-nine men, including many fathers, offered to go onboard. Responding in large part to their sense of paternal obligation, the men departed the village without offering any resistance, and as a result Winslow had fewer than two hundred prisoners left in his camp.

In the meantime, for the next several weeks, the women and children continued to work in the fields. Armed teams of soldiers were dispatched to watch and assist them. Until the day they left Nova Scotia, the women continued to bring food to the prisoners. Those with family members in the camp brought baskets of produce directly to the churchyard; those with family members on shipboard brought food to the waterside. Each prison ship sent a dinghy ashore daily. One prisoner would be onboard to receive the packages, who would then direct the food to the right men back on the ship.

In the first week of October, in preparation for the final embarkation, Winslow asked the women to gather their families.[36] To secure their further assistance, he offered to keep the residents of each village together when he assigned the families to transport ships. Happily or not, most of the women cooperated with him. As Winslow described it, the women came "carrying off their children in their arms, others carrying their decrepit parents in their carts."[37] The process took longer than expected, but the last ship left Minas in the third week of December.[38]

Winslow's description of the evacuation of Minas is the most detailed account available, but it is not the only record of the process. Other accounts document similar operations throughout the region of the Bay of Fundy that fall.[39] Deportation invariably involved a process of family breakup and reunion. The adult men were taken away from their mothers, wives, and children, who were then required to struggle to find them, support them, and ultimately leave Nova Scotia with them. This was the way the procedure had been planned in Halifax, and Winslow and the other commanders carried out the design.[40]

There are several possible explanations as to why the British adopted this family-breakup-and-reunion tactic in moving the Acadians. The deportation was bound to take time, and long-term incarceration was not a common punishment for women in eighteenth-century New England or Great Britain.[41] When men were held in jail for extended periods it was common for the authorities to expect their families to feed them—British colonial jailers felt no compulsion to keep their prisoners well fed.[42] The tactic of having the families of the male Acadians feed them may have seemed particularly expedient given the circumstances of Nova Scotia during the weeks of the deportation. It was harvest time, and the British needed the crop. Soldiers might have done the work of the harvest, but it was much more efficient to let the farm families do it. By requiring the Acadians to make sacrifices for their family members, however, the British exploited and reinforced the Acadians' sense of familial loyalty. The Acadian women were told, at least implicitly, that their first obligation was to their fathers, husbands, and children, which ran counter to the colonial authorities' long-term plans.

In every community that the army reached, after the soldiers had evacuated the inhabitants they set fire to the town. Patrols also traveled through miles of countryside and gutted every farmhouse.[43] In the area of Cobequid some of the troops set their fires early, but in most districts they waited until the inhabitants were gone.[44] In order to maintain food supplies and provide shelter for the women and children, they delayed the burning until everyone had boarded the ships.[45]

According to the best current estimates, approximately 7,000 persons were deported from the coasts of the Bay of Fundy. More than 2,000 Acadians were removed from Minas, 1,500 from Annapolis Royal, 1,100 from Pisiquid, 1,100 from Beauséjour, and hundreds from the St. John River valley and Cape Sable.[46] Several historians have traced the voyages of these exiles.[47] Their work has produced the following estimates of where they went:

COLONY	# OF EXILES
Massachusetts	2,000
Virginia	1,100
Maryland	1,000
Connecticut	700
Pennsylvania	500
North Carolina	500
South Carolina	500
Georgia	400
New York	250
Total	6,950

Though some colonial governors resisted the resettlement of the Acadians, most agreed to accept them and reluctantly followed Lawrence's advice to disperse them widely.[48]

In New York the colonial assembly placed Acadian exiles in several communities near the mouth of the Hudson River. The legislature specifically chose towns with significant French Protestant populations, including Staten Island and New Rochelle. The justice of the peace in each of these towns was authorized to bind the Acadians' children to local families as indentured servants.[49] In Maryland the governor sent his quota of deportees to every county in the colony east of the Allegheny Mountains; the Pennsylvania legislature spread Acadians throughout Philadelphia, Bucks, Lancaster, and Chester Counties and assigned them to the overseers of the poor in at least twenty-seven different townships.[50]

Nowhere was the policy of dispersal more enthusiastically embraced than in southern New England. The legislatures of Connecticut and Massachusetts sent the exiles to at least 122 different townships (see figure 15).[51] Larger towns received larger quotas. A few small communities took responsibility for only three or four Acadians.[52] Once assigned to a locality, the Acadians were prohibited by law from crossing town borders.[53] The overseers of the poor in each town were directed to support them or find them jobs.[54]

In the meantime on the peninsula of Nova Scotia, the destruction of the Acadian villages had created a landscape of burned houses, untended livestock, overgrown orchards, and fields going to seed.[55] British patrols used the shells of farm buildings as landmarks and continued to identify abandoned places by the local farmer's name, though the farmers were gone (see figure 16).[56] It was a good terrain for hit-and-run military activity, and Mi'kmaq warriors and their Algonkian allies were still able to harass the British after 1755.[57] The French on Ile Royale encouraged the Mi'kmaq in their endeavors, and indeed in 1756 the French governor at Louisbourg paid Jean-Baptiste Cope for two British scalps.[58]

One of the main objectives of the native warriors during this period was to rescue Acadian refugees from the British or to assist them when they tried to escape. In the first week of October 1755, eighty-six men fled from the British fort on the isthmus of Chignecto after digging a tunnel thirty feet long under the walls. They crawled out at night and made their way immediately westward toward the valley of the St. John River.[59] Similarly in February 1756, thirty-six Acadian families (226 prisoners) escaped from the hold of the ship that was carrying them to North Carolina, overcame the captain, and sailed into the mouth of the St. John. They ran aground, disembarked, and set fire to their ship. A band of local native people met them and directed them upstream, where they joined an expanding Acadian community.[60]

The St. John River valley and the lands immediately to the east of it became the center of Acadian and Algonkian resistance to the British military in the region. At least until the fall of Québec in 1759, the British repeatedly tried to capture and expel the Acadians from the banks of the St. John.[61] But with the aid of the Mi'kmaq, the Wuastukwiuk, and their Algonkian allies, the Acadians evaded capture. Cope likely participated in the defense of the newly expanded Acadian settlements. The last record

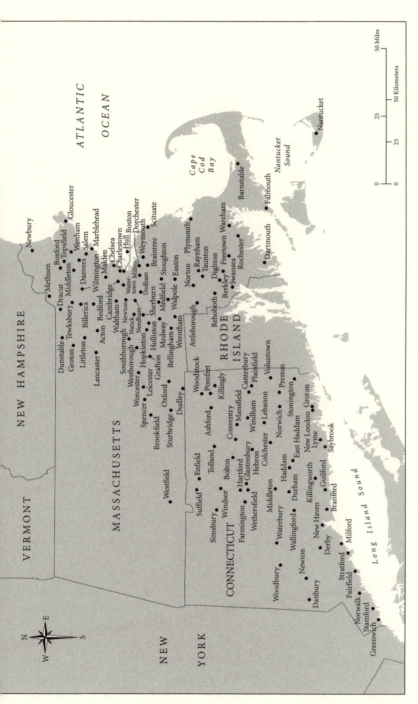

Figure 15. Towns in Massachusetts and Connecticut receiving Acadian exiles. The Connecticut towns are listed in Charles J. Hoadly, ed., *The Public Records of the Colony of Connecticut*, vol. 10 (Hartford, Conn.: Case, Lockwood and Brainard, 1877), 452–53. The Massachusetts towns have been identified through a survey of the *Journals of the House of Representatives of Massachusetts* (Boston: Massachusetts Historical Society, 1901–), vols. 32–37.

of his existence is a report of a conversation he had with a French military officer in the mid-1750s at Miramichi, in present-day New Brunswick on the coasts of the Gulf of St. Lawrence.[62]

In the fall of 1755 Jacques Maurice Vigneau was boarded onto the ship *Prince Frederick* and carried to Georgia.[63] As soon as he disembarked in Savannah he set to work trying to convince the authorities to allow him to return home. Unlike some other Acadian exiles who asserted that they had always remained neutral in the imperial contest, Vigneau presented himself as a vigorous subject who had actively supported the interests of Britain.[64] As he put it, he had "always showed great regard for the English, by saving them frequently from being scalped."[65]

He may have argued more strenuously than necessary. The governor of Georgia had never been happy about receiving Acadian exiles. When the *Prince Frederick* first arrived in Savannah he had refused to allow the passengers to disembark. It was only after the governor received repeated petitions warning him that the Acadians were ill and running out of food that he had allowed them to come ashore. He did not want them in Georgia, but allowing them to return to Nova Scotia might have been construed as an act of defiance against higher imperial authorities. Vigneau offered the governor a way around this dilemma. He did not ask to be sent anywhere, and certainly not to Nova Scotia. He only asked for permission to leave Georgia. On March 10, 1756, the governor acknowledged Vigneau's record of loyal service and presented him with a pass authorizing him to take his "family" out of the province.[66]

After Vigneau obtained this pass his "family" grew. He had arrived in Georgia with his wife and sixteen children and grandchildren.[67] He left with ninety-eight dependents.[68] The governor wanted to rid himself of all the refugees, and the Acadians went along with the ruse. With the merchant at their head they left by canoe and proceeded up the Atlantic coast to South Carolina. After their arrival in Charlestown, Vigneau reported to the governor, who had already received a large quota of exiles and was not pleased to see more. On April 8, 1756 the governor of South Carolina gave Vigneau a pass to proceed to North Carolina.[69] In North Carolina the group was arrested, but Vigneau kept talking, and on May 7, 1756 the provincial council gave his "family" permission to continue up the coast. The councilmen gave Vigneau two sides of beef and ten bushels of corn to support the group on its northward journey.[70] By midsummer the exiles had reached New York, where they were temporarily detained.[71] But Vigneau found the ear of the provincial governor, who gave him permission to proceed.[72]

It was only then that his luck turned. A sailing ship might have by-passed New England and proceeded directly to Nova Scotia, but there was no way for a flotilla of canoes to cut across the open sea. The travelers made it through Connecticut and Rhode Island, but as they approached Cape Cod they made the mistake of entering Barnstable Bay. The local inhabitants surrounded and detained them.[73] Upon learning who the canoeists were, the sheriff of Barnstable County transferred them to the custody of the sheriff in Boston. The entire group remained in the Massachusetts capital for several days while the General Court debated what to do with them. Vigneau did not wait idly for a decision. He petitioned the legislature and won passage of a special bill allowing him, along with his actual blood relatives, to remain within ten miles of Boston.[74]

In September the Vigneau family were released from close custody and they moved north across the Charles River to Charlestown, Massachusetts. In effect, ever so slowly, they were continuing their progress toward Nova Scotia. The selectmen of Charlestown recognized the implications of the move, and in a formal letter to the legislature they warned that it would be "unsafe to the Publick" to allow the Vigneau family to stay so near the Atlantic coast.[75] After receiving this warning the legislators thought better of their earlier leniency. Before the month was out they had enacted another special bill that voided the earlier one and directed Vigneau and his family to settle near Worcester, away from the ocean.[76] His other traveling companions were sent to other communities, most of them not as far inland.[77]

Vigneau could not support his family in the town where the legislature sent him, and the town authorities, hoping to get the family off their relief rolls, petitioned the governor of Massachusetts to move the Vigneaus again.[78] In 1758 the Massachusetts legislature transferred Vigneau, his wife, their children, and grandchildren to the town of Brookfield, where they could not at first find employment. In 1759 Vigneau

Following Pages. Figure 16. Detail of a map prepared in 1755 or 1756 of the central region of Nova Scotia. The designation "Fort Cumberland," the name the British assigned to Fort Beauséjour after the French surrender, indicates that this map was made after June 16, 1755, and the English names assigned to farmsteads in the region indicate that the redistribution of confiscated lands and the renaming of the landscape had already begun. On other parts of the map, however, Acadian names were used to designate landmarks. Pisiquid, a village the British would eventually rename "Windsor," is still labeled Pisiquid, and the farms around that village are still identified by the Acadian owners' names. Reproduced by permission of the Huntington Library, San Marino, California.

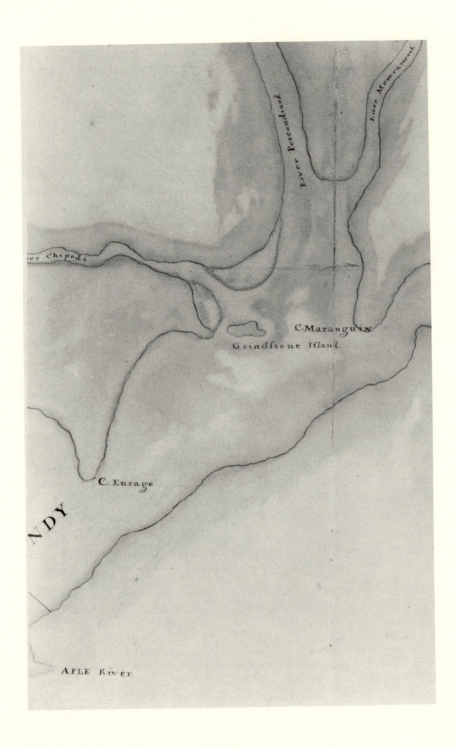

River Menaramcook

River Peteoudiack

er Chipodi

C. Maranguin

Grindstone Island

C. Enrage

NDY

APLE River

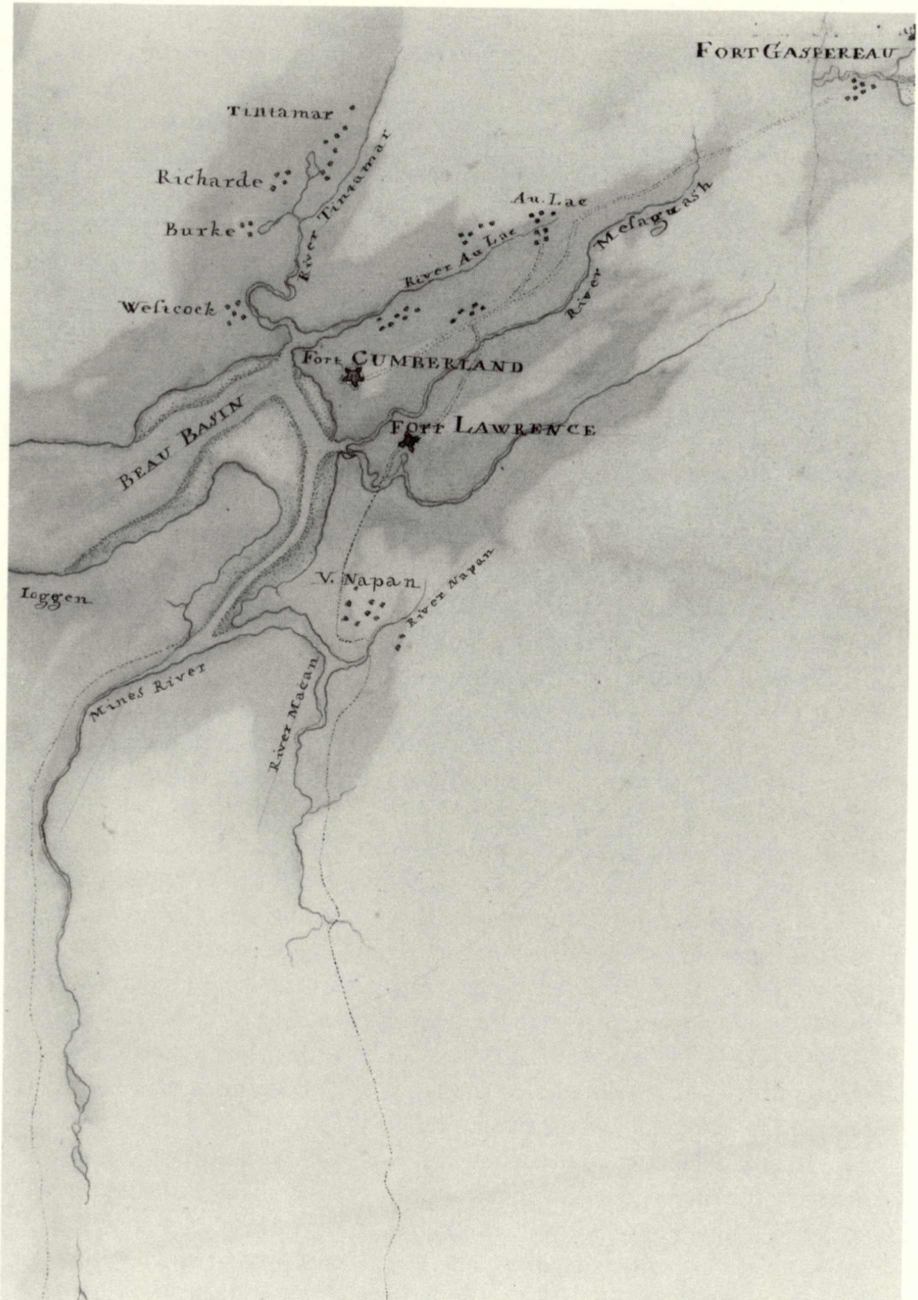

FORT GASPEREAU

Tintamar

Richarde

Burke

Au Lae

River Melaguash

River Tintamar

River Au Lae

Welicock

Fort CUMBERLAND

BEAU BASIN

FORT LAWRENCE

Ioggen.

V. Napan

River Napan

Mines River

River Macan

petitioned the provincial government to reimburse him for the value of his impounded canoes. He received seven pounds, eight shillings, and two pence.[79]

Sometime over the next four years, by a method that is now impossible to determine, Jacques obtained a seaworthy craft. He christened the vessel the *St.-Jacques*, and in 1763, when under the terms of the Treaty of Paris the Acadians were granted permission to return to French-ruled territory, Vigneau took the *St.-Jacques* and his family to Miquelon.[80] He went in a convoy with other ships, and at least 110 Acadian exiles traveled with him. After arriving in Miquelon he returned at least once to the coast of Nova Scotia to transport a number of other Acadians to the French-ruled island.

Along with Vigneau on this journey was a man named Perrault, a former French Canadian official who planned to assemble as many Acadians as he could on Miquelon in order to transport them to Cayenne, in the Caribbean. Vigneau helped Perrault bring the exiles to Miquelon, but when Perrault asked him to cooperate with the next stage of the plan he balked. Along with his brother Joseph, who had recently joined him on the island, Vigneau protested vehemently, and the two men became informal leaders of the new Acadian community on Miquelon.[81] In a carefully drafted letter to Perrault they assured him that they were faithful servants of France, but they argued that the Caribbean would be too warm for them and that they were acclimatized for life on the coasts of the North Atlantic.[82]

The Vigneaus' protests in 1764 worked. They and the other exiles temporarily won the right to reside on Miquelon. But the Acadians had difficulty adapting to life on the island. The fishing methods to which most of them were accustomed were unsuitable for the open Atlantic, and by default many of the exiles became charges of the local French colonial government. In 1767 the governor of the island decided to send them all to France.[83] Vigueau went to Nantes along with the others.[84] There is no record that he protested against the move, but within a year he had returned to Miquelon, where in 1772 he died.[85]

Jacques Maurice Vigneau was in many ways extraordinary. Thanks in part to his language skills and his position as a merchant, he had greater access to military and political leaders than most of his contemporaries. He was also unusually outspoken, and he gathered around him a body of Acadian supporters who lent him prominence as a political leader, first at Beauséjour, later among the Acadian exiles who insisted on traveling north, and finally on Miquelon.

Nonetheless, though Vigneau was hardly typical, an evaluation of his career raises questions relevant to the experience of all the Acadians of his generation. At various times during his lifetime he described himself as a supporter of the British, a stubborn subject of France, and a believer in Acadian independence. An array of pressures and opportunities influenced each of these statements, and there was no way for his contemporaries to determine the sincerity of his declared political beliefs. The problem persists for historians today, and it may be that the best evidence of Vigneau's convictions is not the complex amalgam of statements he made, but the record of his behavior. There can be no doubt that Vigneau and the men, women, and children who traveled with him loved the northeastern coasts of North America. They made tremendous sacrifices, and worked as a team, to return to the region of their ancestral homes. More than any other factor, it was this that undermined the British effort to incorporate the Acadians into the life of the thirteen colonies: the struggles the exiles faced after the deportation only strengthened their sense of community and defined them as a people apart.

Conclusion

Several issues intrinsic to any assessment of the long-term impact of the events discussed here can be illustrated by events in the career of Colonel Jeffery Amherst. Amherst arrived in Nova Scotia in the summer of 1758 to help lead the final British attack against the French on Ile Royale. Within days of his arrival in Halifax he gave a speech to his troops in which he warned them that the local "Indians" were "brutes and cowards" unsurpassed in all creation in their cruelty.[1] The colonel was not basing this assertion on firsthand experience; he had spent his life in England, and therefore we can assume that he was repeating what he had been told.

Amherst was not the first English officer to arrive in Nova Scotia with a bleak preconception of the Mi'kmaq. Nine years earlier Edward Cornwallis had come to the province ready to "root" them out. Cornwallis had employed New England's tactics in fighting them, paying bounties for scalps, and Amherst similarly encouraged scalping after he landed on Ile Royale.[2]

After the seizure of Louisbourg, Amherst participated in the subsequent, successful British attacks on Québec and Montréal. He rose in the military ranks, became a general, and, following the fall of Montréal, assumed a leading role in the formulation of British policy in the Ohio valley and Great Lakes region. In his dealings with the Algonkian and Iroquoian peoples he encountered in those areas he refused to engage in gift exchange or otherwise respect the traditions of local diplomacy, and his obstinacy contributed to the outbreak of war.[3] Amherst may be most famous today for the draconian measures he adopted in the ensuing conflict. Hoping to precipitate an epidemic, he gave native peoples blankets that had been used by smallpox patients.[4] Though the evidence is inconclusive, it is possible that along with his hostility toward "Indians" he acquired the specific idea of infecting them with disease during his short visit to Nova Scotia.[5]

In the early 1760s the violent policies adopted by Amherst disrupted life across broad sections of North America, foreshadowing in many ways events in the decades to come. But other contemporary colonial officials, such as New York's William Johnson, favored more conciliatory measures, and in the interest of security Amherst's tactics were soon abandoned. Amherst was replaced, and after he left the British pursued a more accommodating set of policies toward the Algonkian and Iroquoian peoples of Canada and the transappalachian west.

Events in Nova Scotia in the 1750s had a strong impact on subsequent developments elsewhere in North America, and the pattern of relations that were established there between the colonial authorities and the Mi'kmaq reshaped the thinking of British officials across a wide region. Nonetheless, because the nature of the relationship between the British and the native peoples of North America was constantly changing, Nova Scotia's influence on the future of Anglo-Algonkian relations becomes increasingly difficult to measure when one considers periods beyond the immediate aftermath of the Seven Years' War.

In assessing the long-term effect on British policymaking of the colonial government's efforts to assimilate the Acadians, a similar pattern appears. After the Acadians were sent to the thirteen colonies, dozens of colonial officials and thousands of ordinary British colonists were recruited into the assimilation effort, and in the short term, at least, the project altered the pattern of settlement in much of British North America. But the policy of scattering exiles was pursued with vigor for only a short period, in part because of opposition from British officials and Anglo-Americans.

Massachusetts governor Thomas Hutchinson, looking back after a few decades on the effort to incorporate Acadians within Massachusetts society, argued that the program demonstrated that the "people of New England had more just notions of toleration than their ancestors."[6] Few twenty-first-century commentators would interpret the relocation of the Acadians as a sign of "toleration"—the officials who ordered the program intended to use coercive measures to Anglicize the exiles and convert them to Protestantism. Nonetheless, Hutchinson was right to argue that bringing the Acadians to New England signaled a change in the outlook of those New Englanders who supported the program. They had to overcome a well-ingrained, comfortable tendency to keep to themselves before they could receive the exiles as neighbors. Almost everywhere the Acadians went in British North America, the arrival of French-speaking, Catholic families, especially in small communities, violated the expectations of Anglo-Americans and changed, at least in a small way, their manner of thinking about their communities.

Just as the advocates of massive violence against native peoples faced opposition within the imperial administration, the proponents of integrating the Acadians into colonial society failed to achieve a consensus in support of their assimilationist program. The authorities in London had been skeptical from the outset, and many colonists also opposed the settlement of French-speaking Catholics in their midst.[7] By the time Amherst landed on Ile Royale, the policy of relocating Catholic, French-speaking colonists in the thirteen colonies had already been discarded. The settlers in the territories the British seized in 1758, Ile Royale, Ile-Saint-Jean and the coasts of the Gulf of St. Lawrence, were deported directly to France. Subsequently, in yet another change in policy, after the fall of Québec and Montréal, the French colonists in Canada were allowed to remain in their homes and continue to practice the Catholic faith. Many British colonial officials retained the hope of eventually converting the French-speaking inhabitants of Canada to Protestantism, teaching them English, and transforming them culturally and politically into British colonial subjects, but the forcible removal or relocation of conquered colonial populations had been dropped as a policy option.[8]

The Acadian removal belongs to a particular moment in the evolution of British imperial policy. Throughout most of the eighteenth century, at least since the Treaty of Union between Scotland and England in 1707, controversy had surrounded two interrelated issues: the definition of British subjecthood and the measures that the imperial authorities could take in an effort to confer that status on culturally diverse populations. These issues remained compelling and unresolved throughout the first half of the eighteenth century, not only because of continuing uncertainties surrounding the relationship between the English and the Scots, but also as a result of imperial expansion, ever-increasing trade, migration, and communication between different parts of the empire, as well as changes in the pattern of immigration into Britain and its colonies. The mid-century wars with France and the Jacobite uprising in 1745 gave the question of British subjecthood even greater urgency. Some policymakers, particularly those who, like Cornwallis, had been involved in the pacification of the Scottish Highlands, came to believe that some of the culturally distinct communities residing within the nominal boundaries of the empire were inherently subversive. They concentrated particularly on Catholic communities and those in areas isolated from the economic, political, and cultural life of England, arguing that drastic measures might be needed to reform such groups. These ideas were never universally shared, but they played an important role in shaping British policy in Nova Scotia.

Similarly, the leading political figures of the British Empire never fully agreed with one another about North America's native peoples, but a clear pattern emerges when one views the first half of the eighteenth century as a whole. Early in the century the dream of liberating Algonkian and Iroquoian peoples from French Catholic dominance helped inspire support for expeditions of conquest, particularly among the peoples of Great Britain. By mid-century, however, years of brutal warfare and close contact between British officials and Anglo-Americans had led to a common apprehension that villainized native peoples and authorized the use of almost indiscriminate violence against them. The scalp-bounty policies of mid-century were not new; the only novelty lay in the fact that imperial officials newly arrived from England were pursuing them.

The policies adopted by the government in Nova Scotia in the 1750s —to separate the Mi'kmaq from the Acadians and transform the Acadian villagers into "English Protestants"—reflected two aspects of a single vision of the future. The proponents of these projects imagined that they could create a society of increasingly undifferentiated colonists who would be industrious, Protestant, and English-speaking. Native peoples had no place in this prospective, hypothetical cultural landscape.

When the colonial administrators of the post-1749 period tried to realize this vision for Nova Scotia, they were cognizant of the difficulties that their predecessors had faced in trying to reorder life in the province. Prior to 1749 the colonial government had received relatively little financial assistance from London, and in the absence of government subsidies or other strong inducements, virtually no civilian Protestant settlers could be recruited to move to Nova Scotia. Faced with the problem of governing a colony populated only by Mi'kmaq and Acadians, Samuel Vetch, Richard Philipps, and most other early colonial administrators had tried to pursue policies that distinguished between the two groups and directed them on distinct paths of political, cultural, and economic development. But the conditions of life in Nova Scotia undermined their efforts. Close ties between the Mi'kmaq and the Acadians made it difficult to distinguish the affairs of one group from those of the other, and Mi'kmaq bands and Acadian villages often stood ready to support each other in times of conflict. Additionally, the French on nearby Ile Royale maintained strong religious and commercial ties to both the Mi'kmaq and the Acadians, and in times of armed hostility they were almost always ready to offer logistical support.

From the time of the British conquest, warfare and its legacies had repeatedly upset the balance of relations among the British, the Mi'kmaq, and the Acadians. The Acadians and the Mi'kmaq remembered the violence that New Englanders had inflicted upon them early in the century, and those memories were renewed in the 1720s when New Englanders arrived again to fight. The Anglo-French war that began in 1744 presented the government of Nova Scotia with a strong military threat, and it also created nearly insoluble problems in governance. Since the Acadians, in particular, faced an array of powerful, competing coercive pressures, there was no easy way for the British to assess the behavior of individual villagers, judge them, and allocate merit or blame, which made the administration of justice often difficult and sometimes impossible.

Cornwallis and his successors in the colonial administration in the 1750s faced similar challenges, but by the end of the decade many of these difficulties had been ameliorated. Parliament had taken a stronger interest in Nova Scotia, and with the inducement of a government subsidy thousands of Protestant settlers had arrived, and more would come following the Acadian removal. Furthermore, after 1755 most of the Acadians had been physically separated from most of the Mi'kmaq, and by 1759 the French military had been driven from the region. The problems that Vetch and Philipps had faced had not disappeared entirely, but to an unprecedented degree the provincial authorities in the 1750s managed to make Nova Scotia a home for Protestant settlers and redefine the structure of life for both the Mi'kmaq and the Acadians.

The expulsion of the French from Ile Royale left the Mi'kmaq without a secure base of operations in their war effort and also deprived them of their most important source of material support.[9] Fourteen years of intermittent combat, combined with the ravages of disease, had weakened their capacity to fight and exacted an enormous toll on their communities. The Mi'kmaq needed to change their material circumstances, and the remaining years of the Anglo-French war, from 1759 through 1763, represented a potentially short-lived opportunity for them to salvage the means of their subsistence.

Though the Mi'kmaq were suffering in the years after 1758, the British still feared them. Even small-scale violence could impede the arrival of Protestant settlers on the lands vacated by the Acadian removal. And, at least until 1763, the French still maintained a claim to land in the region and the British colonial authorities still worried that the French military might return, either through a reversal of fortune on the ground or (more likely) through an operation of European diplomacy. By 1760 both the Mi'kmaq and the British had reason to move quickly to negotiate a peace agreement. The bands sent representatives to the British authorities separately, and by 1762 they had all achieved a formal peace.[10] The documents summarizing the peace agreements failed to establish specific territorial limits on the expansion of British settlements, but they assured the Mi'kmaq access to the natural resources that had long sustained them along the region's coasts and in the woods.[11]

After that agreement was concluded some of the Mi'kmaq managed to retain contact with French-speaking colonists by staying near the Acadians in present-day New Brunswick or after 1763 by migrating eastward to St. Pierre and Miquelon. Hundreds of others moved to the west coasts of Newfoundland where they could live more autonomously, far from any centers of British settlement, and the Newfoundland Mi'kmaq were able frequently to visit the French and the Acadians on St. Pierre and Miquelon.[12]

Nonetheless, these strategies were hardly enough to rebuild the world that the Mi'kmaq had lost. Nearly fifteen years of fighting had reduced their numbers, the local game stocks were depleted, and the arrival of thousands of new settlers on the peninsula of Nova Scotia dislodged the Mi'kmaq from many of their customary centers of habitation. Those who remained on the peninsula discovered that their survival depended on their ability to live amicably with their former enemies.

One of the newcomers, John Seccomb, came from New England to settle on the Atlantic coast of Nova Scotia in the summer of 1759. He recorded in his diary, soon after his arrival, that a group of Mi'kmaq families had camped a few miles away from the newly constructed settlement where he planned to live. The Mi'kmaq performed dances for the English-speaking, Protestant immigrants and traded with them. Mi'kmaq women arrived at the town almost weekly in canoes, offering fish and furs for sale. Seccomb recognized a bargain; on one afternoon he recorded that he had purchased several mink skins and a bearskin from a group of Mi'kmaq women for a quart of wine.[13]

That episode reflects a pattern of painful readjustment common among the Mi'kmaq in the late 1750s and early 1760s, especially along the Alantic coast of Nova Scotia.[14] Many members of the Mi'kmaq bands were hungry, increasingly alienated from their lands, and adapting with difficulty to a new colonial world. Hundreds visited Halifax on a regular basis, where the provincial government, eager to maintain peaceful relations, supported them at a rate of two shillings per capita a day.[15] The Mi'kmaq on the Atlantic coast had become economically subordinate to the British, and though it is impossible to date the transition precisely, in the future those among them who acquired a second language were likely to learn English.[16] The process would take longer in other regions, but by the early nineteenth century this was probably true among almost all of the Mi'kmaq bands.

Nonetheless, the Mi'kmaq retained a strong sense of themselves as a separate people. They still had their own language, a distinct material culture, tribal institutions, and a spiritual life informed by Mi'kmaq tradition and an ongoing attachment to the Catholic Church. The disrespect they often received from British colonists only served to emphasize their status as separate nation. The British had not converted them to Protestantism or British colonial culture, much less "rooted" them out of the region. But in the 1750s the colonial authorities had succeeded in separating most of them from the Acadians and the French.

In the early 1760s it was still illegal for Acadians to reside on the peninsula of Nova Scotia; families and individuals who had eluded the British in 1755 continued to be apprehended and detained. Between June 1763 and March 1764, at Minas alone, the British authorities took 343 Acadians into custody at the local fort.[17] To assist the New England planters who had arrived in the region, the commanders at the fort hired some of their prisoners out for agricultural work. The Protestant settlers appreciated the assistance, and in a petition in March 1764 they asked the government to continue the practice. The "french acadians," they wrote, "have been of great use as labourers in assisting the carrying on of our Business in agriculture and improvements in general, but particularly in the repairing and making dykes, a work which they are accustomed to, and experienced in, and we find that without their further assistance many of us cannot continue our improvements, nor plough nor sowe our Lands."[18]

Like many English-speaking colonists before them, the new settlers imagined that they could create a mixed community with the Acadians on the peninsula of Nova Scotia in which they, the English-speaking Protestants, would dominate. It was not to be. Once released from custody, most of the Acadians left Minas.[19] Rather than stay and work for the newcomers as day laborers, they joined their compatriots elsewhere, probably north of the isthmus of Chignecto, or on St. Pierre or Miquelon. Far from incorporating the Acadians into British colonial society, the immediate effect of the events of the 1750s had been to strengthen the Acadians' resolve to remain apart.

Documentation is scarce concerning the lands that became New Brunswick in the period immediately after the Acadian removal. Acadians had lived in the St. John valley almost continuously since the early seventeenth century, but as late as 1748 perhaps only twelve French-speaking families lived on the river.[20] More came during the 1750s, and by the 1760s the area had become what it still is, the center of Acadian life in the maritime region. Through a process that has not yet been adequately studied, Acadian refugees in the St. John valley and to the east established new villages with a strong sense of tradition and communal memory.[21] They were more isolated than they had been on the peninsula of Nova Scotia. They were detached completely from the French Empire, and especially after the wars of the American Revolution and the arrival of loyalist settlers in the region in the 1780s, they were increasingly cut off from the local native peoples and the French-speaking Canadians. It was during the post-removal period that the word "Acadian" came into common usage in English, and the widespread use of the term reflected a growing sense of the insular position of the Acadian exiles in New Brunswick and elsewhere.

In 1763, when the terms of the Treaty of Paris were announced and the Acadian exiles in the thirteen colonies learned that they would be allowed to leave the British Empire, most departed. Some traveled illicitly to the St. John region, the coasts of the Gulf of St. Lawrence or Québec; others went to French-ruled St. Pierre and Miquelon; but a large group made its way indirectly to Louisiana, some by way of St. Domingue and others after years in France.[22] In Louisiana they maintained a distinctive French-speaking community that has thrived to this day, despite the purchase of their colony in 1803 by the United States.

*   *   *

In 1847 Henry Wadsworth Longfellow wrote "Evangeline: A Tale of Acadie," the most influential account of the Acadian removal ever published.[23] The title character of his poem was an Acadian woman separated from her fiancé as a consequence of the removal in 1755. She stayed loyal, searched for her lover constantly, and stoically awaited the time when they might meet again. Evangeline found him in Philadelphia, decades after the deportation, only moments before he died. They professed love for each other and their reunion represented a kind of melancholy victory.

In creating the character of Evangeline, Longfellow drew on nineteenth-century romantic ideals of womanhood.[24] But he also referred to eighteenth-century sources, particularly the writings of Colonel John Winslow.[25] In "Evangeline" Longfellow gave an account of the Acadian removal very similar to the one contained in Winslow's journal, particularly in its emphasis on family breakup and reunion. But rather than recount the experiences of a family divided for weeks, he chose instead to concentrate on a couple separated almost for life. The long period Evangeline spent apart from her fiancé added drama to Longfellow's story, and it helped him present the Acadian removal in the worst possible light. But the extended separation, along with the political revolution that made it easier for Anglo-Americans in the United States to disassociate themselves from their old colonial governments, also allowed the poet to resolve the contradiction that troubled British policymakers and officials in the eighteenth century. Longfellow found a way to celebrate both familial loyalty and cultural assimilation.

Evangeline remained faithful to the man she loved. But relocation changed that man; when she met him again he was no longer simply an Acadian. He had become someone else, a person Longfellow's original readers would have immediately recognized as an "American." In Longfellow's poem the Acadians hated leaving Nova Scotia, but they loved the United States.[26] The poet quotes an exile in Louisiana, untold years after the American Revolution and presumably after his territory had been annexed to the new nation:

Here . . . numberless herds run wild and unclaimed in the prairies;
Here, too, lands may be had for the asking, and forests of timber
With a few blows of the axe are hewn and framed into houses.
After your houses are built, and your fields are yellow with harvests,
No King George of England shall drive you away from your homesteads[27]

Gabriel, Evangeline's beloved, was not content to build a homestead in Louisiana. Instead he became a hunter and tradesman and traveled the full extent of the new republic.[28] In pursuit of buffalo, beaver, mules, and trade, he crossed the Ozark Mountains on Indian trails, took the Oregon trail to the Wind River range, explored "the Nebraska," and wandered the forests of Michigan.[29] As the poem follows Gabriel across the country, it resembles a lyrical U.S. geography book. The unhappy lover even reached the northern provinces of Mexico, lands that the country was in the process of conquering in the weeks when Longfellow was writing the poem.[30] In his adventures Gabriel became an American, and so, by extension, did Evangeline.

Read in the spirit of its age, "Evangeline" is an anthem celebrating the transformation of the Acadians into archetypical Americans. But in the years after it was published the poem acquired a significance never anticipated by its author. The character Evangeline has become more famous and more deeply loved among the Acadians than any historical figure from the Acadian past. More than anyone else, she is their shared ancestor, a central symbol in the culture that makes the Acadians unique.[31]

The ironies surrounding Longfellow's poem must underlie any assessment of the historical significance of the events in Nova Scotia in the 1750s. During much of the decade British policy in the province was animated by a starkly simple vision of the future, in which peoples of diverse European backgrounds would join together in a single society, and all native peoples would be driven away. It was a vision (not unique to Nova Scotia) that would resonate across the continent and influence Anglo-American thinking for generations. But the project could never be realized, and indeed the British actions in Nova Scotia in many ways redefined and strengthened the ethnic boundaries that set the Mi'kmaq and the Acadians apart. The British succeeded, for the most part, in separating the two groups. But both became proud peoples, living on a continent dominated by Anglo-Americans and stubbornly remaining distinct.

Notes

Introduction

1. Council minutes, May 22, 1725, in MacMechan, *Minutes*, 100–101.

2. See Basque, *Des Hommes de pouvoir*, 59–84.

3. Robichaud's career will be discussed in more detail in Chapter 4 below.

4. See Council minutes, October 26, 1722, September 21, 1723, May 22, 1725, in MacMechan, *Minutes*, 47–48, 50, 100.

5. A large array of scholars, including literary theorists, political scientists, and historians, have examined changing concepts of nationality in the Atlantic world in the eighteenth century. See Anderson, *Imagined Communities*; Gellner, *Encounters with Nationalism*; Hobsbawm, *Nations and Nationalism*; Colley, *Britons*; Kettner, *The Development of American Citizenship*. For other discussions particularly relevant to Nova Scotia, see Paquet and Wallot, "Nouvelle-France/Québec/Canada"; Bumstead, "The Cultural Landscape of Early Canada"' Sahlins, "Fictions of a Catholic France"; Godechot, "Nation, patrie, nationalisme et patriotisme."

6. Such views were not always expressed in self-congratulatory terms. From the sixteenth century forward, many European commentators voiced concern that the Europeans would be corrupted by power. These same commentators frequently depicted the indigenous peoples of the colonies as innocents, in many ways morally superior to the colonizers. For an overview of European reactions to the Americas, see Pagden, *European Encounters with the New World* and Kupperman, *America in European Consciousness*.

7. Colley, *Britons*.

8. For indications of this process in North America, see White, *The Middle Ground*, 186–222; Dowd, *A Spirited Resistance*. But see also Calloway, *The American Revolution in Indian Country*.

9. See especially Anderson, *Imagined Communities*. See also Hobsbawm, *Nations and Nationalism* and the essays contained in Canny and Pagden, eds., *Colonial Identity*. Naomi Griffiths and others have worked extensively to identify and describe a distinctive sense of group identity that developed among the Acadians in the first half of the eighteenth century. See Griffiths, *The Contexts of Acadian History*; Griffiths, "The Golden Age"; Griffiths, *The Acadians: Creation of a People*. For an analysis of this issue among English-speakers in the British Empire, see Bumstead, "'Things in the Womb of Time.'"

10. Colley, *Britons*.

11. See Butler, *Huguenots in America*; Fogleman, *Hopeful Journeys*; Roeber, *Palatines, Liberty and Property*; Roeber, "'Origin of Whatever Is Not English.'"

12. See especially White, *Middle Ground*; Hinderaker, *Elusive Empires*; Usner, *Indians, Settlers and Slaves in a Frontier Exchange Economy*. For an introduction to the extensive literature on the Spanish borderlands, see Weber, *The Spanish Frontier in North America*.

13. Buckner and Reid, *The Atlantic Region to Confederation* provides the best introduction to scholarship on the period. Clark, *Acadia: The Geography of Early Nova Scotia* and MacNutt, *The Atlantic Provinces* are older, single-authored overviews.

14. Naomi Griffiths's works, including *The Contexts of Acadian History*, "The Golden Age," *The Acadians: Creation of a People*, and *The Acadian Deportation* provide the most accessible general introduction to the study of the Acadians. William C. Wicken's dissertation, "Encounters," is the best source of detailed information on the Mi'kmaq. See also Daigle, *Acadia of the Maritimes*; Daigle, *Acadians of the Maritimes*; Sauvageau, *Acadie*; Cazaux, *L'Acadie*; Nietfeld, "Determinants"; Martijn, *Les Micmacs et la mer*; Upton, *Micmacs and Colonists*; Dickason, "Amerindians Between French and English in Nova Scotia"; Dickason, "La 'Guerre navale'"; Dickason, "Louisbourg and the Indians." For a Mi'kmaq author's analysis of the events covered by this book, see Paul, *We Were Not the Savages*.

15. Baker and Reid, *New England Knight*, esp. chapter 5; Johnson, *John Nelson*; Daigle, "Nos amis"; Moody, "A Just and Disinterested Man"; Basque, *Des Hommes des pouvoir*; Basque, "Conflits et solidarités familiales"; Godfrey, *Pursuit of Profit*; Waller, *Samuel Vetch*; Alsop, "Age of the Projectors"; Alsop, "Samuel Vetch's 'Canada Survey'd.'"

16. Rawlyk, *Nova Scotia's Massachusetts* complements the earlier work of John Bartlett Brebner, *New England's Outpost*, in analyzing the long-term, large-scale pattern of relations between New Englanders and Nova Scotia. See also Rawlyk, *Yankees at Louisbourg*; Reid, *Acadia, Maine and New Scotland*; Chard, "Canso"; Chard, "The Impact of French Privateering."

17. Barnes, "'The Daily Cry for Justice'"; Brown, "Foundations of British Policy in the Acadian Expulsion"; Bell, *"Foreign Protestants"*.

18. See "Réglement des limites" (1753), in Casgrain, *Collection*, 3: 60–87, 82.

19. See Pencack and Wright, eds., *Authority and Resistance in Early New York*; Roeber, "'Origin of Whatever Is Not English.'" For an account of early New York emphasizing seventeenth-century Dutch resistance to assimilation see Merwick, *Possessing Albany*.

20. See Plank, "A More Modest Proposal?"

21. See Prins, "Tribulations of a Border Tribe," 171–76. For indications of intermarriages between Mi'kmaq speakers and Acadians see Griffiths, "1600–1650," 59; Daigle, "1650–1686," 65; Reid, "1686–1720," 88.

Chapter One

1. See Johnson, *John Nelson*, 46.

2. Claydon, *William III and the Godly Revolution*.

3. Lovejoy, *The Glorious Revolution in America*; see also Johnson, *Adjustment to Empire*.

4. *Journal of the Proceedings of the Late Expedition to Port-Royal*; see also *Report of the Archives Branch for 1912*, 54–63; "Relation de la prise du Port Royal," in *Report of the Archives Branch for 1912*, 67–73; Charles de Monseignat, "Narrative of the Most Remarkable Occurrences in Canada, 1689, 1690," in O'Callaghan, *Documents*, 9: 462–91, 474–75; "Extracts of dispatches from the Governors," in O'Callaghan, *Documents*, 9: 917–33, 921; Baker and Reid, *New England Knight*, 88–92; Johnson, *John Nelson*, 64–65.

5. Louis Phélypeaux, comte de Pontchartrain to Louis de Buade, comte de Frontenac et de Paulluau, April 1692, in O'Callaghan, *Documents*, 9: 530–31; Frontenac to Pontchartrain, n.d., in O'Callaghan, *Documents*, 9: 531–34; Jean-Baptiste de Lagny to Pontchartrain, January 20, 1697, in O'Callaghan, *Documents*, 9: 659–62.

6. *Journal of the Proceedings*, 6.

7. De Monseignat, "Narrative," 9: 462–91, 475.

8. Joseph Robineau de Villebon to the Marquis de Chevry, 1690, in Webster, ed., *Acadia at the End of the Seventeenth Century*, 30.

9. Reid, "1686–1720," 82.

10. De Monseignat, "Narrative," 475; Baker and Reid, *New England Knight*, 92–94; Johnson, *John Nelson*, 65; Rawlyk, *Nova Scotia's Massachusetts*, 71; "Narrative of the Most Remarkable Occurrences in Canada, 1690, 1691," in O'Callaghan, *Documents*, 9: 526; see also unsigned memorial on the state of Acadia, February 5, 1691, RG1, vol. 2, doc. 47, Public Archives of Nova Scotia (hereafter PANS).

11. M. Tibierge, "Memoir on the Present State of the Province of Acadia," in Webster, *Acadia at the End of the Seventeenth Century*, 154.

12. "The Humble Address of Diverse Gentry, Merchants and Others," in Moody and Simmons, *The Glorious Revolution in Massachusetts*, 416–18; Savage, *An Account of the Late Action of the New Englanders*, 11–12; see also Dummer, *A Letter to a Noble Lord*, 12; "The Humble Address of the Publicans of New England," in Whitmore, *Andros Tracts*, 2: 231–69, 237–38; Abstract of a letter from James Lloyd, January 8, 1691, in *Report of the Archives Branch for 1912*, 64.

13. "Further Queries upon the Present State of New English Affairs," in Whitmore, *Andros Tracts*, 1: 193–208, 201.

14. See Baker and Reid, *New England Knight*, 94.

15. See Johnson, *John Nelson*, 64; Baker and Reid, *New England Knight*, 90.

16. See Morrison, *The Embattled Northeast*, 102–32.

17. Mather, *Present State of New England*, 34–35; see also Mather, "The

Mystery of Providence," manuscript sermon, February 14, 1690, Mather Family Papers, Octavo Volume 77.

18. Baker and Reid, *New England Knight.*

19. See Chard, "The Impact of French Privateering."

20. Johnson, *John Nelson*, 27, 39; see also Reid, "1686–1720," 81.

21. Rawlyk, *Nova Scotia's Massachusetts*, 59.

22. Heyrman, *Commerce and Culture*, 233; see also Vickers, *Farmers and Fishermen*, 152–53, 192; Innis, *The Cod Fisheries*, 160–61.

23. Johnson, *John Nelson*, 59.

24. John Cotton to John Cotton (father and son), August 5, 1690, Curwen Family Papers, box 1, folder 4.

25. See Buffington, "The Puritan View of War;" see also George, "War and Peace in the Puritan Tradition;" Johnson, *Ideology, Reason and the Limitation of War*; Walzer, *Revolution of the Saints*, 268–70.

26. Kupperman, *Settling with the Indians*, 185.

27. Consider, for example, the biblical analogy contained in the title of the Reverend John Williams's account of his captivity in New France: *The Redeemed Captive Returning to Zion*. See generally Plank, "The Culture of Conquest," chapter 1. For an overview of New England's foreign relations in the seventeenth century, see Cohen, "Colonial Leviathan."

28. For eighteenth-century expressions of these doctrines, see Colman, *Faith Victorious*, 5; Appleton, *Origin of War*, 16; Williams, *Martial Wisdom Recommended*, 16.

29. Cressy, *Coming Over*, 36, 63; McCusker and Menard, *Economy of British America*, 103, 211–35.

30. Bailyn, *New England Merchants in the Seventeenth Century.*

31. See Johnson, *John Nelson*, 66–69.

32. Mather, *Magnalia Christi Americana*, 1: 168, 172; Mather, *Decennium Luctuosum*, 59–60.

33. See Jacques-René Brislay, marquis de Denonville to Seignelay, January 1690, in O'Callaghan, *Documents*, 9: 440–47; Joseph Robineau de Villebon, "Memoir on the Present Condition of Port Royal," in Webster, *Acadia at the End of the Seventeenth Century*, 128; Joseph Robineau de Villebon, "Memoir on the Settlements and Harbors from Minas at the Head of the Bay of Fundy to Cape Breton," in Webster, *Acadia at the End of the Seventeenth Century*, 132–33.

34. See Dunn, *The Acadians of Minas.*

35. Reid, "1686–1720," 86.

36. See Reid, "The Scots Crown"; Griffiths and Reid, "New Evidence on New Scotland."

37. Eccles, *France in America*, 68; Daigle, "Nos amis," 36–37.

38. Daigle, "1650–1686," 70.

39. Arsenault, *Histoire et généalogie*, 6: 2255.

40. Richard Philipps to Joseph de Monbeton de Brouillan dit St. Ovide, August 10, 1720, RG1, vol. 14, PANS.

41. Bock, "Micmac," 117.

42. Nietfeld, "Determinants."

43. See generally Martijn, *Les micmacs et la mer.*

44. Morrison, *The Embattled Northeast,* 33; Martin, "European Impact on the Culture of a Northeastern Algonquian Tribe," 8.

45. See Axtell, *The Invasion Within,* 7–8; Miller and Hamell, "New Perspective on Indian-White Contact," 321.

46. Pastore, "The Sixteenth Century."

47. See Martin, "Four Lives of a Micmac Copper Pot"; Martin, *Keepers of the Game,* 40–65. But see Krech, *Indians, Animals, and the Fur Trade.*

48. See Lescarbot, *History of New France,* 2: 311–12.

49. Walker, Conkling, and Bussin, "Wabanaki Confederacy"; Speck, "The Eastern Algonkian Wabanaki Confederacy."

50. Nietfeld, "Determinants."

51. See Wicken, "Encounters," 128–37; Morrison, *The Embattled Northeast,* 62–66.

52. See, for example, Jacques de la Place, "Of What Occurred at Miskou," 1645–46, in Thwaites, *Jesuit Relations,* 30: 127–43, 142.

53. Joseph Howe Letter-Book, November 1841–June 21, 1843, RG 432, doc. 15, PANS.

54. Edward Chappell, *Voyage of His Majesty's Ship Rosmond to Newfoundland* (London, 1818), 82, quoted in Wicken, "Encounters," 133.

55. See "Relation de la mission du P. Antoine Gaulin dans le pays des Mikmaks et en Acadie vers 1720," MG3, series K, doc. 114, National Archives of Canada (hereafter NAC).

56. "Memoire sur l'Isle Royale," 1750, MG1, C11C, vol. 16, NAC; Pierre Maillard, "Lettre de m. l'abbé Maillard," in Casgrain, *Les Soirées canadiennes,* 289–426, 388–404.

57. "Récensement général," November 1708, Ayers mss. 751, p. 2, Newberry Library (hereafter NL); Whitehead, *The Old Man Told Us,* 78.

58. "Société St. Jean Baptiste," in Wallace, *Encyclopedia of Canada,* 6: 43.

59. Thwaites, *Jesuit Relations,* 1: 109–11.

60. Ibid., 3:201–7.

61. See Brooks, "Effect of Catholic Missionaries."

62. Hubbard, *Narrative of the Troubles with the Indians,* 29–30.

63. Leach, *Flintlock and Tomahawk,* 243.

64. See Pulsipher, "Massacre at Hurtlebury Hill."

65. Hubbard, *Narrative of the Trouble with the Indians,* 29–30; Dickason, "Guerre navale," 237.

66. Rawlyk, *Nova Scotia's Massachusetts,* 43.

67. Morrison, *The Embattled Northeast,* 72. See also Baker, "New Evidence."

68. Mather, *A Brief History of the War,* iii.

69. "Report on the Affairs of Canada, Acadia and Newfoundland," in

O'Callaghan, *Documents*, 9: 527-30; Champaigny, "Narrative of Military Operations in Canada, 1691-1692," in O'Callaghan, *Documents*, 9: 534-38; "Memoir on the Projected Attack on Canada, 1692," in O'Callaghan, *Documents*, 9: 543-46; Morrison, *The Embattled Northeast*, 125-26; Reid, "1686-1720," 83.

70. Joseph Robinau de Villebon to Pontchartrain, October 12, 1691, in O'Callaghan, *Documents*, 9: 506-7.

71. See "Narrative of the Most Remarkable Occurrences in Canada, 1692, 1693," in O'Callaghan, *Documents*, 9: 555-73, 571.

72. Proclamation, May 27, 1696 (Boston, 1696).

73. Hirsche, "Collision of Military Cultures"; Malone, *The Skulking Way of War*.

74. "Narrative of the Most Remarkable Occurrences in Canada, 1696, 1697," in O'Callaghan, *Documents*, 9: 664-77, 664; "Events in Acadia Since the Departure of the English from the Saint John River," in Webster, *Acadia at the End of the Seventeenth Century*, 94-95; Rawlyk, *Nova Scotia's Massachusetts*, 82; see Bock, "Micmac," 112.

75. On English providentialism, see Claydon, *William III and the Godly Revolution*.

76. Villebon to William Stoughton, September 15, 1698, in Baxter, ed., *Documentary History of the State of Maine*, 30-32; see also Reid, "1686-1720," 86.

77. "Extracts of Dispatches from the Governors," in O'Callaghan, *Documents*, 9: 917-33, 923; Rawlyk, *Nova Scotia's Massachusetts*, 93.

78. Ranlet, "Dudley, Joseph."

79. Johnson, *Adjustment to Empire*, 333-38; Olson, *Making the Empire Work*, 82-86; see also Kimball, *Joseph Dudley*.

80. See Demos, *The Unredeemed Captive*, 11-25.

81. Quoted in Church, *Entertaining Passages*, 105.

82. *Boston Newsletter*, June 5, August 7, August 21, 1704; Church, *Entertaining Passages*, 105, 114-16; Memorial on the English Expedition to Acadia, 1704, RG1, vol. 3, doc. 22, PANS; Penhallow, *History of the Wars of New England*, 18; Douglass, *Summary*, 1: 307; Dunn, *The Acadians of Minas*, 12; Rawlyk, *Nova Scotia's Massachusetts*, 82.

Chapter Two

1. Waller, *Samuel Vetch*, 3-15.

2. Armitage, "The Scottish Vision of Empire"; Armitage, "The Darien Venture."

3. O'Callaghan, ed., *Journal of the Voyage of the Sloop Mary*; Samuel Vetch, "The Case of Samuel Vetch," 1707, in *Calendar of State Papers, Colonial Series*, 23: 379-82, 379; Waller, *Samuel Vetch*, 53, 59, 62; Leder, *Robert Livingston*, 175-76.

4. Alsop, "Age of the Projectors."

5. Philippe de Rigaud, marquis de Vaudreuil, to Pontchartrain, April 28, 1706, in O'Callaghan, *Documents*, 9: 775–76.

6. Waller, *Samuel Vetch*, 79–89; Abstract of Joseph Dudley to Board of Trade, October 8, 1706, in *Calendar of State Papers, Colonial Series*, 23: 258–59; Dudley to William Popple, October 21, 1706, in *Calendar of State Papers, Colonial Series*, 23: 278; Petition of Samuel Vetch and others, 1707, in *Calendar of State Papers, Colonial Series*, 23: 379; Vetch, "The Case of Samuel Vetch," 23: 379–82.

7. Philopolites [Cotton Mather], *A Memorial of the Present Deplorable State of New England*, reprinted in *Collections of the Massachusetts Historical Society* 5th ser. 6 (1879): 31–64. For the attribution of this pamphlet to Mather, see Silverman, *Life and Times of Cotton Mather*, 213–14. See also Mather, *The Deplorable State of New England*, reprinted in *Collections of the Massachusetts Historical Society* 5th ser. 6 (1879): 96–131. For Dudley's response, see Joseph Dudley, *A Modest Inquiry into the Grounds and Occasions of a Late Pamphlet* (London, 1707), reprinted in *Collections of the Massachusetts Historical Society* 5th ser. 6 (1879): 65–95.

8. Olson, "Hobby, Sir Charles."

9. John Barnard, "Autobiography," in *Collections of the Massachusetts Historical Society* 3d ser. 5 (1836): 178–243, 190–93; Mather, *The Deplorable State of New England*, 32, reprinted in *Collections of the Massachusetts Historical Society* 5th ser. 6 (1879): 127; Bonaventure Mason to ?, July 5, 1707, RG1, vol. 3, doc. 32, PANS; Dudley to Charles Spencer, earl of Sunderland, March 5, 1708, HM 22287, Huntington Library.

10. Penhallow, *History of the Wars of New England*, 43; Barnard, "Autobiography," 196; Mather, *The Deplorable State of New England*, 34, reprinted in *Collections of the Massachusetts Historical Society* 5th ser. 6 (1879): 129.

11. Barnard, "Autobiography," 195.

12. Mather, *The Deplorable State of New England*, 33, reprinted in *Collections of the Massachusetts Historical Society* 5th ser. 6 (1879): 128.

13. See especially "Canada Survey'd," an essay Vetch wrote for Charles Spencer, earl of Sunderland, Britain's secretary of state for the Southern Department, in 1708. The full text of the essay can be found in Samuel Vetch's Letter-Book, pp. 46–60, in the collections of the Museum of the City of New York (hereafter MCNY). Excerpts from "Canada Survey'd" can be found in *Calendar of State Papers, Colonial Series*, 24: 41–51, 147–50. For scholarly discussions of the essay, see Waller, *Samuel Vetch*, 106–9; Bond, *Queen Anne's American Kings*, 22–24; and Alsop, "Samuel Vetch's 'Canada Survey'd'"; see also Alsop, "Age of the Projectors," 43–44.

14. See, for example, Vetch to Sunderland, June 29, 1709, Samuel Vetch Letter-Book, p. 28; Vetch to the Lord Treasurer, December 9, 1709, Samuel Vetch Letter-Book, p. 111; Vetch to Sunderland, May 15, 1710, in *Calendar of State Papers, Colonial Series*, 25: 101–2; see also Alsop, "Samuel Vetch's 'Canada Survey'd,'" 51–52.

15. See, for example, D'Avenant, *Political and Commercial Works*, 2: 9. See also Alsop, "Age of the Projectors," 44–46; Alsop, "Samuel Vetch's 'Canada Survey'd,'" 49.

16. Dudley to Board of Trade, October 2, 1706, HM 9916, Huntington Library.

17. Vetch, "Canada Survey'd," Samuel Vetch Letter-Book, p. 55, reprinted in *Calendar of State Papers, Colonial Series*, 24: 51.

18. See Bartlett, *Gerald of Wales*, 202–3. Jordan, *White over Black*, 11–20; Vaughn, "From White Man to Redskin"; but see Nancy Shoemaker, "How Indians Got To Be Red." See also Robert Hale's Notebook, circa 1720, pp. 370–402, Hale Family Papers.

19. Vetch, "Canada Survey'd," p. 50, reprinted in *Calendar of State Papers, Colonial Series*, 24: 46; see also Memorial of a Council of War to Queen Anne, October 1710, in Casgrain, *Collection*, 1: 149–51.

20. See, for example, Vetch to General McKarly, March 10, 1709, Samuel Vetch Letter-Book, p. 2. See also Alsop, "Samuel Vetch's 'Canada Survey'd,'" 41.

21. Vetch, "Canada Survey'd," p. 55, reprinted in *Calendar of State Papers, Colonial Series*, 24: 51. See also Dudley to Board of Trade, 1707, in *Calendar of State Papers, Colonial Series*, 23: 590–92.

22. Vetch, "Canada Survey'd," p. 58; "Examination of Ensign Samuel Whiting," June 2, 1709, in O'Callaghan, *Documents*, 9: 835–36; Memorial of a Council of War to Queen Anne, October 1710, in Casgrain, *Collection*, 1: 149–51; Vetch to William Legge, Lord Dartmouth, January 22, 1711, in *Calendar of State Papers, Colonial Series*, 25: 344.

23. Vetch, "Canada Survey'd," p. 50, reprinted in *Calendar of State Papers, Colonial Series*, 24: 46.

24. Memorial of a Council of War to Queen Anne, October 1710, in Casgrain, *Collection*, 1: 149–51; Vetch to Popple, June 15, 1711, in *Calendar of State Papers, Colonial Series*, 25: 551–52; Vetch to Board of Trade, November 26, 1711, CO 217/1, doc. 1, Public Record Office (hereafter PRO). See also Samuel Vetch, "Some Reasons and Proposals Humbly Offered for Settling the Main [Atlantic] Coast of Nova Scotia with All Imaginable Speed," 1714, CO 217/1, doc. 100, PRO.

25. Vetch to Sunderland, June 29, 1709, Samuel Vetch Letter-Book, p. 28; Vetch to Duke of Dover, June 29, 1709, Samuel Vetch Letter-Book, p. 32.

26. Vetch, "Canada Survey'd," p. 51, reprinted in *Calendar of State Papers, Colonial Series*, 24: 47.

27. Vetch would continue to petition the Tories insistently and often obsequiously until they fell from power after the death of Queen Anne in 1714. See, for example, Vetch to Robert Harley, earl of Oxford, July 22, 1714, Add. 70207, British Library (hereafter BL).

28. Rawlyk, *Nova Scotia's Massachusetts*, 53–54.

29. Alsop, "Samuel Vetch's 'Canada Survey'd,'" 43; see also Waller, *Samuel Vetch*, 121–23; Alsop, "Age of the Projectors," 45. For background information on

Nicholson, see McCully, "Governor Francis Nicholson"; Webb, "Strange Career of Francis Nicholson."

30. Instructions for Samuel Vetch, reprinted in *Collections of the Nova Scotia Historical Society* 4 (1884): 64–68.

31. For a list of the eleven officers, see Alsop, "Distribution of British Officers."

32. See Samuel Vetch Letter-Book, pp. 1–3; Vetch to Sunderland, June 29, 1709, HM 22286, Huntington Library.

33. Examination of Ensign Samuel Whiting, June 2, 1709, in O'Callaghan, *Documents*, 9: 835–36.

34. Waller, *Samuel Vetch*, 142–57.

35. See Shannon, "Dressing for Success on the Mohawk Frontier."

36. Vetch to Francis Nicholson, September 22, 1709, Samuel Vetch Letter-Book, p. 68; Minutes of a council at Rehoboth, Massachusetts, October 14, 1709, Samuel Vetch Letter-Book, p. 93; Vetch to Sunderland, January 9, 1710, Samuel Vetch Letter-Book, p. 113. See also Bond, *Queen Anne's American Kings* and Hinderaker, "The 'Four Indian Kings.'" For a detailed inventory and close analysis of the printed material and other visual artifacts occasioned by the visit of the four "kings," see Garratt, *The Four Indian Kings*.

37. Vetch to Nicholson, August 12, 1709, Samuel Vetch Letter-Book, p. 60.

38. Hinderaker, "The 'Four Indian Kings,'" 489–90. See Abstract of Dudley and Vetch to Sunderland, February 3, 1710, in *Calendar of State Papers, Colonial Series*, 25: 40.

39. Instructions for Richard, Viscount Shannon, July 13, 1710, in *Calendar of State Papers, Colonial Series*, 25: 135. Shannon was directed to relay these instructions to Vetch and Nicholson. See also Nicholson and a Council of War to Board of Trade, October 1710, in *Calendar of State Papers, Colonial Series*, 25: 245–47.

40. Holmes, *British Politics in the Age of Anne*, 69, 105–6; Dickinson, "The Poor Palatines and the Parties."

41. Overviews of British policy in Minorca can be found in Homs, *Las Instituciones de Menorca*; Gregory, *Minorca*; and Laurie, *Life of Richard Kane*. For the provisions of the Treaty of Utrecht governing the French colonists on Newfoundland, see Israel, *Major Treaties of Modern History*, 210. For evidence on the Tories' Newfoundland policy in action, see John Moody to Board of Trade, June 22, 1714, CO 194/5, doc. 133, PRO; Moody to William Tavener, July 5, 1714, CO 194/5, doc. 166, PRO; Proclamation, July 12, 1714, CO 194/5, doc. 168, PRO; Moody to Henry St. John, Viscount Bolingbroke, August 25, 1714, CO 194/5, doc. 256, PRO. For overviews of British policy in Gibraltar, see Conn, *Gibraltar in British Diplomacy*; Jackson, *Rock of the Gibraltarians*.

42. Vetch to Dartmouth, January 22, 1711, in *Calendar of State Papers, Colonial Series*, 25: 343–44.

43. Vetch to Dartmouth, November 6, 1711, Sloane 3607, doc. 9; Vetch to Thomas Caulfield, 1711, Sloane 3607, doc. 8; Vetch to Charles Hobby, 1711, in *Collections of the Nova Scotia Historical Society* 4 (1884): 104–5.

44. For one indication of New England's response to the failure of the 1711 expedition, see Dudley's proclamation printed in the *Boston Newsletter*, October 29, 1711.

45. "The Case of Colonel Vetch," 1714, CO 217/1, doc. 185, PRO.

46. Mather, *A Memorial of the Present Deplorable State of New England*, 9, reprinted in *Collections of the Massachusetts Historical Society* 5th ser. 6 (1879): 41.

47. Mather, *Diary*, 2:30.

48. Cotton Mather to Samuel Penhallow, May 22, 1710, in Mather, *Diary*, 2:36.

49. Concerning the clergymen's joining the aborted 1709 expedition, see Dudley to Vetch, September 8, 1709, Samuel Vetch Letter-Book, p. 64. The letter indicates that the province hired chaplains to serve on the expedition. It does not say who they were, but it is likely that they were New Englanders, because the British forces that were expected to join in the expedition never arrived (the reason the expedition was canceled). For an indication of the New Englanders' proclivity to blame Vetch personally for the cancellation of the 1709 expedition, see De Ramzay to Vaudreuil, October 19, 1709, in O'Callaghan, *Documents*, 9: 838–40.

50. Instructions for Nicholson, March 18, 1710, Peter Force Collection, series 8D, item 6, p. 2; Petition of Hobby et al., October 13, 1710, Peter Force Collection, Series 8D/6; Address of General Nicholson and the Council of War, October 14, 1710, in *Calendar of State Papers, Colonial Series*, 25: 229; Vetch to Hobby, July 5, 1711, in *Collections of the Nova Scotia Historical Society* 4 (1884): 104–5; Vetch to Board of Trade, 1714, CO 217/1, doc. 97, PRO; Petition of Hobby to the King in council, received January 14, 1715, CO 217/1, doc. 167, PRO; John Gorham to Paul Mascarene, November 24, 1748, CO 217/9, doc. 45, PRO.

51. See Murrin, "Anglicizing an American Colony;" Breen, "An Empire of Goods"; Steele, *The English Atlantic*.

52. For indications of the merchants' stance, see Vetch to Privy Council, October 16, 1712, Sloane 3607, p. 23; Vetch to Peter Mason, May 22, 1713, CO 217/31, doc. 35, PRO; Caulfield to Nicholson, November 5, 1713, CO 217/1, doc. 64, PRO; Petition of Vetch, winter 1714, CO 217/1, doc. 104, PRO; Samuel Vetch, "The Case of Colonel Vetch" (1714), CO 217/1, doc. 105, PRO. See also Chard, "Canso," 55–56.

53. Petition of Hobby to the King in council, received January 14, 1715, CO 217/1, doc. 167, PRO.

54. See, for example, Vetch to Dartmouth, May 1711, CO 217/1, doc. 122, PRO.

55. *Boston Newsletter*, November 6, 1710.

56. Vetch to Dartmouth, June 14, 1711, Gay Papers, Nova Scotia, vol. 1, doc. 100.

57. Christopher Cahonet to ?, July 20, 1711, RG1, vol. 3, doc. 51, PANS; Antoine Gaulin to ?, September 5, 1711, RG1, vol. 3, doc. 48, PANS.

58. Minutes of a Council of War, June 15, 1711, CO 217/1, doc. 124, PRO.

59. Vetch to Dartmouth, November 6, 1711, Sloane 3607, doc. 9.

60. Petition of Hobby, January 14, 1715, CO 217/1, doc. 167, PRO.

61. See, for example, the addresses of a Council of War, October 1710, in *Calendar of State Papers, Colonial Series*, 25: 229, 245–47; "The Council of War's Memorial to the Queen about Settling Nova Scotia," 1711, Samuel Vetch Letter-Book, pp. 128–130; Vetch to Board of Trade, November 26, 1711, CO 217/1, doc. 1, PRO; Samuel Vetch, "Some Reasons and Proposals Humbly Offered for Settling the Main Coast of Nova Scotia," 1714, CO 217/1, doc. 100, PRO; Petition of Vetch and others, May 13, 1720, CO 217/3, doc. 12, PRO; Petition of officers, received April 17, 1722, CO 217/4, doc. 178, PRO.

62. Memorial of a Council of War, October 14, 1710, in Casgrain, *Collection*, 1: 149–51.

63. See Fischer, *Albion's Seed*, 605–782; Landsman, "Legacy of British Union."

64. Sewall, *Diary* 2: 652.

65. George Vane to John Hill, May 5, 1712, CO 217/31, doc. 29, PRO; Vane to ?, May 5, 1712, CO 217/31, doc. 24, PRO.

66. Vetch's answers to inquiries posed by the Board of Trade, spring 1714, CO 217/1, doc. 97, PRO. See also Vetch to Board of Trade, November 24, 1714, in Akins, *Selections*, 5; Vetch to Board of Trade, March 9, 1715, in Akins, *Selections*, 7.

67. Colley, *Britons*.

68. Durand de la Garenne to ?, November 6, 1710, RG1, vol. 4, doc. 12(a), PANS; Philippe de Pastour de Costabelle to ?, November 6, 1710, RG1, vol. 4, doc. 12(b), PANS.

69. Mascarene to Nicholson, November 6, 1713, in *Collections of the Nova Scotia Historical Society* 4 (1884): 76–77.

70. *Boston Newsletter*, July 25, 1711; Gaulin to ?, September 5, 1711, RG1, vol. 3, doc. 48, PANS; Vetch to Robert Hunter, June 19, 1711, Sloane 3607, doc. 42; Vetch to Board of Trade, June 24, 1711, Sloane 3607, doc. 3; Vaudreuil to Pontchartrain, October 25, 1711, in O'Callaghan, *Documents*, 9: 858; Dickason, "Louisbourg and the Indians," 73.

71. Vetch to Dartmouth, June 14, 1711, Gay Papers, Nova Scotia, vol. 1, doc. 100; Vetch to ?, June 24, 1711, in *Collections of the Nova Scotia Historical Society* 4 (1884): 94–95; Vaudreuil to Pontchartrain, October 25, 1711, in O'Callaghan, *Documents*, 9: 858.

72. See Basque, "Genre et gestion"; Basque, *Des Hommes de pouvoir*, 62. See also Basque, "Conflits et solidarités familiales."

73. Statement of the "principal inhabitants of Acadia or Nova Scotia," November 28, 1711, CO 217/1, doc. 184, PRO.

74. Samuel Sewall, "Diary," in *Collections of the Massachusetts Historical Society* 5th ser. 6 (1879): 298–99.

75. Vetch to Nathaniel Blackmore, May 3, 1711, Samuel Vetch Letter-Book, pp. 155–56.

76. Vane to Hill, May 5, 1712, CO 217/31, doc. 29, PRO.

77. "Les principaux habitants de Port Royal" to Vaudreuil, November 13, 1710, RG1, vol. 3, doc. 46, PANS; see Waller, *Samuel Vetch*, 196.

78. Declaration of Vane et al., May 31, 1714, CO 217/1, doc. 187, PRO; Statement of the "principal inhabitants of Acadia or Nova Scotia," November 28, 1711, CO 217/1, doc. 184, PRO.

79. Appointment of John Harrison, October 11, 1710, A/9, doc. 391, Records of the Society for the Propagation of the Gospel (SPG). See also John Harrison to Nicholson, November 30, 1713, A/8, doc. 575, Records of the SPG; Memorials concerning the state of the church at Annapolis Royal, November 23, 1713, A/8, doc. 568, Records of the SPG.

80. Order of Caulfield, November 7, 1713, A/8, doc. 568, Records of the SPG.

81. Caulfield to Vetch, November 2, 1715, in Casgrain, *Collection*, 1:113–14; Abstract of Caulfield to Board of Trade, November 2, 1715, in MacMechan, ed., *Calendar*, 27; Abstract of Caulfield to Vetch, November 1, 1715, in MacMechan, *Calendar*, 29; Caulfield to ?, November 2, 1715, in Shortt, Johnston, and Lactot, *Documents*, 96; Order of council, September 29, 1714, CO 217/2, doc. 33; Statement of Francis Spelman and Andrew Simpson, September 2, 1715, CO 217/2, doc. 45, PRO; Vetch to Board of Trade, September 2, 1715, in Shortt, Johnston, and Lactot, *Documents*, 95.

82. See Moogk, "Reluctant Exiles."

83. Le Blant, *Un Colonial sous Louis XIV*, 170–71.

84. Caulfield to Nicholson, November 13, 1713, CO 217/1, doc. 64, PRO; List of inhabitants who left the province on the sloop *Marie Joseph*, August 18, 1714, CO 217/1, doc. 201, PRO; List of goods taken by inhabitants leaving Minas on the *St. Louis*, CO 217/1, doc. 224, PRO; Petition of inhabitants of Annapolis Royal, August 25, 1714, CO 217/1, doc. 196, PRO; Petition of inhabitants of Minas and Cobequid, September 17, 1714, CO 217/1, doc. 226, PRO; Abstract of Caulfield to Board of Trade, November 23, 1715, in MacMechan, *Calendar*, 34; Pothier, "Acadian Emigration to Ile Royale."

85. McNeill, *Atlantic Empires of France and Spain*, 20, 22.

86. See Rawlyk, "1720–1744."

87. This controversy will be discussed in more detail in Chapter 4, below.

88. John Doucette to Secretary of State, November 5, 1717, in Akins, *Selections*, 12; Doucette to Board of Trade, November 6, 1717, CO 217/2, doc. 175, PRO.

89. Philipps to St. Ovide, August 10, 1720, RG1, vol. 14, PANS.

90. Minutes of the Marine Council, October 4, 1719, August 1720, in Casgrain, *Collection*, 2: 5, 6–8.

91. See Le Blant, *Un Colonial sous Louis XIV*, 169–70.

92. ". . . ils avoient Les Bois dont jamais personne ne seroit capable de les débusquer." Quoted in Dickason, "Louisbourg and the Indians," 68.

93. "Memoir Respecting the Abenaquis of Acadia, 1718" in O'Callaghan, *Documents*, 9: 878–80.

94. Letter to St. Ovide, September 18, 1726, C11B, vol. 8, doc. 34, NAC; see also Antoine Gaulin, "Relation de la mission du P. Antoine Gaulin dans le pays des Mikmaks et en Acadie vers 1720," MG3, series K, pp. 108–9, NAC; Costabelle to ministry, November 5, 1715, C11B, vol. 1, doc. 145, NAC; "Sur les sauvages," December 4, 1716, C11B, vol. 2, doc. 44, NAC; Minutes of the Marine Council, November 24, 1719, November 15, 1721, December 10, 1722, C11B, vol. 5, docs. 20, 340, and 43, NAC.

95. See Plank, "The Two Majors Cope," 29n.41.

96. Dickason, "Louisbourg and the Indians."

97. Vetch, "Canada Survey'd," p. 46, reprinted in *Calendar of State Papers, Colonial Series*, 24: 42.

98. Memorial of a Council of War, October 9, 1710, A/10, doc. 288, Records of the SPG.

99. See Pierre Maillard, "Lettre de m. l'abbé Maillard," in Casgrain, *Les Soirées canadiennes*, 291–426, 377; Report of Jean-Louis Le Loutre, July 29, 1749, RG1, C11C, vol. 9, doc. 130, NAC.

100. See Wicken, "Encounters."

Chapter Three

1. Sutherland, "Philipps, Richard."

2. Akins, *Selections*, 18–19, n; Piers, "The Fortieth Regiment."

3. Moody, "A Just and Disinterested Man," 55.

4. See Pagden, *European Encounters with the New World*; Pagden, *Lords of All the World*.

5. See Vaughn, "From White Man to Redskin." But see also Shoemaker, "How Indians Got To Be Red." Among British colonists, New England's Dr. William Douglass, an immigrant to Massachusetts from Scotland, was precocious in attributing the distinctiveness of "Indian" peoples to biology. See Douglass, *Practical Essay*, 37–38; Douglass, *Summary*, 1: 116,n., 151–61.

6. Israel, *Major Peace Treaties*, 1: 209–11.

7. For a rare use of the word "mulatto," see Council minutes, January 4, 1745, in Fergusson, ed. *Minutes*, 55–56. See also Chapter 5, below.

8. See, for example, Griffiths, "1600–1650," 58–59; Daigle, "1650–1686," 65; Reid, "1686–1720," 88.

9. Instructions for Philipps, July 14, 1719, Tredegar Park Mss., box 79, doc. 25; Report of the Board of Trade, September 8, 1721, King's Mss. 205, doc. 4.

10. The garrison at Annapolis Royal experienced frequent desertions. Some of the men who left were later discovered among the French at Louisbourg or the Acadians, but others apparently escaped without a trace. See Vetch to Dartmouth, June 14, 1711, Gay Papers, vol. 1, doc. 100; Vetch to Dartmouth, August 8, 1712, Sloane Mss. 3607, doc. 19; "The Case of Samuel Vetch," 1714, CO 217/1, doc. 105, PRO.

11. Instructions to the Governor of Newfoundland and Nova Scotia, April 30, 1719, CO 217/31, doc. 89, PRO; Philipps to James Craggs, July 1720, in Akins, *Selections*, 35–37; Philipps to Board of Trade, August 16, 1721, CO 217/4, doc. 42, PRO; Philipps to Board of Trade, November 30, 1734, CO 217/7, doc. 136, PRO.

12. Instructions to the Governor of Newfoundland and Nova Scotia, April 30, 1719; Philipps to Craggs, July 1720, in Akins, *Selections*, 35–37.

13. Philipps to Board of Trade, November 30, 1734, CO 217/7, doc. 136, PRO.

14. Upton, *Micmacs and Colonists*, 39.

15. Chard, "Canso," 59; Flemming, *The Canso Islands*, 4.

16. See Chard, "Southack, Cyprian."

17. Instructions for Cyprian Southack, March 11, 1713, CO 217/2, doc. 244, PRO; Southack to Samuel Shute, January 22, 1719, CO 217/2, doc. 252, PRO; Abstract of a memorial of Southack, December 9, 1713, in *Calendar of State Papers, Colonial Series*, 27: 258.

18. Samuel Vetch, "Some Reasons and Proposals Humbly Offered for Settling the Main [Atlantic] Coast of Nova Scotia with All Imaginable Speed," 1714, CO 217/1, doc. 100, PRO.

19. The Acadian man was probably François Tourangeau, a seventy-three-year-old resident of Cape Sable, or one of his sons. For a reference to Tourangeau, see "Resensement général," 1708, Ayers Mss. 751, p. 40.

20. Dudley to Southack, April 8, 1715, CO 217/2, doc. 245, PRO; Southack to Shute, January 22, 1719, CO 217/2, doc. 252, PRO.

21. David Jeffries and Charles Shoprove to Robert Mours, July 6, 1715, CO 217/2, doc. 5, PRO; Jean Loyard to Caulfield, 1715, CO 217/2, doc. 55, PRO; Caulfield to the "Cape Sable Indians," 1715, CO 217/2, doc. 56, PRO; Abstract of Instructions for Peter Capoon, August 16, 1715, in MacMechan, *Calendar*, 21; Abstract of Caulfield to Board of Trade, December 14, 1715, in MacMechan, *Calendar*, 35; *Boston Newsletter*, July 25, August 1, August 8, 1715; Reid, "Mission to the Micmac." See also Chard, "Canso."

22. Jeffries and Shoprove to Mours, July 6, 1715, CO 217/2, doc. 5, PRO.

23. See Prins, "Tribulations of a Border Tribe," 274–313; Bourque, "Ethnicity on the Maritime Peninsula." For an indication of the long-running scholarly controversy over Mi'kmaq territoriality, see Martin, "Four Lives of a Micmac Copper Pot."

24. Cyprian Southack, "Memorandum," CO 217/2, doc. 249, PRO; Southack went onboard as a representative of the council of Massachusetts. Flemming, *The Canso Islands*, 12–13; Chard, "Canso," 62; *Some Considerations on the Consequences of the French Settling Colonies on the Mississippi*, 32–33; Cyprian Southack, "Journal," January 13, 1719, CO 217/2, doc. 250, PRO.

25. Philipps to Board of Trade, January 3, 1719/20, in Akins, *Selections*, 16–17; Petition of 24 inhabitants of Annapolis Royal and 27 "officers civil and military, together with the inhabitants [of Canso]" to the Board of Trade, August 1,

1734, CO 217/39, doc. 120, PRO; Mascarene to Board of Trade, December 1, 1743, Add. Mss. 19,071, doc. 41.

26. Philipps to Board of Trade, October 1, 1721, CO 217/4, doc. 45, PRO.

27. Statement of "Prudent Robichaux," August 24, 1720, in Shortt, Johnston, and Lactot, *Documents*, 131.

28. Statement of Michael Richard, August 24, 1720, CO 217/3, doc. 140, PRO.

29. See Savelle, *Diplomatic History of the Canadian Boundary*, 7–8; Fleming, *The Canso Islands*, 164n. 29.

30. For accounts of the war and the treaties that ended it, see Upton, *Micmacs and Colonists*, 40–45; Morrison, *Embattled Northeast*, 185–90; Dickason, "Amerindians Between French and English in Nova Scotia," 39–41; Dickason, "'Guerre navale,'" 244; Wicken, "Mi'kmaq and Wuastukwiuk Treaties." To place the war in a broader Native American context see Walker, Conkling, and Buesing, "Wabanaki Confederacy"; Speck, "Eastern Algonkian Wabanaki Confederacy."

31. Dickason, "Louisbourg and the Indians," 77; Dickason, "'Guerre navale,'" 244.

32. Vaudreuil to ministry, November 28, 1724, in O'Callaghan, *Documents*, 9: 936–39; Abstract of letters of Vaudreuil and Pierre La Chasse, April 24, 1725, in O'Callaghan, *Documents*, 9: 945–47.

33. Abstract of Vaudreuil to ministry, October 31, 1725, in O'Callaghan, *Documents*, 9: 955; Abstract of Vaudreuil to ministry, August 7, 1725, in O'Callaghan, *Documents*, 9: 947–49.

34. Abstract of dispatches from Canada, March 16, 1728, in O'Callaghan, *Documents*, 9: 990–94.

35. Abstract of Vaudreuil to ministry, October 31, 1725, in O'Callaghan, *Documents*, 9: 955–56.

36. Declaration of Doucette, June 29, 1722, CO 217/4, doc. 123, PRO.

37. Steele, "Surrendering Rites," 147–48; Proclamation of Massachusetts government, May 27, 1696 (Boston, 1696); Penhallow, *History of the Wars of New England*, 93–94; Doucette to Board of Trade, June 29, 1722, CO 217/4, doc. 112, PRO; William Winniet to Doucette, July 1, 1722, CO 217/4, doc. 128, PRO; Douglass, *Summary*, 1: 317–18; Council minutes, July 8, 1724, in MacMechan, *Minutes*, 56–57; Report of Felix Pain, RG1, vol. 3, doc. 86, PANS.

38. "Treaty No. 239," in Cumming and Mickenberg, *Native Rights in Canada*, 302–6; Treaty of June 4, 1726, CO 217/4, doc. 320, PRO. See Wicken, "Encounters," 411–38; Wicken, "Mi'kmaq and Wuastukwiuk Treaties."

39. See Dickason, "Louisbourg and the Indians," 27.

40. Le Normant to ministry, December 10, 1722, MG1, C11B, vol. 6, doc. 74, NAC; St. Ovide to ministry, November 24, 1724, MG1, C11B, vol. 7, doc. 28, NAC.

41. Upton, *Micmacs and Colonists*, 34; Minutes of the Marine Council, Au-

gust 1720, in Casgrain, *Collection*, 2: 6–8; Letter to St. Ovide, September 18, 1726, C11B, vol. 8, doc. 34, NAC; see also Antoine Gaulin, "Relation de la mission du P. Antoine Gaulin dans le pays des Mikmaks et en Acadie vers 1720," MG3, series K, pp. 108–9, NAC; Costabelle to ministry, November 5, 1715, C11B, vol. 1, doc. 145, NAC; "Sur les sauvages," December 4, 1716, C11B, vol. 2, doc. 44, NAC; Minutes of the Marine Council, November 24, 1719, November 15, 1721, December 10, 1722, C11B, vol. 5, docs. 20, 340, and C11B, vol. 6, doc. 43, NAC.

42. Council minutes, August 12, 1724, in MacMechan, *Minutes*, 70.

43. Doucette to Gaulin, March 14, 1722, CO 217/4, doc. 134, PRO; St. Ovide to ministry, December 10, 1725, C11B, vol. 7, doc. 191, NAC.

44. Abstract of dispatches from Longueil and Michel Begon, May 7, 1726, in O'Callaghan, *Documents*, 9: 955–65; Louis XV to Charles de la Boische, marquis de Beauharnois and Dupuy, April 29, 1727, in O'Callaghan, *Documents*, 9: 989; Council minutes, November 1, November 11, 1731, in MacMechan, *Minutes*, 199–200, 204.

45. See *Trials of Five Persons*.

46. *Boston Gazette*, September 5, 1726; see also Wicken, "26 August 1726."

47. *Boston Gazette*, October 10, 1726.

48. *Trials of Five Persons*, 13, 14; Arsenault, *Histoire et généalogie*, 1593, 1597–98.

49. *Trials of Five Persons*, 14–15.

50. For discussions of this system among the Mi'kmaq, see Wicken, "Encounters," 145–51; see also Plank, "Changing Country of Anthony Casteel"; Lescarbot, *History of New France*, 3: 263–72; Maillard, *Customs and Manners of the Mickmackis*, 19–33.

51. *Trials of Five Persons*, 7.

52. See Flaherty, "Criminal Practice in Provincial Massachusetts," 219; Millender, "Transformation of the American Criminal Trial," 36.

53. Erasmus James Phillips to Lawrence Armstrong, March 24, 1727, CO 217/38, doc. 143, PRO.

54. Erasmus James Phillips, the man who read the records to the Acadians, secured an appointment to a proposed court of admiralty for Nova Scotia in 1729. In that capacity he hoped to apply the same legal procedures that were reflected in the court records he read aloud to the Acadians. See Godfrey, "Phillips, Erasmus James."

55. *Trials of Five Persons*, 30.

56. For examples of the restitution system in practice, see Council minutes, June 20, 1737, CO 217/31, doc. 118, PRO; Armstrong to Thomas Hollis-Pelham, duke of Newcastle, July 8, 1737, CO 217/39, doc. 175, PRO; Mascarene to Alexander Bourg, April 12, 1742, CO 217/39, doc. 254, PRO; Letter from Mascarene, April 13, 1742, CO 217/39, doc. 255, PRO; Mascarene to Jean-Louis Le Loutre, June 2, 1742, CO 217/39, doc. 252, PRO.

57. See Plank, "The Two Majors Cope."

58. See Dunn, *The Acadians of Minas*, 18.

59. Winaguadesh (the transcription of the name varies) appears on a 1708 census of the Mi'kmaq. He was an orphan, seventeen years old, in 1708. He had one brother named Antoine, aged ten. The census lists two "sauvages des Mines" named Andres, a father and a son, aged twenty-six and one respectively. In 1732 Jacques would have been forty-one, Antoine thirty-four, and Andres twenty-five or fifty (unless someone else named "Andres" was involved). The best French account of this incident indicates that four Mi'kmaq men spoke with the carpenter, but it does not name them. Council minutes, July 25, 1732, in MacMechan, *Minutes*, pp. 238–41; "Récensement général," November 1708, Ayers Mss. 751, pp. 11–13; St. Ovide to ministry, November 14, 1732, MG1, C11B, vol. 12, doc. 256, NAC; Minutes of the French marine council, February 9, 1733, MG1, C11B, vol. 14, doc. 12, NAC.

60. Philipps to Newcastle, November 15, 1732, in Akins, *Selections*, 101.

61. See generally Barnes, "'Daily Cry for Justice.'"

62. Charles Davison, Peter Capon, and W. Edwards, "A Scheme for Settling of a Colony at Le Havre in Nova Scotia," received by the Board of Trade August 23, 1723, CO 217/4, doc. 189, PRO.

63. See especially Philipps to Board of Trade, October 2, 1729, CO 217/5, doc. 170, PRO. See also letter from Philipps, October 2, 1729, in Innis, *Select Documents*, 134–35. For reports on other years, see Charles Morris's description of Nova Scotia, January 9, 1762, King's Mss. 205, doc. 192; Armstrong to Board of Trade, October 29, 1733, CO 217/7, doc. 28, PRO. See also Robert Ffytche, "Scheme of the Fishery, 1732, at Canso," in Innis, *Select Documents*, 160–62.

64. "Reasons for the Immediate Peopling of Nova Scotia," June 1735, CO 217/39, doc. 138, PRO; William Catterell's answers to the Board of Trade's inquiries about the fishery at Canso, 1734, CO 217/7, doc. 107, PRO. See also Bell, *"Foreign Protestants"*, 25.

65. Thomas Waterhouse's answers to queries from the Board of Trade relating to the fishery at Canso for the year 1730, in Shortt, Johnston, and Lactot, *Documents*, 179; "Answers to the Several Queries from the Lords Commissioners for Trade and Plantations Relating to the Fishery of Canso," 1739, in Innis, *Select Documents*, 62; Captain J. Towery's report on the fishery at Canso for 1735, CO 217/7, doc. 148, PRO.

66. Philipps to Christopher Aldridge, April 12, 1733, Tredegar Park Mss. 284, doc. 20. For more general statements about territorial expansion and settlement, and its effect on the ability of fishermen to recruit and retain workers, see Innis, *Cod Fisheries*, 100, 146–47; Lounsbury, *British Fishery at Newfoundland*, 193–94. For an extensive discussion of this problem in practical terms, see Vickers, *Farmers and Fishermen*.

67. St. Ovide to ministry, November 14, 1732, MG1, C11B, vol. 12, doc. 254, NAC.

68. Pierre Maillard, "Lettre de m. l'abbé Maillard," in Casgrain, *Les Soirées*

canadiennes, 289-426, 388-404. See Maillard to How, November 3, 1746, in Gaudet, "Généalogie," 102-3; Pincombe, "How, Edward." See also Ferguson, *Report*, 5; Flemming, *Canso Islands*, 38-39.

Chapter Four

1. See Report of Philipps, April 26, 1718, CO 217/2, doc. 170, PRO.

2. Black, *British Foreign Policy*; see also Holmes, *British Politics in the Age of Anne*.

3. See Roy, "Settlement and Population Growth."

4. Bock, "Micmac," 117.

5. Caulfield to Nicholson, November 13, 1713, CO 217/1, doc. 64, PRO; List of inhabitants who left the province on the sloop *Marie Joseph*, August 18, 1714, CO 217/1, doc. 201, PRO; List of goods taken by inhabitants leaving Minas on the *St. Louis*, CO 217/1, doc. 224, PRO; Petition of inhabitants of Annapolis Royal, August 25, 1714, CO 217/1, doc. 196, PRO; Petition of inhabitants of Minas and Cobequid, September 17, 1714, CO 217/1, doc. 226, PRO; Pothier, "Acadian Emigration to Ile Royale."

6. Vetch to Board of Trade, November 24, 1714, in Akins, *Selections*, 5.

7. See Michel Begon to Jean-Frédéric Maurepas, September 25, 1715, in O'Callaghan, *Documents*, 9: 932; Instructions for Capoon and Thomas Button, January 1715, in Akins, *Selections*, 3; Aldridge to Nicholson, January 15, 1715, CO 217/2, doc. 47, PRO; Caulfield to Secretary of State, May 3, 1715, in Akins, *Selections*, 7.

8. For early expressions of this stance, see the statements of January 22, 1715 (N.S.), CO 217/1, docs. 353, 355, PRO; see also Basque, *Des Hommes de pouvoir*, 60-61.

9. Statement of the Acadians, 1717, in MacMechan, *Calendar*, 52-53.

10. Vetch to Dartmouth, November 6, 1711, Sloane Mss. 3607, doc. 9; Vetch's instructions to Hobby, 1711, in *Collections of the Nova Scotia Historical Society* 4 (1884): 104-5; Vetch's proclamation to the inhabitants living outside the banlieu, January 11, 1711, in Samuel Vetch Letter-Book, p. 125; Doucette to Secretary of State, November 5, 1717, in Akins, *Selections*, 12; Doucette to Board of Trade, November 6, 1717, CO 217/2, doc. 175, PRO.

11. Galerme, *A Relation of the Misfortunes*; *Pennsylvania Archives* 8th ser., vol. 5, p. 4190.

12. Caulfield to Vetch, November 2, 1715, in Casgrain, *Collection*, 1: 113-14.

13. Report of Philipps, April 26, 1718, CO 217/2, doc. 170, PRO.

14. Israel, *Major Peace Treaties*, 1: 210.

15. For a discussion of the Irish "penal laws" in practice, see Connolly, *Religion, Law, and Power*, 263-313.

16. Dinkin, *Voting in Provincial America*, 31-32, 51; Laurie, *Life of Richard*

Kane; Homs, *Las Instituciones de Menorca*. For a discussion of the unsettled legal precedents governing the status of Catholics in the empire, see Lawson, *The Imperial Challenge*, 44-45.

17. See letter from Philipps (no date, 1720), CO 217/3, doc. 103, PRO.

18. Mascarene's description of Nova Scotia, September 27, 1720, CO 217/4, doc. 329, PRO; Armstrong to Board of Trade, June 23, 1729, in Akins, *Selections*, 82; Armstrong to Board of Trade, June 19, 1736, CO 217/31, doc. 115, PRO; Mascarene, "Proclamation Regarding Romish Priests," July 3, 1740, in MacMechan, *Calendar*, 242-43; Mascarene to Jean Des Enclaves, June 29, 1741, in Akins, *Selections*, 111; Chris Kirby to Secretary of State, August 30, 1743, CO 217/31, doc. 187, PRO; *The Importance of Settling and Fortifying Nova Scotia*, 8.

19. Philipps to Board of Trade, January 3, 1719, in Akins, *Selections*, 16.

20. Mascarene to Nicholson, November 6, 1710, in *Collections of the Nova Scotia Historical Society* 4 (1884): 70-72; Proclamation of Mascarene, November 16, 1710, in Shortt, Johnston, and Lactot, *Documents*, 20-21. See also Council minutes, April 29, 1720, in MacMechan, *Minutes*, 4. The best sources of information on the deputy system are MacMechan, *Minutes*, and Fergusson, *Minutes*.

21. Very early on, the British hoped that the deputies would serve as tax collectors, but the Acadians consistently refused to pay taxes. See Proclamation of Mascarene, November 16, 1710, in Shortt, Johnston, and Lactot, *Documents*, 20-21.

22. See Philipps to the inhabitants of Annapolis Royal, May 20, 1720, in MacMechan, *Calendar*, 59. See also Philipps to the inhabitants of Annapolis Royal, May 7, 1720, in MacMechan, *Calendar*, 167; Council minutes, May 4, 1720, in MacMechan, *Minutes*, 7.

23. See Abstract of Philipps to Inhabitants of Annapolis Royal, April 10, 1721, in MacMechan, *Calendar*, 74.

24. Proclamation of Philipps, April 12, 1720, RG1, vol. 4, doc. 23, PANS.

25. Council minutes, April 29, 1720, in MacMechan, *Minutes*, 4; Inhabitants of Nova Scotia to St. Ovide, May 6, 1720, in Akins, *Selections*, 25; Minutes of the Marine Council, August 1720, in Casgrain, *Collection*, 2: 6.

26. Council minutes, September 19, 1720, in MacMechan, *Minutes*, 14.

27. Council minutes, May 4, 1721, in MacMechan, *Minutes*, 30.

28. Paul Mascarene, "Description of Nova Scotia," September 27, 1720, CO 217/4, doc. 329, PRO.

29. Board of Trade to Philipps, December 28, 1720, in Akins, *Selections*, 58; Report of the Board of Trade, September 8, 1721, King's Mss. 205, doc. 4.

30. Instructions for James Stanhope, received May 9, 1715, CO 194/5, doc. 334, PRO; Christopher Codrington to Board of Trade, June 28, 1702, CO 152/4, doc. 104(i), PRO; Codrington to Board of Trade, July 6, 1702, CO 152/5, doc. 2, PRO; Capitulation agreement, 1702, CO 152/5, doc. 8, PRO; Jonathan Johnson to Board of Trade, September 17, 1705, CO 152/6, doc. 37, PRO; Daniel Parke to Board of Trade, August 28, 1706, CO 152/6, doc. 63, PRO.

31. Black, *British Foreign Policy*.

32. See, for example, Council minutes, May 22, 1725, in MacMechan, *Minutes*, 100–101.

33. See Council minutes, September 21, 1723, in MacMechan, *Minutes*, 47–48; Council minutes, October 26, 1722, in MacMechan, *Minutes*, 50; Council minutes, May 22, 1725, in MacMechan, *Minutes*, 100.

34. Report of Felix Pain, RG1, vol. 3, doc. 86, PANS.

35. Statement of the "principal inhabitants of Acadia or Nova Scotia," November 28, 1711, CO 217/1, doc. 184, PRO.

36. Oath, January 22, 1715, in Casgrain, *Collection*, 1: 110; Basque, *Des Hommes de pouvoir*, 61.

37. Doucette to Pain, March 26, 1718, in Casgrain, *Collection*, 1: 118; Basque, *Des Hommes de pouvoir*, 72; Philipps to the inhabitants of Annapolis Royal, May 20, 1720, in MacMechan, *Calendar*, 59. See also Philipps to the inhabitants of Annapolis Royal, May 7, 1720, in MacMechan, *Calendar*, 167; Council minutes, May 4, 1720, in MacMechan, *Minutes*, 7.

38. See Council minutes, August 24, 1720, in MacMechan, *Minutes*, 12; Statement of Prudent Robichaud, August 24, 1720, in Whitehead, *The Old Man Told Us*, 93–94; Robichaud's son would report on Mi'kmaq warriors again in 1731. See Council minutes, March 11, 1731, in MacMechan, *Minutes*, 175–76; see also Council minutes, April 25, 1731, in MacMechan, *Minutes*, 178.

39. Basque, *Des Hommes de pouvoir*, 72.

40. Council minutes, September 21, 1723, in MacMechan, *Minutes*, 47–48; Basque, *Des Hommes de pouvoir*, 72.

41. Council minutes, May 22, 1725, in MacMechan, *Minutes*, 100–101; Basque, *Des Hommes de pouvoir*, 72.

42. Commission, April 5, 1727, in MacMechan, *Calendar*, 172; Brebner, *New England's Outpost*, 147; Council minutes, September 11, 1732, in MacMechan, *Minutes*, 255; see also Council minutes, August 11, 1733, CO 217/7, doc. 79, PRO; Order to "Prudane Robishau," December 1, 1733, in MacMechan, *Calendar*, 197; Council minutes, January 25, 1734, in MacMechan, *Minutes*, 292; Statement of Prudent Robichaud, January 26, 1740, in Fergusson, *Minutes*, 24–25; Brebner, *New England's Outpost*, 152.

43. Doucette to Gaulin, March 14, 1722, CO 217/4, doc. 134, PRO; Council minutes, July 8, 1724, in MacMechan, *Minutes*, 56–57; Council minutes, August 29, 1724, in MacMechan, *Minutes*, 73–74; Council minutes, October 31, 1724, in MacMechan, *Minutes*, 77–78; Council minutes, January 21, 1725, in Mac-Mechan, *Minutes*, 90–91.

44. Council minutes, February 5, 1724, in MacMechan, *Minutes*, 52; Council minutes, November 5, 1724, in MacMechan, *Minutes*, 81–82; Council minutes, January 4, 1725, in MacMechan, *Minutes*, 84–86.

45. Council minutes, April 20, 1726, in MacMechan, *Minutes*, 111–12; see also Council minutes, August 29, 1724, in MacMechan, *Minutes*, 73–74; Council

minutes, January 6, 1725, in MacMechan, *Minutes*, 90; Council minutes, January 26–27, 1725, in MacMechan, *Minutes*, 91–92; Council minutes, June 12, 1725, in MacMechan, *Minutes*, 102–3.

46. Armstrong to St. Ovide, June 17, 1732, CO 217/6, doc. 227, PRO; St. Ovide to Armstrong, September 19, 1732, CO 217/6, doc. 254, PRO; Armstrong to Newcastle, December 2, 1725, in Akins, *Selections*, 64; see also Louis XV to Beauharnois and Dupuy, May 16, 1728, in O'Callaghan, *Documents*, 9: 1003.

47. Council minutes, September 25, 1726, in MacMechan, *Minutes*, 129; Report of Robert Wroth, November 18, 1727, CO 217/38, doc. 186, PRO.

48. Council minutes, November 13, 1727, in MacMechan, *Minutes*, 168.

49. Statement of Charles DeGoladie and Alexandre Nouville, April 29, 1730, in Gaudet, "Acadian Genealogy and Notes," 24.

50. Philipps to Board of Trade, January 3, 1730, in Gaudet, "Acadian Genealogy and Notes," 67; Oaths of allegiance, 1729 and 1730, in Gaudet, "Généalogie," 131–32, 134–38.

51. Council minutes, April 28, 1735, in MacMechan, *Minutes*, 322.

52. Abstract of commissions, April 5, 1727, in MacMechan, *Calendar*, 171–72; Basque, *Des Hommes de pouvoir*, 74.

53. Order signed by Armstrong, July 19, 1733, CO 217/7, doc. 55, PRO.

54. Council minutes, March 4, 1734, in MacMechan, *Minutes*, 293–94; Council minutes, April 26, 1735, in MacMechan, *Minutes*, 322; Mascarene to Board of Trade, received November 19, 1740, in Akins, *Selections*, 110–11; Council minutes, September 11, 1734, in MacMechan, *Minutes*, 302.

55. Abstract of an order of the council, September 13, 1734, in MacMechan, *Calendar*, 201.

56. Philipps to Charles Wager, September 22, 1737, Tredegar Park Mss., doc. 284; Memorial of the council of Nova Scotia to the king, June 10, 1738, Tredegar Park Mss. box 79, doc. 43.

57. Council minutes, April 19–20, 1721, in MacMechan, *Minutes*, 28–29; see Barnes, "'Daily Cry for Justice,'" 17–18.

58. No census was taken in these years, but see Clark, *Acadia*, 157; Raymond, *River St. John*, 96.

59. See Prins, "Tribulations of a Border Tribe," 274–313; Bourque, "Ethnicity on the Maritime Peninsula."

60. See Statement of Jean Loyard, April 26, 1714, Gay Papers, Nova Scotia, vol. 1, doc. 121.

61. Armstrong to the settlers on the St. John River, March 28, 1732, CO 217/6, doc. 216, PRO; Abstract of Armstrong to the settlers on the St. John River, March 28, 1732, in MacMechan, *Calendar*, 188; Armstrong to Board of Trade, June 10, 1732, CO 217/6, doc. 117, PRO; see also Council minutes, July 26, 1732, in MacMechan, *Minutes*, 241; Council minutes, September 4, 1732, in MacMechan, *Minutes*, 252. Statement of Rene LeBlanc, March 20, 1732, CO 217/6, doc. 135, PRO; Council minutes, July 15, 1732, in MacMechan, *Minutes*, 239–240.

62. Armstrong to Jonathan Belcher, September 11, 1732, CO 217/6, doc. 228, PRO.

63. Upton, *Micmacs and Colonists*, 38; Armstrong to Board of Trade, January 14, 1735, in *Calendar of State Papers, Colonial Series*, 41: 353.

64. Armstrong to Board of Trade, June 19, 1736, CO 217/7, doc. 174, PRO.

65. Council minutes, April 21, 1720, in MacMechan, *Minutes*, 2–3; Council minutes, July 6, 1725, in MacMechan, *Minutes*, 104; Armstrong to Secretary of State, April 30, 1727, in Akins, *Selections*, 70; Armstrong to Board of Trade, November 17, 1727, CO 217/5, doc. 39, PRO; Rawlyk, *Yankees at Louisbourg*, xvi–xvii; Chard, "Canso," 56–57.

66. "Estimate of Quit Rents in Sterling and New England Money," 1740, in Shortt, Johnston, and Lactot, *Documents*, 220–21.

67. Armstrong to Board of Trade, June 23, 1729, in Akins, *Selections*, 82–83; Council minutes, July 8, 1736, in MacMechan, *Minutes*, 359–60.

68. Arsenault, *Histoire et généalogie*, 6: 2255; Webster, ed., *Thomas Pichon*, 153.

69. DeGoladie to Armstrong, April 8, 1732, CO 217/6, doc. 129, PRO: DeGoladie to Armstrong, April 29, 1732, CO 217/6, doc. 131, PRO; Armstrong to Board of Trade, June 10, 1732, in Akins, *Selections*, 94; Council minutes, June 19, 1732, in MacMechan, *Minutes*, 225–26.

70. Letter from Le Loutre, September 3, 1740, in Casgrain, *Collection*, 1:25–27.

71. Letter from Mascarene, August 10, 1740, CO 217/8, doc. 68, PRO; Council minutes, July 1, 1740, in Fergusson, *Minutes*, 29; Mascarene to Deputies, July 4, 1740, CO 217/8, doc. 95, PRO; see also Abstract of Armstrong to DeGoladie, January 14, 1738, in MacMechan, *Calendar*, 115.

72. Paul Mascarene, "A Return of what artificers are in the five companies here in garrison belonging to his Excellency General Philipps' regiment at Annapolis Royal," April 20, 1720, Add. Mss. 19,071, doc. 2.

73. Council minutes, March 7, 1744, Add. Mss. 19,071, doc. 78.

74. Mascarene to John Melledge, November 21, 1723, Add. Mss. 19,071, doc. 33. See also Council minutes, June 24, 1731, in MacMechan, *Minutes*, 178; John Leddel to Philipps, June 25, 1731, Tredegar Park Mss. box 79, No. 36; Armstrong to Henry Cope et al., November 16, 1731, CO 217/6, doc. 223, PRO; Council minutes, June 19–20, 1732, in MacMechan, *Minutes*, 227–30.

75. William Bontein, "Annapolis Royal, Fort and what is called the Town, Survey'd in October, 1754," Map Division H/9 240, NAC.

76. Mascarene to John Washington, March 30, 1721, Add. Mss. 19,071, doc. 9.

77. Washington to Mascarene, October 10, 1721, Add. Mss. 19,071, doc. 16.

78. Council minutes, May 11, 1724, in MacMechan, *Minutes*, 54; Council minutes, March 27, 1732, in MacMechan, *Minutes*, 217.

79. Petitions for compensation for destroyed houses, May 1745, CO 217/9, doc. 17, PRO.

80. See Basque and Brun, "La Neutralité à l'épreuve," 114–15; Fergusson, "Winniett, William"; Godfrey, *Pursuit of Profit*, 3.

81. Council minutes, August 6, 1734, in MacMechan, *Minutes*, 300.

82. Petition of Richard Watts, 1727, A/20, doc. 25; Watts to the Lord Bishop of London, May 31, 1728, A/21, doc. 408; Certificate of Alexander Cosby, November 18, 1728, A/21, doc. 476; Certificate of Philipps, May 20, 1730, A/23, doc. 150; Certificate of Erasmus James Phillips, November 24, 1730, A/23, doc. 154; Petition of Margaret Watts, 1730, A/23, doc. 404, all in Records of the SPG; King Gould to Joshua Harrison, August 17, 1738, Tredegar Park Mss. 286, doc. 32.

83. See Philipps to Board of Trade, May 25, 1727, in Casgrain, *Collection*, 1:174.

84. Moody, "A Just and Disinterested Man," 47, 90, 110.

85. Ibid., 25.

86. *Boston Gazette*, January 22, 1728; for Mascarene's poetical reply, see *Boston Gazette*, February 26, 1728.

87. *Boston Gazette*, January 5, 1730. See also *Boston Gazette*, January 8, 1728, November 27, 1732.

88. Andrew Le Mercier's proposal for settling a colony of French Protestants in the province of Nova Scotia, September 28, 1729, CO 217/38, doc. 227, PRO. See also CO 217/5, doc. 185, PRO; Bell, *"Foreign Protestants"*, 43, 51–53; Advertisement to attract settlers from Boston, CO 217/6, doc. 218, PRO; Instructions for Mascarene, September 11, 1732, CO 217/6, doc. 219, PRO.

89. Council minutes, December 13, 1732, in MacMechan, *Minutes*, 257; Armstrong to deputies at Annapolis Royal, December 13, 1732, CO 217/39, doc. 85, PRO; Abstract of Armstrong to the deputies of Annapolis Royal, December 13, 1732, in MacMechan, *Calendar*, 88; for the arrival of St. Poncy, see St. Ovide to Armstrong, September 19, 1732, CO 217/6, doc. 254, PRO; Armstrong to Bishop of Québec, November 21, 1732, in Akins, *Selections*, 99.

90. Abstract of order of June 9, 1735, in MacMechan, *Calendar*, 209; Council minutes, June 8, 1736, in MacMechan, *Minutes*, 352; Council minutes, June 12, 1736, in MacMechan, *Minutes*, 354–55; Council minutes, May 18, 1736, in MacMechan, *Minutes*, 345; Council minutes, June 8, 1736, in MacMechan, *Minutes*, 352.

91. Council minutes, October 20, 1736, in Fergusson, *Minutes*, 8.

92. Council minutes, November 10, 1736, in Fergusson, *Minutes*, 10; Petition of inhabitants of Annapolis Royal, November 10, 1736, CO 217/7, doc. 210, PRO.

93. Council minutes, December 4, 1736, in Fergusson, *Minutes*, 11; Armstrong to Board of Trade, July 8, 1737, CO 217/8, doc. 10, PRO.

94. Council minutes, September 18, 1740, in Akins, *Selections*, 107; Inhabitants of Beaubassin to Mascarene, July 6, 1742, CO 217/39, doc. 257, PRO; Mascarene to Deputies at Chignecto, July 12, 1742, in Akins, *Selections*, 120.

95. Mascarene to Claude de la Vernede de St. Poncy, April 22, 1739, Mas-

carene Papers; St. Poncy to Mascarene, May 1, 1740, Mascarene Papers; see also Moody, "A Just and Disinterested Man," 155–61.

96. Council minutes, April 23, 1740, in Fergusson, *Minutes*, 27; Abstract of Mascarene to St. Poncy, April 23, 1740, in MacMechan, *Calendar*, 132; Passport, April 23, 1740, in MacMechan, *Calendar*, 233–34.

97. Abstract of Mascarene to Bourg, September 17, 1740, in MacMechan, *Calendar*, 139–40; Council minutes, September 18, 1740, in Fergusson, *Minutes*, 32.

98. Abstract of Mascarene to Pierre Bergeau, September 1740, in MacMechan, *Calendar*, 140; Jean P. Miniac to Mascarene, November 2, 1742, Mascarene Papers.

99. Abstract of Mascarene to DeGoladie, January 12, 1742, in MacMechan, *Calendar*, 160.

100. Mascarene to Ladeuze, November 11, 1752, Add. Mss. 19,071, doc. 61.

101. The first English-language reference to "French neutrals" (or "neutral French") that I have located is a story in the *Boston Postboy* of May 6, 1745. The piece identified the "Nova Scotians" as "neutral French" and was subsequently reprinted in the *Boston Gazette*, May 7, 1745, *Boston Newsletter*, May 9, 1745, *New York Postboy*, May 20, 1745, and *South Carolina Gazette*, June 22, 1745. The use of "neutral French" as a collective noun to describe the Acadians appears in a September 22, 1745, letter from William Shirley to the Duke of Newcastle, RG1, vol. 13, doc. 10, PANS. The quoted parenthetical phrases come from the *Boston Evening Post*, July 17, 1749, and July 14, 1755. See also *Pennsylvania Gazette*, November 29, 1755.

Chapter Five

1. See Wilson, "Empire, Trade and Popular Politics"; Jordan and Rogers, "Admirals as Heroes."

2. See *Boston Evening Post*, July 8, July 15, 1745; *Boston Postboy*, July 8, 1745; Charles Chauncey to William Pepperell, July 4, 1745, in *Collections of the Massachusetts Historical Society* 1st ser. 1 (1792): 49; Thomas Hubbard to Pepperell, in *Collections of the Massachusetts Historical Society* 6th ser. 10 (1899): 308–9; Daniel Edwards to Roger Wolcott, July 9, 1745, in *Collections of the Connecticut Historical Society* 11 (1907): 334–37.

3. Moore, "The Other Louisbourg"; McNeill, *Atlantic Empires of France and Spain*, 20–24.

4. McNeill, *Atlantic Empires of France and Spain*, 84.

5. See Rawlyk, *Yankees at Louisbourg*, 6.

6. Ibid., 2–4.

7. For accounts of the attack, see Flemming, *The Canso Islands*, 45; William Shirley to Newcastle, July 7, 1744, in Lincoln, ed., *Correspondence of William Shirley*, 1: 133; McLennan, *Louisbourg*, 111; Mascarene to Philipps, June 9, 1744, Add. Mss. 19,071, doc. 45; *Boston Postboy*, June 11, 1744.

8. For accounts of New England vessels taken, see *Boston Evening Post*, June 11, June 25, 1744; *Boston Newsletter*, September 20, 1744; *South Carolina Gazette*, July 4, 1744. For New England's attacks on the French fishery, see *Boston Evening Post*, September 24, October 22, November 26, 1744; *Boston Gazette*, August 21, 1744; *Boston Newsletter*, August 16, September 20, September 27, October 25, 1744; *Boston Postboy*, September 24, October 22, 1744; *New York Gazette*, October 1, 1744; Douglass, *Summary*, 1:339.

9. See Hamilton, "The Itinerarium," 261. See also Rawlyk, *Yankees at Louisbourg*, 37, 38; Schutz, *William Shirley*, 90. It was a fisherman who first alerted Boston of the attack on Canso, but the printer of the *Boston Evening Post* chose not to publish the story because it was "looked upon as fishermen's news." Only after a merchant confirmed the report was it placed in the paper. *Boston Evening Post*, May 28, 1744. For the reaction of the legislature, see *Journals of the House of Representatives of Massachusetts* 21: 8–11, 29, 42; *Boston Postboy*, June 4, 1744; *Boston Newsletter*, June 14, 1744.

10. See Schutz, *William Shirley*.

11. Ibid., 23–44; Remer, "Old Lights and New Money."

12. See, for example, Schutz, *William Shirley*, 80–103; Bailyn, *Origins of American Politics*, 116–17; but see Pencak, *War, Politics, and Revolution*, 115–47.

13. Hatch, "Origins of Civil Millennialism in America."

14. *Boston Gazette*, June 26, 1744.

15. See, for example, *Boston Newsletter*, June 6, 1745; *Boston Evening Post*, July 29, 1745.

16. *Boston Evening Post*, October 22, 1744.

17. *Journals of the House of Representatives of Massachusetts* 21: 99, 106–7; *Boston Evening Post*, November 5, 1744.

18. *Boston Evening Post*, November 11, 1744; using a contemporary term, Shirley called the St. Croix the Passamaquodi River.

19. Rogers, "Abbé Le Loutre"; Jean-Louis Le Loutre, "Autobiography," translated by John Clarence Webster, in Webster, ed., *Career of the Abbé Le Loutre*, 33–50, 35; See also Rawlyk, *Yankees at Louisbourg*, 7–11.

20. Pierre Maillard, "Lettre," in Casgrain, *Les Soirées canadiennes*, 289–426, 322–28; Webster, *Career of the Abbé Le Loutre*, 10.

21. "Motifs des sauvages mickmaques et marichites des continuer la guerre contre les Anglois depuis la dermière paix," in De Beaumont, *Les Derniers jours*, 248–53, 251.

22. This is the only use of the word "mulatto" I have seen in connection with Nova Scotia in the first half of the eighteenth century.

23. Council minutes, January 4, 1745, in Fergusson, *Minutes*, 55–56.

24. Steele, "Surrendering Rites," 152–53; *Boston Evening Post*, July 15, July 22, August 5, September 2, October 21, 1745; *Boston Postboy*, July 22, September 9, September 30, 1745; *Boston Newsletter*, September 12, 1745.

25. Mascarene to Shirley, December 7, 1745, CO 217/39, doc. 316, PRO; Shirley to Newcastle, December 23, 1745, RG1, vol. 13, doc. 21, PANS; Shirley to

Newcastle, February 11, 1746, RG1, vol. 13A, doc. 5, PANS; see Moody, "A Just and Disinterested Man," 334–42.

26. "State of the Province of Nova Scotia," November 8, 1745, CO 217/39, doc. 320, PRO.

27. For accounts of the general wartime migration to French-controlled territory, see Clark, *Acadia*, 278, 285, 291; Roy, "Settlement and Population Growth," 151–52; Jean Daigle, "Acadia from 1604 to 1763," 36.

28. There is no record of Robichaud's whereabouts after 1744, but several members of his family moved to the isthmus of Chignecto and present-day New Brunswick, regions that were controlled by the French during the war. Raymond, *River St. John*, 86, 94, 117; Mascarene to Frances Belleisle Robishau, October 13, 1744, in Akins, *Selections*, 136; Robichaud, *Les Robichaud*, 153–54. According to Donat Robichaud, who recorded the Robichaud family's history in the 1960s, the elder Prudent was still alive in 1756 and boarded the ship *Pembroke* for transportation south. The *Pembroke* left Annapolis Royal in late January or early February 1756, bound for North Carolina, but the 226 Acadian prisoners onboard took control of the ship, ran it aground in the mouth of the St. John River, and burned it. The Acadians were greeted on the banks of the river by Mi'kmaq or Wuastukwiuk warriors, who guided them to Québec. Prudent Robichaud, according to the family history, died on the trail and never reached New France. The newspaper accounts of this incident indicate that the *Pembroke* embarked from Chignecto, but Lawrence's letter states that it left Annapolis Royal, and he probably had better intelligence than the newspaper writers did. None of the documents cited above, other than the Robichaud family history, mention Prudent Robichaud by name. See Abstract of Dispatches from Canada, in O'Callaghan, *Documents*, 10: 427; Claude Godfrey Coquard to his brother, 1757, in O'Callaghan, *Documents*, 10: 528; Charles Lawrence to Shirley, February 18, 1756, in Akins, *Selections*, 297; *Boston Evening Post*, March 15, 1756; *Pennsylvania Gazette*, March 18, 1756; Knox, *Journal*, 1: 115.

29. Report of Jean Luc de La Corne, September 28, 1747, RG1, vol. 3, doc 89, PANS; Statement of Honore Gautrol, December 13, 1749, in Akins, *Selections*, 177; *Boston Evening Post*, January 15, 1750; Salusbury, *Expeditions of Honour*, 76; Edward Cornwallis to Board of Trade, March 19, 1750, CO 217/9, doc. 188, PRO.

30. Mascarene to Philipps, June 9, 1744, Add. Mss. 19,071, doc. 45; Mascarene to Secretary of State, June 15, 1748, CO 217/40, doc. 22, PRO; Mascarene to Gorham, August 6, 1748, Add. Mss. 19,071, doc. 119; Mascarene to ?, September 29, 1749, Add. Mss. 19,071, doc. 99.

31. Mascarene to Shirley, spring 1745, in Gaudet, "Acadian Genealogy and Notes," 38; Council minutes, May 2–4, 1745, in Fergusson, *Minutes*, 68–70; Council minutes, November 14, 1746, in Fergusson, *Minutes*, 94; Shirley to Newcastle, May 22, 1746, in Lincoln, *Correspondence of William Shirley*, 1: 150; see also O'Callaghan, *Documents*, 10: 155; "Relation d'une expédition faite sur les anglois

dans le pays de l'Acadie, le 11 fevrier 1747, par un détachement de canadiens," in Casgrain, *Collection*, 2: 10-16, 15; "Journal de la compagne du détachement de Canada à l'Acadie et aux mines, en 1746-47" in Casgrain, *Collection*, 2: 16-75, 47, 51-52. For evidence of the merchant's earlier cooperation with the government, see Mascarene to William Douglass, July 1740 and August 20, 1741, Mascarene Family Papers; Casgrain, *Pèlegrinage*, 519; Council minutes, August 17, 1736, in MacMechan, *Minutes*, 361-62.

32. Proclamation of the provincial council of Nova Scotia, May 19, 1746, RG1, vol. 21, doc. 81, PANS.

33. Pothier, *Course à L'Accadie*, 70-71, 73, 87-88, 139; Instructions for François Dupont Duvivier, MFM 12082, French Records, Acadia 1711-88, reel 8, 100, PANS; "Ordre et instruction de Duquesnel pour Duvivier, 1744," in Pothier, *Course à L'Accadie*, 159.

34. "Journal de la campagne," 1746-47, in Casgrain, *Collection*, 2: 16-75, 28.

35. See Mascarene to Deputies of Mines, Pisiquid and River Canard, October 13, 1744, in Akins, *Selections*, 137; Shirley to Board of Trade, October 16, 1744, in Lincoln, *Correspondence of William Shirley*, 1:150; Shirley to Newcastle, October 16, 1744, RG1, vol. 12, doc 37, PANS.

36. Shirley to Pepperell, May 25, 1745, in *Collections of the Massachusetts Historical Society* 6th ser. 10 (1899): 219.

37. "Journal de la campagne," 1746-47, in Casgrain, *Collection*, 2: 16-75, 44, 48; *Boston Evening Post*, December 1, 1746; see also *Boston Evening Post*, November 3, November 17, 1746; Wicken, "Encounters," 184-205. For a vivid description of the epidemic, see "Journal," July 25, 1748-September 14, 1748, AC, F3, vol. 50, doc. 447, NAC.

38. *Boston Evening Post*, May 28, 1744.

39. See, for example, Shirley to Newcastle, October 20, 1747, RG1, vol. 13A, doc. 32, PANS; Shirley to Newcastle, November 21, 1746, RG1, vol. 13, doc. 33, PANS; Charles Knowles and Shirley to Newcastle, April 28, 1747, RG1, vol. 13A, doc. 25, PANS; Shirley to Newcastle, July 8, 1747, RG1, vol. 13A, doc. 27, PANS.

40. See "Journal de la campagne," 1746-47, in Casgrain, *Collection*, 2: 16-75, 48.

41. Shirley to Newcastle, October 20, 1747, RG1, vol. 13A, doc. 32, PANS.

42. Shirley to Newcastle, November 21, 1746, RG1, vol. 13, doc. 33, PANS; Knowles and Shirley to Newcastle, April 28, 1747, RG1, vol. 13A, doc. 25, PANS; Shirley to Newcastle, July 8, 1747, RG1, vol. 13A, doc. 27, PANS.

43. See Macinnes, *Clanship, Commerce, and the House of Stuart*, 210-41; Withers, *Gaelic Scotland*.

44. "On the subject of civilising the Highlands," 1748, GD248654/1, Scottish Record Office.

45. Laughton, "Knowles, Sir Charles," 11: 293; see also Laughton, "Martin, William," 12: 1185; Black, *Culloden and the '45*, 89, 124-25.

46. Shirley to Newcastle, November 21, 1746, RG1, vol. 13, doc. 33, PANS.

See Duncan Forbes, "Some Considerations on the Present State of the Highlands of Scotland," in Warrand, *More Culloden Papers*, 5: 98–103; Speck, *The Butcher*, 168; Prebble, *Culloden*, 232.

47. Dunn, *The Acadians of Minas*, 19; *Boston Evening Post*, November 24, 1746, March 2, March 9, September 28, 1747; *Pennsylvania Gazette*, December 16, 1746, March 3, March 10, 1747; Report of Pierre de Chapt, Chevalier de la Corne, September 28, 1747, RG1, vol. 3, doc. 89, PANS; Report of Jean Baptiste Le Guardier de Repentigny, November 1, 1747, RG1, vol. 3, doc. 90, PANS; *Journals of the House of Representatives of Massachusetts*, 23: 313–15, 319; Knowles and Shirley to Newcastle, April 28, 1747, RG1, vol. 13A, doc. 25, PANS; see also Knowles to Shirley, May 24, 1747, HM 9712, Huntington Library.

48. Knowles and Shirley to Newcastle, April 28 1747, RG1, vol. 13A, doc. 25, PANS; see also Knowles to Shirley, May 24 1747, HM 9712, Huntington Library.

49. Shirley to Newcastle, July 8, 1747, RG1, vol. 13A, doc. 27, PANS.

50. Shirley to Newcastle, July 8, 1747, RG1, vol. 13A, doc. 27, PANS.

51. John Russell, duke of Bedford, to Newcastle, September 11, 1747, RG1, vol. 13A, doc. 30, PANS; Newcastle to Shirley, October 3, 1747, RG1, vol. 13A, doc. 31, PANS.

52. Sosin, "Louisbourg and the Peace of Aix-la-Chapelle." The final decision to cede Ile Royale back to France was not made until the end of the negotiations in 1748, but the ministry had considered the island a bargaining chip from the moment it learned of New England's conquest. See Newcastle to ?, August 18, 1745, Add. Mss. 32,705, doc. 65.

53. More than one thousand New England men died, most of disease after an epidemic struck the New England garrison at Louisbourg after the French surrendered. See Rawlyk, *Nova Scotia's Massachusetts*, 177; Nash, *The Urban Crucible*, 172; Pencak, *War, Politics, and Revolution*, 127; Nash, "Failure of Female Factory Labor." For London newspaper pieces urging the retention of Ile Royale, see *General Advertiser*, February 21, 1746 (quoted in the *Boston Evening Post*, June 2, 1746); *General Evening Post*, July 26, 1746 (quoted in the *Boston Evening Post*, October 13, 1746); *Daily Gazetteer*, October 16, 1746 (quoted in the *Boston Evening Post*, March 2, 1747); *British Spy*, October 25, 1746 (quoted in the *New York Evening Post*, January 19, 1747); *London Magazine*, December 1746 (quoted in the *Maryland Gazette*, July 28, 1747).

54. The value of the province's notes dropped by one-half. See Douglass, *Summary*, 1: 357; *Boston Evening Post*, September 25, 1749.

55. Mascarene to Joseph Gorham, August 6, 1748, in Shortt, Johnston, and Lactot, *Documents*, 274–76.

56. "Report by Captain Morris to Governor Shirley," 1749, in *Report of the Archives Branch for 1912*, 79–83; Shirley to Bedford, February 18, 1749, RG1, vol. 13, doc. 45, PANS; see also Mascarene to Board of Trade, October 17, 1748, CO 217/32, doc. 103, PRO.

57. See especially Douglass, *Summary*; *Independent Advertiser*.

58. See, for example, *Independent Advertiser*, February 8, 1748; William Douglass, "To the Publishers of the *Independent Advertiser*," *Independent Advertiser*, July 4, 1748; *Independent Advertiser*, February 13, 1749. Political economists had been advancing this argument against imperial expansion at least since 1670. See Coke, *Discourse of Trade*, 7; *Royal Fishery Revived*.

59. See Bumstead, "Doctor Douglass's Summary."

60. See the Fortieth Regiment's ledger books, Tredegar Park Mss., Manuscript 272, p. 71, Manuscript 275, pp. 12–19, 59.

61. His anger may have been shared by Mascarene himself, who complained to Shirley in 1744 that he had been left out of the discussions leading up to the decision to attack Ile Royale. See Mascarene to Shirley, September 22, 1744, Add. Mss. 19,071, doc. 54.

62. Douglass, *Summary*, 1: 509n., 2: 6–9. Shirley had commissioned Otis Little, a New England officer who had served in the garrison of Annapolis Royal, to write a treatise in favor of the settlement plan. The resulting work, *State of the Trade*, 12, 47–50, contained the most extensive public arguments in favor of Shirley's settlement scheme.

63. See, for example, *London Evening Post*, March 27–29, 1746.

64. Henretta, "*Salutary Neglect*," 287–90. See also *Pennsylvania Gazette*, October 28, 1748; *Boston Evening Post*, May 1, 1749; Instructions for Edward Cornwallis, May 2, 1749, in Gaudet, "Acadian Genealogy and Notes," 49–51.

65. *Boston Evening Post*, May 1, 1749.

66. *Boston Evening Post*, June 5, 1749; Cornwallis to Bedford, March 9, 1750, CO 217/33, doc. 17, PRO.

67. Bell, *"Foreign Protestants"*, 284.

68. Instructions for Cornwallis, May 2, 1749, in Gaudet, "Acadian Genealogy and Notes," 49–51.

69. Ibid., 49.

70. Ibid., 51; see also Board of Trade to the SPG, C/Can NS 1, iv, Records of the SPG.

71. Instructions for Cornwallis, May 2 1749, in Gaudet, "Acadian Genealogy and Notes," 51.

72. Colley, *Britons*.

Chapter Six

1. Moore, "The Other Louisbourg"; McNeill, *Atlantic Empires of France and Spain*, 19–22, 139, 186.

2. See "Lu au roy," August 29, 1749, in Gaudet, "Généalogie," 354–56.

3. Le Loutre to the bishop, July 29, 1749, MG1, C11C, vol. 9, doc. 130, NAC; Charles Des Herbiers to Antoine-Louis Rouillé, August 9, 1749, MG1, C11B, vol. 28, doc. 78, NAC; Des Herbiers to Rouillé, December 6, 1750, MG1,

C11B, vol. 29, doc. 66, NAC; William Anne Keppel, earl of Albemarle, to Louis-Philogene Brulart de Sillery, Marquis de Puysieulx, July 7, 1750, in O'Callaghan, *Documents*, 10: 216; George Fothringham to John Campbell, earl of Loudon, September 15, 1750, LO 224, Huntington Library; *Boston Evening Post*, June 19, July 17, 1749; Cornwallis to John Rous, July 23, 1749, CO 217/40, doc. 107, PRO (reprinted without date in Akins, *Selections*, 371–72). For background on the imperial border dispute, see Savelle, *Diplomatic History of the Canadian Boundary*, 21–43. For a sampling of the debate over the boundary, see *Genuine Account of Nova Scotia*; Jefferys, *Conduct of the French*; Jefferys, *Remarks on the French Memorials*; see also *Boston Evening Post*, June 4, 1750.

4. Letter from Le Loutre, October 1, 1738, in Casgrain, *Collection*, 1:19–25.

5. Le Loutre to ministry, July 29, 1749, Gaudet, "Généalogie," 346–47; Patterson, "1744–1763," 132.

6. Salusbury, *Expeditions of Honour*, 90–91; Examination of Jean Battiste Petre and Pierre Beboir, May 8, 1750, RG1, vol. 342, doc. 6, PANS; Journal of Lawrence, beginning April 20, 1750, in Webster, ed., *Building of Fort Lawrence*, 17–19; Cornwallis to Bedford, May 1, 1750, CO 217/9, doc. 240, PRO.

7. See Hopson to Board of Trade, December 6, 1752, Add. Mss. 19,072, doc. 9.

8. Shirley to Newcastle, November 21, 1746, RG1, vol. 13, doc. 33, PANS.

9. Patterson, "1744–1763," 127.

10. Treaty of August 15, 1749, RG1, vol. 163, doc. 10, PANS.

11. Receipt, August 24, 1751, RG1, vol. 430, doc. 2, PANS.

12. Des Herbiers to Rouillé, August 9, 1749, MG1, C11B, vol. 28, doc. 77, NAC.

13. Proclamation of Council, October 1, 1749, in Akins, *Selections*, 581; Cornwallis to Board of Trade, October 17, 1749, in Akins, *Selections*, 591; *Boston Evening Post*, October 2, 1749; Salusbury, *Expeditions of Honour*, 61n., 65–66.

14. Cornwallis to Board of Trade, July 24, 1749, CO 217/9, doc. 70, PRO; Hugh Davidson to Richard Aldworthy, July 24, 1749, CO 217/40, doc. 112, PRO; *Boston Evening Post*, September 11, 1749; see also extract of a letter from Halifax, Nova Scotia, March 20, 1750, in Shortt, Johnston, and Lactot, *Documents*, 290; Council minutes, August 14, 1749, in Akins, *Selections*, 573–74; *Boston Evening Post*, September 11, 1749; Salusbury, *Expeditions of Honour*, 59; Report of Le Loutre, July 29, 1749, C11C, vol. 9, doc. 130, NAC.

15. Cornwallis to Board of Trade, September 11, 1749, in Gaudet, "Acadian Genealogy and Notes," 53–55; Davidson to Aldworthy, September 11, 1749, CO 217/40, doc. 172, PRO.

16. Mascarene to Cornwallis, September 29, 1749, Belknap 61.C.94c.

17. Proclamation of Cornwallis, October 2, 1749, in Akins, *Selections*, 581–82.

18. Council minutes, October 1, 1749, in Akins, *Selections*, 581; Shortt, Johnston, and Lactot, *Documents*, 281. For indications of the practical effect of

this policy, see Salusbury, *Expeditions of Honour*, 68; Council minutes, October 1, 1749, in Akins, *Selections*, 581-82; Instructions for Ezekiel Gilman, October 4, 1749, RG1, vol. 163, doc. 16, PANS; Cornwallis to Sylvanus Cobb, January 13, 1750, CO 217/9, doc. 209, PRO; Proclamation of Cornwallis, June 21, 1750, RG1, vol. 163, doc. 41, PANS; *Boston Evening Post*, July 16, 1750; Instructions for Patrick Sutherland, May 29, 1751, RG1, vol. 163, doc. 75, PANS; Pierre de Rigaud, marquis de Vaudreuil, to ministry, October 18, 1755, in Gaudet, "Généalogie," 237-39; *Boston Gazette*, July 5, 1756; Robert Hale's Chronicle, folio 1, vol. 1, pp. 26, 43, entries for August 14, 1756, May 27 and May 30, 1757, French and Indian War Manuscripts.

19. Bigot to Ministry, September 30, 1749, in Gaudet, "Généalogie," 351.

20. "Sur l'Acadie, 1748," MG1, C11D, vol. 10, doc. 154, NAC; Dickason, "Louisbourg and the Indians," 99; *Gentleman's Magazine*, January 1747, quoted in Shortt, Johnston, and Lactot, *Documents*, 248; Prévost to Rouillé, August 16, 1753, MG1, C11B, vol. 33, doc. 197, NAC; "Divers dépense," Louisbourg, December 31, 1756, MG1, C11B, vol. 36, doc. 241, NAC; Le Courtois des Bourbes to Michel de Courtois de Surlaville, April 18, 1756, in De Beaumont, *Les Derniers jours*, 185-88, 187; De Fresne du Motel to Surlaville, December 1, 1756, in De Beaumont, *Les Derniers jours*, 204-6, 205.

21. See McLennan, *Louisbourg*, 189-90.

22. *Boston Evening Post*, December 4, 1749. See also Upton, *Micmacs and Colonists*, 51; Dickason, "Louisbourg and the Indians," 131; Salusbury, *Expeditions of Honour*, 65-66; Johnson, *Apôtres ou agitateurs*, 113-14; Casgrain, *Documents*, 1: 17-19; Cornwallis to Des Herbiers, September 21, 1749, in Gaudet, "Généalogie," 356-57.

23. The quotation is from CO 217/9, doc. 202, PRO. See also CO 217/40, doc. 145, PRO.

24. Cornwallis to Bedford, December 7, 1749, CO 217/40, doc. 176, PRO; see also Thomas Pichon and Michel de Courtois de Surlaville, "Memoir on the Establishment of the Beausejour Frontier in Acadia," in Webster, *Thomas Pichon*, 32; *Boston Evening Post*, July 30, 1750; see also Cornwallis to Board of Trade, March 19, 1750, in Akins, *Selections*, 606; Cornwallis to Bedford, March 19, 1750, in Akins, *Selections*, 183; Report of Benjamin Green, John Salusbury and William Steele, September 20, 1750, in Shortt, Johnston, and Lactot, *Documents*, 309.

25. *Boston Evening Post*, July 24, 1749; Salusbury, *Expeditions of Honour*, 75.

26. Cornwallis to Board of Trade, March 19, 1750, CO 217/9, doc. 188, PRO.

27. La Corne to Des Herbiers, 1750, in Gaudet, "Généalogie," 386-87; "A Journal of the Proceedings," 1750, in Gaudet, "Acadian Genealogy and Notes," 320-23; Salusbury, *Expeditions of Honour*, 90-91; Examination of Petre and Beboir, May 8, 1750, RG1, vol. 342, doc. 6, PANS; Journal of Lawrence, beginning April 20, 1750, in Webster, *Building of Fort Lawrence*, 17-19; Cornwallis to Bedford, May 1, 1750, CO 217/9, doc. 240, PRO.

28. Albemarle to Puysieulx, July 7, 1750, in O'Callaghan, *Documents*, 10: 216; Fothringham to Loudon, September 15, 1750; LO 224, Huntington Library. See also Peregrine Hopson to Board of Trade, July 23, 1753, in Akins, *Selections*, 200; Lawrence to Board of Trade, August 1, 1754, in Akins, *Selections*, 213.

29. Pierre-Jacques de Taffanel, marquis de la Jonquière to Ministry, May 1, 1751, in Gaudet, "Généalogie," 402–6; Ordinance of De la Jonquière, April 12, 1751, summarized in Gaudet, "Acadian Genealogy and Notes," 496. See also Griffiths, *The Acadian Deportation*, 83.

30. Thomas Pichon to John Hussey, January 3, 1755, in Webster, *Thomas Pichon*, 79.

31. Charles Lawrence, "Journal," in Webster, *Forts of Chignecto*, 105–8; Joshua Winslow, *Journal*; Fothringham to Loudon, September 15, 1750, LO 224, Huntington Library; Cornwallis to Board of Trade, September 22, 1750, CO 217/33, doc. 100, PRO; *Boston Evening Post*, October 1, October 8, November 12, 1750; Cornwallis to Board of Trade, November 27, 1750, CO 217/33, doc. 123, PRO; Salusbury, *Expeditions of Honour*, 100, 102.

32. Pierre Maillard, "Lettre," in Casgrain, *Les Soirées canadiennes*, 404–7; Louis Le Neuf de la Valliere, "Journal of Events in Chignecto and Other Parts of the Frontiers of Acadie from Sept. 15, 1750 to July 28, 1751," in Webster, *Forts of Chignecto*, 135–36; "A short account of what passed at Cape Breton, from the beginning of the last War until the taking of Louisbourg in 1758, by a French Officer," in Akins, *Selections*, 195–96. See also Webster, *Building of Fort Lawrence*, 12–13; Cornwallis to Bedford, November 27, 1750, in Akins, *Selections*, 194–95. This incident has sparked the interest of several historians. See, for example, Parkman, *Montcalm and Wolf*, 99; Casgrain, *Pèlegrinage*, 505–7.

33. "A short account," in Akins, *Selections*, 195–96. For an alternative theory, see "Journal de ce qui s'est passé," in Gaudet, "Généalogie," 389.

34. *Boston Evening Post*, July 2, 1750, April 20, 1751; Salusbury, *Expeditions of Honour*, 106, 109–10, 111.

35. Bell, *"Foreign Protestants"*, 388–90.

36. Cornwallis to Board of Trade, July 10, 1750, CO 217/33, doc. 81, PRO.

37. Cornwallis to Board of Trade, September 2, 1750, CO 217/10, doc. 95, PRO; Board of Trade to Cornwallis, March 22, 1751, Add. Mss. 19,072, doc. 7; Board of Trade to Cornwallis, March 6, 1752, Add. Mss. 19,072, doc. 8. See Bell, *"Foreign Protestants"*, 321.

38. Hopson to Board of Trade, October 16, 1752, in Akins, *Selections*, 677–78.

39. Lawrence to Board of Trade, December 5, 1753, Add. Mss. 19,072, doc. 18.

40. Board of Trade to Cornwallis, March 22, 1751, Add. Mss. 19,072, doc. 7.

41. See Clark, *Acadia*, 339–40.

42. Lawrence to Board of Trade, December 29, 1753, CO 217/15, doc. 3, PRO.

43. Cornwallis to Mascarene, August 13, 1751, HM 27646, Huntington Library; Mascarene to Cornwallis, August 27, 1751, CO 217/13, doc. 27, PRO.

44. The fullest statement of this strategy can be found in George Scott to Hopson, August 17, 1752, CO 217/12, doc. 292, PRO; see Patterson, "Indian-White Relations," 38.

45. Board of Trade to Cornwallis, October 16, 1749, in Akins, *Selections*, 587–90; Cornwallis to Board of Trade, March 19, 1750, CO 217/9, doc. 188, PRO.

46. Patterson, "Indian-White Relations," 35–36; see also *Boston Evening Post*, July 22, 1751.

47. See Plank, "The Two Majors Cope."

48. Council minutes, September 14, 1752, in Akins, *Selections*, 671; Council minutes, November 22, 1752, in Akins, *Selections*, 682–85; Salusbury, *Expeditions of Honour*, 125; *Halifax Gazette*, November 25, 1752; *Boston Evening Post*, December 11, 1752, February 5, 1753.

49. Report on negotiations between Hopson and Cope, CO 217/13, doc. 306, PRO.

50. Instructions for William Piggot, October 25, 1752, RG1, vol. 163, doc. 25, PANS; Anthony Casteel's journal, in Casgrain, *Collection*, 2: 113–26; Paul, *We Were Not the Savages*, 122–34; Whitehead, *The Old Man Told Us*, 132–36; Casteel's deposition, July 30, 1753, in Akins, *Selections*, 696–98; Salusbury, *Expeditions of Honour*, 128.

51. Patterson, "Indian-White Relations," 43; Prévost to Rouillé, September 10, 1752, MG1, C11B, vol. 32, doc. 165, NAC.

52. Hopson to Board of Trade, December 6, 1752, Add. Mss. 19,072, doc 9; Hopson to Board of Trade, January 4, 1753, CO 217/14, doc. 3, PRO.

53. See Plank, "Changing Country of Anthony Casteel."

54. Casteel's journal, in Casgrain, *Collection*, 2: 113–26, 116; Paul, *We Were Not the Savages*, 122–34, 125; Whitehead, ed., *The Old Man Told Us*, 132–36, 135. Casteel's deposition, July 30, 1753, in Akins, *Selections*, 696.

55. Plank, "Changing Country of Anthony Casteel"; Pote, *Journal*, 49; Le Chevalier de la Houssaye to Surlaville, April 14 and May 12, 1753, in De Beaumont, *Les Derniers jours*, 89.

56. De la Houssaye to Surlaville, April 14 and May 12, 1753, in De Beaumont, *Les Derniers jours*, 89; Pichon to ?, November 9, 1754, in Casgrain, *Collection*, 2: 136–37; Pichon to Hussey, December 24, 1754, in Webster, *Thomas Pichon*, 74.

57. Pichon to Hussey, January 13, 1755, in Webster, *Thomas Pichon*, 81; see also Pichon to ?, November 9, 1754, in Casgrain, *Collection*, 2: 136–37.

58. Casteel's journal, in Casgrain, *Collection*, 2: 113–26, 118. For other accounts of the incident, see Council minutes, April 16, 1753, in Akins, *Selections*, 694–96; *Halifax Gazette*, April 21, April 28, 1753; *Boston Evening Post*, May 7, 1753; see also Upton, *Micmacs and Colonists*, 55.

59. Le Loutre to Lawrence, September 9, 1754, in Akins, *Selections*, 215.

60. William Cotterell to Sutherland, November 16, 1753, RG1, vol. 134, doc. 15, PANS; Lawrence to Hussey, November 18, 1754, RG1, vol. 134, doc. 286, PANS; Upton, *Micmacs and Colonists*, 55–56; Le Loutre to Council, September 9, 1754, in Akins, *Selections*, 215; Lawrence to Robert Monckton, February 16, 1755, Peter Force Collections Series 8D/18; see also Hussey to Lawrence, January 20, 1755, in Webster, *Thomas Pichon*, 85; Hussey to Lawrence, February 21, 1755, in Webster, *Thomas Pichon*, 93–95.

61. Lawrence to Hussey, November 8, 1754, in Akins, *Selections*, 237.

62. Orders of Lawrence, March 16, 1753, LO 440, Huntington Library; Proclamation of Lawrence, September 17, 1754, in Akins, *Selections*, 219–20; Cotterell to John Handfield, July 15, 1754, RG1, vol. 134, doc. 185, PANS; Cotterell to Murray, November 4, 1754, RG1, vol. 134, doc. 264, PANS. The restrictions on internal travel augmented earlier orders, dating from 1749, barring emigration. See Indictment of Petre and Reinbour, August 8, 1750, RG1, vol. 342, doc. 5, PANS.

63. Cotterell to Murray, November 4, 1754, RG1, vol. 134, doc. 264, PANS.

64. In the winter of 1750 the garrison at Chignecto had sent ships to Annapolis Royal for firewood, and much of their food during that first year came from Boston and New York. Soon, however, the commanders realized that armed teams of men on expeditions from the fort could compel nearby Acadian farmers to supply their needs. See Cornwallis to Board of Trade, November 27, 1750, CO 217/33, doc. 123, PRO; Salusbury, *Expeditions of Honour*, 104; Webster, *Building of Fort Lawrence*, 11–12; *Boston Evening Post*, December 31, 1750.

65. Mascarene to Cornwallis, September 29, 1749, Belknap 61.C.94c; Orders for Fort Vieux Logis and Fort Edward, December 15, 1752, in Akins, *Selections*, 197–98; Cotterell to Murray, September 1, 1754, RG1, vol. 134, doc. 134, PANS; Cotterell to Murray, September 27, 1754, RG1, vol. 134, doc. 242, PANS; Cotterell to Handfield, March 17, 1755, RG1, vol. 134, doc. 330, PANS; Cotterell to George Scott, April 12, 1754, in Akins, *Selections*, 209.

66. Lawrence to Matthew Floyer, August 1, 1754, in Akins, *Selections*, 212.

67. See, for example, Cotterell to Murray, December 9, 1754, RG1, vol. 134, doc. 295, PANS.

68. Cotterell to Murray, September 27, 1754, RG1, vol. 134, doc. 242, PANS.

69. Council minutes, October 2, 1754, in Akins, *Selections*, 225–26.

70. Council minutes, October 3, 1754, in Akins, *Selections*, 226–27; Pichon to Surlaville, November 12, 1754, N.S., in De Beaumont, *Les Derniers jours*, 132 (translated and reprinted in Webster, *Forts of Chignecto*, 134); Pichon to Scott, October 14, 1754, in Webster, *Thomas Pichon*, 44.

71. Council minutes, October 21, 1754, in Akins, *Selections*, 235; Cotterell to Murray, October 21, 1754, RG1, vol. 134, doc. 259, PANS; Pichon to Scott, November 2, 1754, in Webster, *Thomas Pichon*, 53–54.

Chapter Seven

1. Shirley to Thomas Robinson, May 8, 1754, in Lincoln, *Correspondence of William Shirley*, 2: 62–68.

2. Graham, "Lawrence, Charles."

3. Cotterell to Hopson, October 1, 1753, in Gaudet, "Acadian Genealogy and Notes," 57–58.

4. Charles Morris, "Memorandum," 1753, in Casgrain, *Collection*, 2: 97–101.

5. Board of Trade to Lawrence, March 4, 1754, in Akins, *Selections*, 207. For a discussion of the role of property law in these discussions, see Brown, "Foundations of British Policy in the Acadian Expulsion."

6. Lawrence to Shirley, November 5, 1754, CO 217/15, doc. 177, PRO.

7. Board of Trade to Lawrence, March 4, 1754, in Akins, *Selections*, 207; Board of Trade to Lawrence, October 29, 1754, Add. Mss. 19,073, doc. 32.

8. Shirley to Robinson, May 8, 1754, in Lincoln, *Correspondence of William Shirley*, 2: 64.

9. See Lawrence to Monckton, January 9, 1755, in Griffiths, *The Acadian Deportation*, 108.

10. Lawrence to Monckton, May 1, 1755, Peter Force Collection, Series 8D/18.

11. Thomas Speakman to John Winslow, June 25, 1755, in *Collections of the Nova Scotia Historical Society* 4 (1884): 184.

12. Griffiths, *Contexts of Acadian History*, 88.

13. For firsthand accounts of these events, see John Winslow, "Journal," in *Collections of the Nova Scotia Historical Society* 3 (1883): 71–195; 4 (1884): 113–246, esp. pp. 145–57; Robert Monckton, "Journal," in Webster, *Forts of Chignecto*, 110–16, esp. pp. 111–13; John Thomas, "Diary," *New England Historical and Genealogical Register* 33 (1879): 383–398, esp. pp. 386–88, reprinted in *Collections of the Nova Scotia Historical Society* 1 (1878): 119–140, esp. pp. 122–25, and in Webster, ed., *Journals of Beauséjour*, 11–32, esp. pp. 14–17; Abijah Willard, "Journal of Abijah Willard of Lancaster, Massachusetts," in *Collections of the New Brunswick Historical Society* 13 (1930): 3–75, esp. pp. 19–25; Louis Thomas Jacau de Fiedmont, "Journal," in Webster, *The Siege of Beauséjour*, 11–35, esp. pp. 23–32; Thomas Pichon, "Journal," in Webster, *Thomas Pichon*, 101–4; Louis de Courville, "Journal," in Webster, *Journals of Beauséjour*, 45–50, esp. pp. 47–49; see also *Boston Evening Post*, June 30, 1755; "Extrait du Journal," in Gaudet, "Généalogie," 236–37.

14. De Fiedmont, "Journal," in Webster, *Siege of Beauséjour*, 33; De Courville, "Journal," in Webster, *Journals of Beauséjour*, 49.

15. Winslow, "Journal," in *Collections of the Nova Scotia Historical Society* 4 (1884): 157–58, 175.

16. Ibid., 4:161, 176.

17. Lawrence to Monckton, May 1, 1755, Peter Force Collections, series 8D/18.

18. Lawrence to Monckton, June 25, 1755, in Griffiths, *The Acadian Deportation*, 109.

19. Willard, "Journal," in *Collections of the New Brunswick Historical Society* 13 (1930): 26.

20. Ibid., 33, 39, 44.

21. Monckton, "Journal," in Webster, *Forts of Chignecto*, 113, 114; Pichon, "Journal," in Webster, *Thomas Pichon*, 105; Thomas, "Diary," in *New England Historical and Genealogical Register* 33 (1879): 389; Lawrence to Robinson, June 28, 1755, in Akins, *Selections*, 243.

22. Lawrence to Robinson, June 28, 1755, in Akins, *Selections*, 243.

23. Council minutes, July 3–4, 1755, in Akins, *Selections*, 247–56; Lawrence to Board of Trade, July 18, 1755, in Akins, *Selections*, 259–60; *Boston Evening Post*, July 14, 1755.

24. Council minutes, July 25, 1755, in Akins, *Selections*, 260–62; Council minutes, July 28, 1755, in Akins, *Selections*, 263–67. Statements of Acadian deputies and opinion of Jonathan Belcher, Jr., July 28, 1755, in Gaudet, "Acadian Genealogy and Notes," 62–65. For other accounts of the deliberations of July 1755, see Cazaux, *L'Acadie*, 314–15; Griffiths, *Contexts of Acadian History*, 83–89.

25. Opinion of Belcher, July 28, 1755, in Gaudet, "Acadian Genealogy and Notes," 63–65.

26. Ibid., 63.

27. Circular letter of Lawrence, August 11, 1755, in *Collections of the Nova Scotia Historical Society* 3 (1883): 82.

28. Opinion of Belcher, 63–65.

29. See Monckton, "Journal," in Webster, *Forts of Chignecto*, 110–16, 115; see also John Winslow, "Journal," in *Collections of the Nova Scotia Historical Society* 4 (1884): 222–27.

30. For biographical information on Winslow, see Pargellis, "Winslow, John."

31. Lawrence to Murray, August 9, 1755, in *Collections of the Nova Scotia Historical Society* 4 (1884): 242.

32. See conclusion, below, especially note 26.

33. See Winslow to Shirley, August 22, 1755, in *Collections of the Nova Scotia Historical Society* 3 (1883): 71–72; Winslow to William Coffin, August 22, 1755, in *Collections of the Nova Scotia Historical Society* 3 (1883): 72–73; Winslow to Monckton, August 23, 1755, in *Collections of the Nova Scotia Historical Society* 3 (1883): 75; Winslow to Murray, August 24, 1755, in *Collections of the Nova Scotia Historical Society* 3 (1883): 76–77.

34. Winslow, "Journal," 3: 90–95; Winslow to Lawrence, September 17, 1755, in *Collections of the Nova Scotia Historical Society* 3 (1883): 126–28.

35. Winslow, "Journal," 3: 109.

36. Ibid., 3: 164.

37. Ibid., 3: 166.

38. Phineas Osgood to Winslow, December 20, 1755, in *Collections of the Nova Scotia Historical Society* 3 (1883): 192.

39. Willard, "Journal," 40–41; Lawrence to Monckton, September 11, 1755, Peter Force Collection, series 8D/18; Winslow to Handfield, September 19, 1755, in *Collections of the Nova Scotia Historical Society* 3 (1883): 134.

40. See Lawrence to Monckton, July 31, 1755, in Gaudet, "Acadian Genealogy and Notes," 8–9.

41. Hull, *Female Felons*, 112; Rothman, *Discovery of the Asylum*, 52–56.

42. See Rothman, *Discovery of the Asylum*, 56; Greenberg, *Crime and Punishment*, 125–27; Porter, *English Society in the Eighteenth Century*, 91, 155; for a sense of how this system might have worked for fortunate prisoners, see Oliver Goldsmith's fictional presentation in *The Vicar of Wakefield*, 136–86.

43. See Lawrence to Monckton, October 20, 1755, Peter Force Collection, series 8D/18.

44. Willard, "Journal," 42; Thomas, "Diary," 392.

45. Winslow to Lawrence, September 29, 1755, in *Collections of the Nova Scotia Historical Society* 3 (1883): 154–56; Winslow to Lawrence, October 31, 1755, in *Collections of the Nova Scotia Historical Society* 3 (1883): 177–81; Winslow, "Journal," 3: 185. See also Willard, "Journal," 37, 41, 49, 51, 54, 66–67, 69; Winslow, "Journal," 3: 100–102; Thomas, "Diary," 392–93; Monckton, "Journal," 115, 116; *Boston Gazette*, September 29, October 6, 1755; *New York Mercury*, September 29, 1755.

46. Clark, *Acadia*, 346.

47. Roy, "Settlement and Population Growth," 153. Lawrence did not send any Acadians to New Jersey, he said, because he did not believe that the colony had the "capacity" to "dispose of them." Lawrence to Charles Hardy, July 5, 1756, Add. Mss. 19,073. In all likelihood he employed a similar logic with respect to the lower counties of the Delaware and Rhode Island. See *Minutes of the Provincial Council of Pennsylvania*, 7: 241. The legislature of New Hampshire maintained that the Acadians were a security risk, and barred any ships carrying them from landing in the province. Report of a committee of the assembly, December 19, 1755, in Bouton, *Provincial Papers*, 6: 452.

48. Virginia refused to cooperate fully with the program. For a discussion of the fate of the Acadians sent there, see Griffiths, "Acadians in Exile."

49. *New York Mercury*, May 10, 1756; *Colonial Laws of New York*, 4: 94–95; Gipson, *Great War for the Empire*, 320. On the Huguenot communities of New Rochelle and Staten Island, see Butler, *Huguenots in America*, 47, 191–92.

50. *Maryland Gazette*, December 11, 1755; *Archives of Maryland*, 52: 333; Gipson, *Great War for the Empire*, 304–7, 309–18; *Pennsylvania Archives* 8th ser. vol. 5, pp. 4196–4207, 4216, 4880–83, 5052–66; see also Brasseaux, *Founding of New Acadia*, 47–52.

51. Hoadly, *Public Records*, 10: 452–53. *Journals of the House of Representatives of Massachusetts*, 32–37.

52. Hoadly, *Public Records*, 10: 452–53.

53. *Acts and Laws*, 239; Hoadly, *Public Records*, 10: 453.

54. *Acts and Laws*, 217; Hoadly, *Public Records*, 10: 453.

55. James Campbell to Louden, December 13, 1755, LO 698, Huntington Library; Crépeau and Dunn, *The Melanson Settlement*, 12.

56. Dan Dyson's journal beginning December 6, 1757, LO 4957, Huntington Library.

57. See, for example, Vaudreuil to ministry, August 6, 1756, in Gaudet, "Généalogie," 241–43; *New York Mercury*, April 5, 1756; *Boston Gazette*, May 10, 1756.

58. "Divers dépense," Louisbourg, December 31, 1756, MG1, C11B, vol. 36, doc. 241, NAC.

59. Monckton to Winslow, October 7, 1755, in *Collections of the Nova Scotia Historical Society* 3 (1883): 177–81; Monckton, "Journal," 115; *Boston Evening Post*, October 27, 1755; *Boston Gazette*, October 27, 1755; Captain Beale's description of the St. John River, August 1756, LO 2363, Huntington Library; Monckton, "Report of the Proceedings of the Troops on the St. John River," in *Collections of the New Brunswick Historical Society* 5 (1904): 165–74, 171.

60. Abstract of dispatches from Canada, in O'Callaghan, *Documents*, 10: 427; Claude Godfrey Coquard to his brother, 1757, in O'Callaghan, *Documents*, 10: 528; *Boston Evening Post*, March 15, 1756; *Pennsylvania Gazette*, March 18, 1756; Vaudreuil to ministry, June 1, 1756, in Gaudet, "Généalogie," 239–41. For accounts of other Acadians who escaped to the St. John valley, see Monckton to Winslow, October 7, 1755, in *Collections of the Nova Scotia Historical Society* 3 (1883): 177–81; Monckton, "Journal," 114–15; *Boston Evening Post*, July 14, July 21, October 27, 1755; *Boston Gazette*, October 27, 1755, March 1, 1756; Captain Bale's description of the St. John River, August 1756, LO 2363, Huntington Library; Monckton, "Report of the Proceedings of the Troops on the St. Johns River," 165–74, 171; Lawrence to Shirley, April 9, 1756, Add. 19,073, Mss. doc. 53; Lawrence to Board of Trade, November 3, 1756, CO 217/16, doc. 61, PRO; Willard, "Journal," 60–65; Thomas, "Diary," 395; Pichon, "Journal," in Webster, *Thomas Pichon*, 106; Winslow, "Journal," 4: 187, 194–95; William Martin, "Description of the St. Johns River in Nova Scotia, March 11, 1758," LO 6939, Huntington Library; Vaudreuil to Jean Baptiste de Machault d'Aronville, September 18, 1755, in O'Callaghan, *Documents*, 10: 358–59.

61. See Jeffery Amherst to William Pitt, April 19, 1759, in *Collections of the New Brunswick Historical Society* 5 (1904): 174–75; Knox, *Journal*, 1: 262, 268, 279–81; Monckton, "Report of the Proceedings of the Troops," 1758, in Gaudet, "Acadian Genealogy and Notes," 236–38; Journal of Enoch Poor, April 16, 1759 to May 12, 1760, HM 610, Huntington Library.

62. "A short account of what passed at Cape Breton, from the beginning of

the last War until the taking of Louisbourg in 1758, by a French Officer, in Akins, *Selections*, 195–96.

63. Candler, *Colonial Records of Georgia*, 7: 301–2, 304; "Passes from the Governors of Georgia, South Carolina, and New York to a French neutral, Jacques Morrice and his family, March 10, 1756," LO 903, Huntington Library.

64. For the statements of Acadians who professed neutrality, see Galerme, *A Relation of the Misfortunes*; *Pennsylvania Archives* 8th ser. vol. 5, p. 4191; statement of "Alexis Tibaudau" et al., 1756, *Pennsylvania Archives* 8th ser., vol. 5, pp. 4293–95; statement of "Oliver Tibaudat" et al., *Pennsylvania Archives* 8th ser. vol. 6, pp. 4509–12; *Colonial Records of South Carolina*, 56; Casgrain, *Pèlegrinage*, 231–37, 236.

65. "Passes from the Governors."

66. Ibid.

67. *Journals of the House of Representatives of Massachusetts*, vol. 33, part 1, p. 142.

68. *Ibid.*, pp. 112–13, 121. A second party of eighty refugees left Georgia a few weeks after the Vigneau party of ninety-nine, and other Acadian exiles made similar journeys. See *Boston Gazette*, August 20, 1756; *New York Mercury*, August 30, 1756; *South Carolina Gazette*, May 1, 1756; Vaudreuil to ministry, August 6, 1756, Vaudreuil to ministry, August 7, 1756, in Gaudet, "Généalogie," 241–44.

69. "Passes from the Governors."

70. Saunders, *Colonial Records of North Carolina*, 5: 655.

71. Charles Hardy to Board of Trade, September 5, 1756, in Gaudet, "Généalogie," xvii–xviii; Robert Hale's Chronicle, French and Indian War Manuscripts, folio 1, vol. 1, p. 26.

72. "Passes from the Governors."

73. *Boston Evening Post*, July 26, 1756.

74. *Journals of the House of Representatives of Massachusetts*, vol. 33, part 1, p. 142.

75. Ibid., p. 176; see also pp. 178, 187.

76. Ibid., p. 177, and vol. 34, part 2, p. 439.

77. *Journals of the House of Representatives of Massachusetts*, vol. 33, part 1, pp. 112–13, 121.

78. Daniel Henshaw et al. to Spencer Phips, March 30, 1757, in Gaudet, "Généalogie," 168–69.

79. *Journals of the House of Representatives of Massachusetts*, vol. 35, pp. 136–37.

80. Poirier, *Les Acadiens*, 46.

81. Letter from Perrault, September 1, 1764, in Gaudet, "Généalogie," 218–20; Poirier, *Les Acadiens*, 72–73.

82. Petition, September 16, 1764, in Gaudet, "Généalogie," 217–18; Poirier, *Les Acadiens*, 49–51.

83. Poirier, *Les Acadiens*, 75–89.
84. Ibid., 230.
85. Arsenault, *Histoire et généalogie*, 6: 2255.

Conclusion

1. Jeffery Amherst, "Address to the officers and men of the army before attacking Louisbourg," June 3, 1758, LO 5847, Huntington Library.
2. Equiano, *Interesting Narrative*, 69.
3. See White, *The Middle Ground*, 257–68.
4. Knollenberg and Kent, "Communications."
5. In 1746 an epidemic had struck the Mi'kmaq, and although it is likely that the native people contracted their disease from French allies, a rumor circulated through the province that the British had intentionally made the Mi'kmaq ill by selling them "poisoned" cloth. "Motifs des sauvages mickmaques et marichites des continuer la guerre contre les Anglois depuis la dernière paix," in De Beaumont, *Les Derniers jours*, 248–53, 251. One of the closest advisors to the acting governor of Nova Scotia at the time of the epidemic was William Douglass, a self-styled expert on smallpox who advocated exploiting the native peoples' vulnerability to disease in wartime. See, for example, Douglass, *Practical Essay*. For Douglass's advocacy of the exploitation of disease in warfare, see Douglass, *Summary*, 1: 550–51.
6. Hutchinson, *Massachusetts-Bay*, 3: 30–31.
7. Robinson to Lawrence, August 13, 1755, in Griffiths, *The Acadian Deportation*, 111; Griffiths, "Acadians in Exile;" Brasseaux, *Founding of New Acadia*, 35–52; Gipson, *Great War for the Empire*, 291–320.
8. Philip Lawson's *Imperial Challenge* provides a comprehensive analysis of the policy debates that followed the conquest of Canada, though it does not refer to earlier episodes in other places in which the deportation of the colonial population was an option considered for conquered colonies.
9. See Bartels and Janzen, "Micmac Migration."
10. Upton, *Micmacs and Colonists*, 57–59.
11. The terms of the agreement were memorialized in a series of documents, and ambiguities surrounding their meaning and binding nature have led to years of litigation in the 1990s. See, for example, the decision of the Supreme Court of Canada in *R. v. Marshall*, file no. 26014, September 17, 1999.
12. Bartels and Janzen, "Micmac Migration."
13. John Seccomb's diary (typescript), pp. 2–4, 7, 10, Seccomb Family Papers.
14. For indications of the difficulties the Mi'kmaq faced, see Prins, "Tribulations of a Border Tribe," 212–16; Dickason, "Louisbourg and the Indians," 123–25.

15. Upton, *Micmacs and Colonists*, 64.

16. For early evidence of the loss of the French language, see Leonard Christopher Rudolf's diary, beginning June 1, 1757, LO 3765, Huntington Library.

17. "Acadian Prisoners at Fort Edward," in Gaudet, "Acadian Genealogy and Notes," 264; Dunn, *The Acadians of Minas*, 25.

18. Memorial of the inhabitants of King's County, March 23, 1765, in Casgrain, *Collection*, 2:93.

19. "Catholiques dans la Nouvelle-Ecosse," January 1, 1767, in Gaudet, "Généalogie," 315.

20. Raymond, *River St. John*, 96.

21. See Thériault, "Acadia from 1763 to 1990."

22. Common estimates place the Acadian population of the thirteen colonies in 1763 between 3,600 and 3,800. The outward migration continued through the 1760s as Acadian exiles left the colonies in small groups and occasionally by the dozens or hundreds. See Roy, "Settlement and Population Growth," 156–59; Brasseaux, *Founding of New Acadia*, 53.

23. See Longfellow, "Evangeline."

24. For a recent literary analysis of Longfellow's work, see Gioia, "Longfellow in the Aftermath of Modernism." See also Pearce, *The Continuity of American Poetry*, 210–14.

25. Winslow, "Journal," in *Collections of the Nova Scotia Historical Society* 3 (1883): 71–195; 4 (1884): 113–246. Longfellow always asserted that he referred to French-language sources as well as English ones when he was composing the poem. He indicated that he had orally received a thirdhand account of an Acadian woman whose experiences paralleled those of Evangeline. No such woman has ever been identified by historians, and if she did exist, Longfellow could not have received much detailed information in the story he heard, because he did not know the route the Acadians took on their journey to Louisiana. Longfellow also read the work of the Abbé Thomas-Guillaume Raynal, but Raynal's interpretation of the Acadian experience does not closely resemble Longfellow's. Raynal provided little narrative detail about the deportation of the Acadians and made no reference to the specific experiences of Acadian women during or after 1755. Furthermore, he argued that the Acadians were stubbornly loyal French subjects. Longfellow strongly suggests that before the relocation they were uninterested in imperial politics. See Raynal, *Histoire philosophique*, 8: 267–78. Raynal's work was available in English as Raynal, *Philosophical and Political History of the Settlements and Trade of the Europeans in the East and West Indies*, 5: 415–29. For a general discussion of Longfellow's sources see Hawthorne and Dana, *The Origin and Development*. The historian Thomas C. Haliburton relied heavily on Winslow's journal in preparing his history of Nova Scotia, and Haliburton's work, in turn, inspired and informed the work of Longfellow. See Haliburton, *Historical and Statistical Account of Nova Scotia*, vii, 176–81; Hawthorne and Dana, *Origin and Development*, 9, 14. Other nineteenth-century works directly or indirectly dependent on

the journal as a source include Williams, *The Neutral French*, and Hawthorne, *Famous Old People*, 122–35.

26. Longfellow suggests that the transformation of the Acadian people into Americans began the moment they heard the deportation order. In that instant, they all shouted, spontaneously and unanimously, "Down with the tyrants of England!" The phrase would be echoed later in the poem. Longfellow, "Evangeline," 47.

27. Longfellow, "Evangeline," 81.

28. "Gabriel it was, who, weary with waiting, unhappy and restless / Sought in the Western wilds oblivion of self and sorrow." Nonetheless, somewhat incongruously, he ended his days in Philadelphia. Longfellow, "Evangeline," 71.

29. Longfellow, "Evangeline," 78, 86, 95.

30. Ibid., 76–78.

31. For a discussion of the cultural impact of the poem, see Griffiths, "Longfellow's *Evangeline*."

Bibliography

Archives Consulted and Selected Paper Collections

American Antiquarian Society, Worcester, Massachusetts
    Curwen Family Papers
    French and Indian War Manuscripts
    Hale Family Papers
    Mather Family Papers
    Seccomb Family Papers
British Library, London
    Additional manuscripts
    King's manuscripts
    Sloane manuscripts
Houghton Library, Harvard University
    Mascarene Papers
Huntington Library, San Marino, California
    Loudon Papers
Library of Congress, Washington, D.C.
    Peter Force Collection
Massachusetts Historical Society, Boston
    Belknap Papers
    Gay Papers
    Mascarene Family Papers
Museum of the City of New York
    Samuel Vetch Letter-Book
National Archives of Canada, Ottawa
    French colonial archives, general North American correspondence (C11C)
    French colonial archives, Ile Royale correspondence (C11B)
    French colonial archives, Acadia correspondence (C11D)
Newberry Library, Chicago
    Ayers Manuscripts
Public Archives of Nova Scotia, Halifax
    Tredegar Park Manuscripts

Public Record Office, Kew, England
  Colonial Office papers, Nova Scotia (CO 217)
  Colonial Office papers, Newfoundland (CO 194)
  Colonial Office papers, St. Christopher's (CO 152)
Rhodes House Library, University of Oxford
  Records of the Society for the Propagation of the Gospel
Scottish Record Office, Edinburgh

Published Primary Sources

Note: "Evans" numbers refer to entry numbers assigned colonial era American publications in Charles Evans, *American Bibliography* (New York: Peter Smith, 1941–59).

Acts and Laws of the Great and General Court. Boston, 1756. Evans 7705.

Akins, Thomas B., ed. *Selections from the Public Documents of the Province of Nova Scotia*. Halifax: Charles Annand, 1869.

Appleton, Nathaniel. *The Origin of War Examined and Applied*. Boston, 1733. Evans 3623.

Archives of Maryland, Vol. 52. Baltimore: Maryland Historical Society, 1935.

Baxter, James Phinney, ed. *Documentary History of the State of Maine*. Portland: Maine Historical Society, 1907.

Bouton, Nathaniel, ed. *Provincial Papers: Documents and Records Relating to the Province of New Hampshire*, Vol. 6. Manchester, N.H.: James M. Campbell, 1872.

Calendar of State Papers, Colonial Series, America and West Indies. London: Public Record Office, 1860–.

Candler, Alan D., ed. *The Colonial Records of the State of Georgia*. Atlanta: Franklin, 1906.

Casgrain, Abbé Henri-Raymond, ed. *Collection des documents inédits sur le Canada et l'Amerique*. 3 vols. Québec: L.-J. Demers and Frère, 1888.

———. *Les Soirées canadiennes*. Québec: Brousseau, 1863.

Church, Thomas. *Entertaining Passages Relating to Phillip's War*. Boston, 1716. Evans 1800.

Coke, Roger. *A Discourse of Trade*. London, 1670. Reprint, New York: Arno Press, 1972.

Collections of the Connecticut Historical Society. Hartford: Connecticut Historical Society, 1860–.

Collections of the Massachusetts Historical Society. Boston: Massachusetts Historical Society, 1815–.

Collections of the New Brunswick Historical Society. St. John: New Brunswick Historical Society, 1894–.

Collections of the Nova Scotia Historical Society. Halifax: Nova Scotia Historical Society, 1878–.

Colman, Benjamin. *Faith Victorious.* Boston, 1702. Evans 1042.

The Colonial Laws of New York from the Year 1664 to the Revolution. 5 vols. Albany, N.Y.: J. B. Lyon, 1894–1896.

The Colonial Records of South Carolina: Journal of the Commons House of Assembly, November 20, 1755–July 6, 1757. Columbia: University of South Carolina Press, 1989.

Cumming, Peter A., and Niel H. Mickenberg, eds. *Native Rights in Canada.* Toronto: General Publishing, 1972.

D'Avenant, Charles. *The Political and Commercial Works of that Celebrated Writer Charles D'Avenant, L.L.D.* Ed. Charles Whitmore. London, 1771.

De Beaumont, Gaston du Boscq, ed. *Les Derniers jours de l'Acadie.* Geneva: Slatkine-Megariotis, 1975.

Douglass, William. *Dr. Douglass's Practical Essay Concerning the Small Pox.* Boston, 1730. Evans 3275.

———. *A Summary, Historical and Political, of the First Planting, Progressive Improvements, and Present State of the British Settlements in North America.* Vol. 1. Boston, 1749. Evans 6307.

———. *A Summary, Historical and Political, of the First Planting, Progressive Improvements, and Present State of the British Settlements in North America.* Vol. 2. Boston, 1751. Evans 6663.

Dummer, Jeremiah. *A Letter to a Noble Lord, Concerning the Late Expedition to Canada.* Boston, 1712. Evans 1542.

Equiano, Olaudah. *The Interesting Narrative of the Life of Olaudah Equiano, Written by Himself.* Ed. Robert J. Allison. Boston: Bedford Books, 1995.

Fergusson, Charles Bruce, ed. *Minutes of His Majesty's Council at Annapolis Royal, 1736–1749.* Halifax: Public Archives of Nova Scotia, 1967.

Galerme, John Baptiste. *A Relation of the Misfortunes of the French Neutrals.* Philadelphia, 1756. Evans 7669.

Gaudet, Placide, ed. "Acadian Genealogy and Notes." In *Report Concerning Canadian Archives for the Year 1905.* Ottawa: National Archives of Canada, 1906.

———, ed. "Généalogie des familles acadiennes." In *Rapport concernant les archives canadiennes pour l'année 1905.* Ottawa: National Archives of Canada, 1906.

A Genuine Account of Nova Scotia. Dublin: Philip Bowes, 1750.

Goldsmith, Oliver. *The Vicar of Wakefield: A Tale, Supposed To Be Written by Himself.* London: Oxford University Press, 1974.

Griffiths, Naomi, ed. *The Acadian Deportation: Deliberate Perfidy or Cruel Necessity?* Toronto: Copp Clark, 1969.

Haliburton, Thomas C. *An Historical and Statistical Account of Nova Scotia*. Halifax: Joseph Howe, 1829.

Hamilton, Alexander. "The Itinerarium of Dr. Alexander Hamilton." In *Colonial American Travel Narratives*, ed. Wendy Martin. New York: Penguin, 1994, 173–327.

Hawthorne, Nathaniel. *Famous Old People: Being the Second Epoch of Grandfather's Chair*. Boston: Tappan and Dennet, 1842.

Hoadly, Charles J., ed. *The Public Records of the Colony of Connecticut*, vol. 10. Hartford, Conn.: Case, Lockwood and Brainard, 1877.

Hubbard, William. *A Narrative of the Troubles with the Indians*. Boston, 1677. Evans 231.

Hutchinson, Thomas. *The History of the Colony and Province of Massachusetts-Bay*. Ed. Lawrence Shaw Mayo. Cambridge, Mass.: Harvard University Press, 1936.

The Importance of Settling and Fortifying Nova Scotia. London, 1751.

Innis, H. A., ed. *Select Documents in Canadian Economic History*. Toronto: University of Toronto Press, 1929.

Instructions for Samuel Vetch. New York, 1709. Evans 1353.

Israel, Fred L., ed. *Major Peace Treaties of Modern History, 1648–1967*. 5 vols. New York: Chelsea House, 1967–1980.

Jefferys, Thomas. *The Conduct of the French with Regard to Nova Scotia*. London, 1754.

———. *Remarks on the French Memorials Concerning the Limits of Acadia*. London, 1756.

A Journal of the Proceedings of the Late Expedition to Port-Royal. Boston, 1690. Evans 513.

Journals of the House of Representatives of Massachusetts. Boston: Massachusetts Historical Society, 1901–.

Knox, John. *An Historical Journal of the Campaigns in North America, for the Years 1757, 1758, 1759 and 1760*. Ed. Arthur G. Doughty. 3 vols. Toronto: Champlain Society, 1914.

Lescarbot, Marc. *History of New France*. Trans. W. L. Gant. 3 vols. Toronto: Champlain Society, 1911–14.

Lincoln, Charles Henry, ed. *Correspondence of William Shirley*. New York: Macmillan, 1912.

Little, Otis. *The State of Trade in the North Colonies Considered; With an Account of the Produce, and a Particular Description of Nova Scotia*. London, 1748.

Longfellow, Henry Wadsworth. "Evangeline: A Tale of Acadie." In *The Poetical Works of Henry Wadsworth Longfellow*. New York: Houghton Mifflin, 1886, 2:19–106.

MacMechan, Archibald M., ed. *A Calendar of Two Letter-Books and One Com-*

mission-Book in the Possession of the Government of Nova Scotia, 1713–1741. Halifax: Public Archives of Nova Scotia, 1900.

———. *Original Minutes of His Majesty's Council at Annapolis Royal, 1720–1739*. Halifax: Public Archives of Nova Scotia, 1908.

Maillard, Pierre. *An Account of the Customs and Manners of the Mickmackis*. London, 1758.

Mather, Cotton. *Decennium Luctuosum: An History of Remarkable Occurrences in the Long War*. Boston, 1699. Evans 873. Reprint, New York: Garland, 1978.

———. *The Deplorable State of New England*. London, 1708.

———. *Diary of Cotton Mather*. Boston: Prince Society, 1912.

———. *Magnalia Christi Americana, or the Ecclesiastical History of New England*, Vol. 1. Hartford, Conn.: Silas Andrus, 1820.

———. *A Memorial of the Present Deplorable State of New England*. Boston, 1707. Evans 1331.

———. *The Present State of New England*. Boston, 1690. Evans 537.

Mather, Increase. *A Brief History of the War*. Boston, 1676. Evans 220.

Minutes of the Provincial Council of Pennsylvania. Vol. 7. Harrisburg, Pa.: Theo. Fenn and Co., 1851.

Moody, Robert Earle, and Richard Clive Simmons, eds. *The Glorious Revolution in Massachusetts*. Boston: Colonial Society of Massachusetts, 1988.

New England Historical and Genealogical Register. Boston: New England Historical and Genealogical Society, 1874–1923.

O'Callaghan, E. B., ed. *Documents Relative to the Colonial History of the State of New York*. 15 vols. Albany, N.Y.: Weed, Parsons, 1850–83.

———, ed. *Journal of the Voyage of the Sloop Mary*. Albany, N.Y.: Private printing, 1866.

Penhallow, Samuel. *The History of the Wars of New England with the Eastern Indians*. Boston, 1726. Evans 2796.

Pennsylvania Archives. Philadelphia: Joseph Severns, 1852–.

Pote, William Jr. *The Journal of Captain William Pote, Jr*. New York: Garland, 1976.

Pothier, Bernard, ed. *Course à L'Accadie: Journal de campagne de François Du Pont Duvivier en 1744*. Moncton, N.B.: Éditions d'Acadie, 1982.

Raynal, Thomas-Guillaume. *Histoire philosophique et politique des establissements et du commerce des européens dans les deux Indes*. 10 vols. Geneva, 1783.

———. *A Philosophical and Political History of the Settlements and Trade of the Europeans in the East and West Indies*. Trans. J. O. Justamond. 6 vols. Dublin, 1784.

Report of the Work of the Archives Branch for the Year 1912. Ottawa: National Archives of Canada, 1913.

The Royal Fishery Revived. London, 1670.

Salusbury, John. *Expeditions of Honour: The Journal of John Salusbury in Halifax, Nova Scotia, 1749–53*. Ed. Ronald Rompkey. Newark: University of Delaware Press, 1980.

Saunders, William L., ed. *The Colonial Records of North Carolina*. 10 vols. Raleigh, N.C.: Public Libraries, 1887.

Savage, Thomas. *An Account of the Late Action of the New Englanders*. London, 1691.

Sewall, Samuel. *The Diary of Samuel Sewall*. Ed. M. Halsey Thomas. New York: Farrar, Straus and Girous, 1973.

Shortt, Adam, V. K. Johnston, and Gustave Lactot, eds. *Documents Relating to Currency, Exchange and Finance in Nova Scotia, with Prefatory Documents, 1675–1758*. Ottawa: J. O. Patenaude, 1933.

Some Considerations on the Consequences of the French Settling Colonies on the Mississippi. London, 1720. Reprint, Cincinnati: Historical and Philosophical Society of Ohio, 1928.

Thwaites, Reuben Gold, ed. *The Jesuit Relations and Allied Documents: Travels and Explorations of the Jesuit Missionaries in New France, 1601–1791*. 73 vols. New York: Pageant, 1959.

The Trials of Five Persons for Piracy. Boston, 1726. Evans 2818.

Warrand, Duncan, ed. *More Culloden Papers*. Vol. Five. Inverness, Scotland: R. Carruthers and Sons, 1930.

Webster, John Clarence, ed. *Acadia at the End of the Seventeenth Century*. Saint John: New Brunswick Museum, 1934.

———. *The Building of Fort Lawrence in Chignecto*. Saint John: New Brunswick Museum, 1941.

———. *The Career of the Abbé Le Loutre in Nova Scotia*. Shediac, N.B.: Private printing, 1933.

———. *The Forts of Chignecto: A Study of the 18th Century Conflict Between Great Britain and France*. Shediac, N.B.: Private printing, 1930.

———. *Journals of Beauséjour*. Sackville, N.B.: Tribune Press, 1937.

———. *The Siege of Beauséjour in 1755*. Sackville, N.B.: New Brunswick Museum, 1930.

———. *Thomas Pichon, the "Spy of Beausejour": An Account of His Career in Europe and America*. Halifax: Public Archives of Nova Scotia, 1937.

Whitehead, Ruth Holmes, ed. *The Old Man Told Us: Excerpts from Micmac History, 1500–1750*. Halifax: Nimbus, 1991.

Whitmore, W. H., ed. *The Andros Tracts*. 3 vols. Boston: T. R. Marving, 1868.

Williams, Catherine Reade. *The Neutral French, or, The Exiles of Nova Scotia*. Providence, R.I.: Private printing, 1841.

Williams, John. *The Redeemed Captive Returning to Zion*. Boston, 1707. Evans 1340. Reprint, New York: Garland, 1978.

Williams, William. *Martial Wisdom Recommended.* Boston, 1737. Evans 4210.

Winslow, Joshua. *Journal of Joshua Winslow, 1750.* Saint John: New Brunswick Museum, 1936.

Secondary Sources

Alsop, James D. "The Age of the Projectors: British Imperial Strategy in the North Atlantic in the War of Spanish Succession." *Acadiensis* 21 (1991): 30–53.

———. "The Distribution of British Officers in the Colonial Militia for the Canada Expedition of 1709." *Journal of the Society for Army Historical Research* 65 (1987): 120–21.

———. "Samuel Vetch's 'Canada Survey'd': The Formation of a Colonial Strategy, 1706–1710." *Acadiensis* 12 (1982): 39–58.

Anderson, Benedict. *Imagined Communities: Reflections on the Origin and Spread of Nationalism.* London: Verso, 1983.

Armitage, David. "The Darien Venture." In *Scotland and the Americas: 1600 to 1800,* ed. Michael Fry. Providence, R.I.: John Carter Brown Library, 1995, 3–15.

———. "The Scottish Vision of Empire: Intellectual Origins of the Darien Venture." In *A Union for Empire: Political Thought and the British Union of 1707,* ed. John Robertson. Cambridge: Cambridge University Press, 1995, 97–120.

Arsenault, Bona. *Histoire et généalogie des acadiens.* 6 vols. Montréal: Éditions Lemémeac, 1978.

Axtell, James. *The Invasion Within: The Contest of Cultures in Colonial North America.* New York: Oxford University Press, 1985.

Bailyn, Bernard. *The New England Merchants in the Seventeenth Century.* Cambridge, Mass.: Harvard University Press, 1955.

———. *The Origins of American Politics.* New York: Vintage, 1967.

Baker, Emerson W., and John G. Reid. *The New England Knight: Sir William Phips, 1651–1695.* Toronto: University of Toronto Press, 1998.

Baker, Emerson W. "New Evidence on the French Involvement in King Phillip's War." *Maine Historical Society Quarterly* 28 (1988): 85–91.

Barnes, Thomas Garden. "'The Daily Cry for Justice': The Juridical Failure of the Annapolis Royal Regime, 1713–1749." In *Essays in the History of Canadian Law,* ed. Philip Girard and Jim Phillips. Toronto: University of Toronto Press, 1990, 3: 10–41.

Bartels, Dennis A., and Olaf Uwe Janzen. "Micmac Migration to Western Newfoundland." *Canadian Journal of Native Studies* 10 (1990): 71–96.

Bartlett, Robert. *Gerald of Wales, 1146–1223.* Oxford: Clarendon Press, 1982.

Basque, Maurice. "Conflits et solidarités familiales dans l'ancienne Acadie: l'affaire Broussard de 1724." *Cahiers de la société historique acadienne* 20 (1989): 60–68.

———. *Des Hommes de pouvoir: histoire d'Otho Robichaud et de sa famille, notables acadiens de Port-Royal et de Néguac.* Néguac, N.B.: Société historique de Néguac, N.B., 1996.

———. "Genre et gestion du pouvoir communautaire à Annapolis Royal au 18e siècle." *Dalhousie Law Journal* 17 (1994): 498–508.

Basque, Maurice, and Josette Brun. "La Neutralité à l'épreuve: des Acadiennes à la défense de leurs intérêts en Nouvelle-Écosse du 18e siècle." In *Entre le quotidien et le politique: facettes de l'histoire des femmes francophones en milieu minoritaire*, ed. Monique Hébert, Phyllis LeBlanc, and Nathalie J. Kermoal. Gloucester, Ont.: Réseau National D'Action Éducation Femmes, 1997, 107–22.

Bell, Winthrop Pickard. *The "Foreign Protestants" and the Settlement of Nova Scotia: The History of a Piece of Arrested Colonial Policy in the Eighteenth Century.* Toronto: University of Toronto Press, 1961.

Black, Jeremy. *British Foreign Policy in the Age of Walpole.* Edinburgh: John Donald, 1985.

———. *Culloden and the '45.* New York: St. Martin's Press, 1997.

Bock, Philip A. "Micmac." In *Handbook of North American Indians*, vol. 15, *Northeast*, ed. Bruce G. Trigger. Washington, D.C.: Smithsonian Institution, 1978, 109–20.

Bond, Richmond P. *Queen Anne's American Kings.* Oxford: Clarendon Press, 1952.

Bourque, Bruce J. "Ethnicity on the Maritime Peninsula, 1600–1759." *Ethnohistory* 36 (1989): 257–84.

Brasseaux, Carl A. *The Founding of New Acadia: The Beginnings of Acadian Life in Louisiana, 1765–1803.* Baton Rouge: Louisiana State University Press, 1987.

Brebner, John Bartlett. *New England's Outpost: Acadia Before the Conquest of Canada.* New York: Columbia University Press, 1927.

Breen, Timothy H. "An Empire of Goods: The Anglicization of Colonial America, 1690–1776." *Journal of British Studies* 25 (1986): 467–99.

Brooks, Katherine J. "The Effect of the Catholic Missionaries on the Micmac Indians of Nova Scotia, 1610–1986." *Nova Scotia Historical Review* 6 (1986): 107–15.

Brown, Desmond H. "Foundations of British Policy in the Acadian Expulsion: A Discussion of Land Tenure and the Oath of Allegiance." *Dalhousie Review* 57 (1977–78): 709–25.

Buckner, Phillip A., and John G. Reid, eds. *The Atlantic Region to Confederation: A History.* Toronto: University of Toronto Press, 1994.

Buffington, Arthur H. "The Puritan View of War." *Colonial Society of Massachusetts Publications* 28 (1930–33): 67–86.

Bumstead, J. M. "The Cultural Landscape of Early Canada." In *Strangers Within the Realm: Cultural Margins of the First British Empire*, ed. Bernard Bailyn and Philip D. Morgan. Chapel Hill: University of North Carolina Press, 1991, 363–92.

———. "Doctor Douglass's Summary: Polemic for Reform." *New England Quarterly* 37 (1964): 242–50.

———. " 'Things in the Womb of Time': Ideas of American Independence, 1633 to 1763." *William and Mary Quarterly* 3d ser. 31 (1974): 533–64.

Butler, Jon. *The Huguenots in America: A Refugee People in New World Society*. Cambridge, Mass.: Harvard University Press, 1983.

Calloway, Colin G. *The American Revolution in Indian Country: Crisis and Diversity in Native American Communities*. Cambridge: Cambridge University Press, 1995.

Canny, Nicholas, and Anthony Pagden, eds. *Colonial Identity in the Atlantic World*. Princeton, N.J.: Princeton University Press, 1987.

Casgrain, Abbé Henri-Raymond. *Un Pèlegrinage au pays d'Evangéline*. Québec: L.-J. Demers and Frère, 1888.

Cazaux, Yves. *L'Acadie: histoire des acadiens du XVIIe siècle à nos jours*. Paris: A. Michel, 1992.

Chard, Donald F. "Canso, 1710–1721: Focal Point of New England-Cape Breton Rivalry." *Collections of the Nova Scotia Historical Society* 39 (1977): 49–77.

———. "The Impact of French Privateering on New England, 1689–1713." *American Neptune* 35 (1975): 153–65.

———. "Southack, Cyprian." In *Dictionary of Canadian Biography*. Toronto: University of Toronto Press, 1966, 3: 596–97.

Clark, Andrew Hill. *Acadia: The Geography of Early Nova Scotia to 1760*. Madison: University of Wisconsin Press, 1968.

Claydon, Tony. *William III and the Godly Revolution*. New York: Cambridge University Press, 1996.

Cohen, Ronald D. "Colonial Leviathan: New England Foreign Affairs in the Seventeenth Century." Ph.D. diss., University of Minnesota, 1967.

Colley, Linda. *Britons: Forging the Nation, 1707–1837*. New Haven, Conn.: Yale University Press, 1992.

Conn, Stetson. *Gibraltar in British Diplomacy in the Eighteenth Century*. New Haven, Conn.: Yale University Press, 1942.

Connolly, S. J. *Religion, Law and Power: The Making of Protestant Ireland, 1660–1760*. Oxford: Clarendon Press, 1992.

Crépeau, Andrée, and Brenda Dunn. *The Melanson Settlement: An Acadian Farming Community (ca. 1664–1755)*. Ottawa: Parks Canada, 1986.

Cressy, David. *Coming Over: Migration and Communication Between England and*

New England in the Seventeenth Century. New York: Cambridge University Press, 1987.

Daigle, Jean. "Acadia from 1604 to 1763: An Historical Synthesis." In *Acadia of the Maritimes: Thematic Studies from the Beginning to the Present*, ed. Jean Daigle. Moncton, N.B.: Chaire d'Études Acadiennes, 1995, 1–43.

———. "Nos amis les ennemis: Les relations commerciales entre l'Acadie et le Massachusetts, 1670–1711." Ph.D. diss., University of Maine, 1975.

———. "1650–1686: 'Un pays qui n'est pas fait'." In *The Atlantic Region to Confederation: A History*, ed. Phillip A. Buckner and John G. Reid. Toronto: University of Toronto Press, 1994, 61–77.

———, ed. *Acadia of the Maritimes: Thematic Studies from the Beginning to the Present*. Moncton, N.B.: Chaire d'Études Acadiennes, 1995.

———. *The Acadians of the Maritimes: Thematic Studies*. Moncton, N.B.: Centre d'Études Acadiennes, 1982.

Demos, John. *The Unredeemed Captive: A Family Story from Early America*. New York: Knopf, 1994.

Dickason, Olive Patricia. "Amerindians Between French and English in Nova Scotia, 1716–1763." *American Indian Culture and Research Journal* 10 (1986): 31–56.

———. "La 'Guerre navale' des micmacs contre les britaniques, 1713–1763." In *Les Micmacs et la mer*, ed. Charles A. Martijn. Montreal: Recherches amérindiennes au Québec, 1986, 233–48.

———. "Louisbourg and the Indians: A Study in Imperial Race Relations." In *History and Archeology/Histoire et Archéologie*, vol. 6. Ottawa: Parks Canada, 1976, 1–132.

Dickinson, H. T. "The Poor Palatines and the Parties." *English Historical Review* 82 (1967): 464–83.

Dinkin, Robert J. *Voting in Provincial America: A Study of Elections in the Thirteen Colonies*. Westport, Conn.: Greenwood Press, 1977.

Dowd, Gregory Evans. *A Spirited Resistance: The North American Struggle for Unity, 1745–1815*. Baltimore: Johns Hopkins University Press, 1992.

Dunn, Brenda. *The Acadians of Minas*. Ottawa: Parks Canada, 1985.

Eccles, W. J. *France in America*. New York: Harper and Row, 1972.

Fergusson, Charles Bruce. "Winniett, William." In *Dictionary of Canadian Biography*. Toronto: University of Toronto Press, 1966, 2: 665–66.

Ferguson, Robert. *Report on the 1979 Field Season at Grassy Island, Nova Scotia*. Ottawa: Parks Canada, 1981.

Fischer, David Hackett. *Albion's Seed: Four British Folkways in North America*. New York: Oxford University Press, 1989.

Flaherty, David H. "Criminal Practice in Provincial Massachusetts." In *Law in*

Colonial Massachusetts. Boston: Colonial Society of Massachusetts, 1984, 191–242.

Flemming, David B. *The Canso Islands: An Eighteenth-Century Fishing Station.* Ottawa: Parks Canada, 1977.

Fogleman, Aaron Spencer. *Hopeful Journeys: German Immigration, Settlement, and Political Culture in Colonial America, 1717–1755.* Philadelphia: University of Pennsylvania Press, 1996.

Garratt, John G. *The Four Indian Kings.* Ottawa: National Archives of Canada, 1985.

Gellner, Ernest. *Encounters with Nationalism.* Oxford: Blackwell, 1994.

George, Timothy. "War and Peace in the Puritan Tradition." *Church History* 53 (1984): 492–503.

Gioia, Dana. "Longfellow in the Aftermath of Modernism." In *The Columbia History of American Poetry*, ed. Jay Parini and Brett C. Millier. New York: Columbia University Press, 1993, 64–96.

Gipson, Lawrence Henry. *The Great War for the Empire: The Years of Defeat, 1754–1757.* New York: Knopf, 1946.

Godechot, Jacques. "Nation, patrie, nationalisme et patriotisme en France au XVIIIe siècle." *Annales historiques de la révolution française* 43 (1971): 481–501.

Godfrey, William G. "Phillips, Erasmus James." In *Dictionary of Canadian Biography.* Toronto: University of Toronto Press, 1966, 3:514.

———. *Pursuit of Profit and Preferment in Colonial North America: John Bradstreet's Quest.* Waterloo, Ont.: Wilfred Laurier University Press, 1982.

Graham, Dominick. "Lawrence, Charles." In *Dictionary of Canadian Biography.* Toronto: University of Toronto Press, 1966, 3:361–66.

Greenberg, Douglas. *Crime and Punishment in the Colony of New York.* Ithaca, N.Y.: Cornell University Press, 1976.

Gregory, Desmond. *Minorca, the Illusory Prize: A History of the British Occupations of Minorca Between 1708 and 1802.* Rutherford, N.J.: Farleigh-Dickinson University Press, 1990.

Griffiths, Naomi. *The Acadians: Creation of a People.* New York: McGraw-Hill Ryerson, 1973.

———. "Acadians in Exile: The Experiences of the Acadians in the British Seaports." *Acadiensis* 4 (1974): 67–84.

———. *The Contexts of Acadian History, 1686–1784.* Montréal: McGill-Queen's University Press, 1992.

———. "The Golden Age: Acadian Life, 1713–1748." *Histoire sociale/Social History* 17 (1984): 21–34.

———. "Longfellow's *Evangeline*: The Birth and Acceptance of a Legend." *Acadiensis* 11 (1982): 28–41.

———. "1600–1650: Fish, Fur and Folk." In *The Atlantic Region to Confederation: A History*, ed. Phillip A. Buckner and John G. Reid. Toronto: University of Toronto Press, 1994, 40–60.

Griffiths, Naomi, and John G. Reid. "New Evidence on New Scotland." *William and Mary Quarterly* 3d. ser. 49 (1992): 492–508.

Hatch, Nathan. "The Origins of Civil Millennialism in America: New England Clergymen, War with France, and the American Revolution." *William and Mary Quarterly* 3d ser. 31 (1974): 407–30.

Hawthorne, Manning, and Henry Wadsworth Longfellow Dana. *The Origin and Development of Longfellow's "Evangeline"*. Portland, Me.: Athoensen Press, 1947.

Henretta, James. *"Salutary Neglect": Colonial Administration Under the Duke of Newcastle*. Princeton, N.J.: Princeton University Press, 1972.

Heyrman, Christine Lee. *Commerce and Culture: The Maritime Communities of Massachusetts, 1690–1750*. New York: Norton, 1984.

Hinderaker, Eric. *Elusive Empires: Constructing Colonialism in the Ohio Valley, 1673–1800*. New York: Cambridge University Press, 1997.

———. "The 'Four Indian Kings' and the Imaginative Construction of the First British Empire." *William and Mary Quarterly* 3d ser. 53 (1996): 487–526.

Hirsche, Adam J. "The Collision of Military Cultures in Seventeenth-Century New England." *Journal of American History* 74 (1987–88): 1187–1212.

Hobsbawm, E. J. *Nations and Nationalism Since 1780: Programme, Myth, Reality*. Cambridge: Cambridge University Press, 1990.

Holmes, Geoffrey. *British Politics in the Age of Anne*. London: Hambledon Press, 1987.

Homs, Roman Piña. *Las Instituciones de Menorca en el sigle XVIII*. Palma, Spain: Sa Nostra, 1986.

Hull, N. E. H. *Female Felons: Women and Serious Crime in Colonial Massachusetts*. Urbana: University of Illinois Press, 1987.

Innis, Harold A. *The Cod Fisheries: A History of an International Economy*. Toronto: University of Toronto Press, 1978.

Jackson, W. G. F. *The Rock of the Gibraltarians*. Rutherford, N.J.: Farleigh-Dickinson University Press, 1986.

Johnson, James Turner. *Ideology, Reason, and the Limitation of War: Religious and Secular Concepts, 1200–1740*. Princeton, N.J.: Princeton University Press, 1975.

Johnson, Micheline Dumont. *Apôtres ou agitateurs: la France missionaire en Acadie*. Trois Rivières, Québec: La Boréal Express, 1970.

Johnson, Richard R. *Adjustment to Empire: The New England Colonies, 1675–1715*. New Brunswick, N.J.: Rutgers University Press, 1981.

————. *John Nelson, Merchant Adventurer: A Life Between Empires*. New York: Oxford University Press, 1991.

Jordan, Gerald, and Nicholas Rogers. "Admirals as Heroes: Patriotism and Liberty in Hanoverian England." *Journal of British Studies* 28 (1989): 210–24.

Jordan, Winthrop. *White over Black: American Attitudes Toward the Negro, 1550–1812*. Chapel Hill: University of North Carolina Press, 1968.

Kettner, James H. *The Development of American Citizenship, 1608–1870*. Chapel Hill: University of North Carolina Press, 1978.

Kimball, Everett. *The Public Life of Joseph Dudley*. New York: Longman's, Green, 1911.

Knollenberg, Bernhard, and Donald H. Kent. "Communications." *Mississippi Valley Historical Review* 41 (1954–55): 489–94, 762–63.

Krech, Sheppard III, ed. *Indians, Animals and the Fur Trade: A Critique of Keepers of the Game*. Athens: University of Georgia Press, 1981.

Kupperman, Karen Ordahl. *Settling with the Indians: The Meeting of English and Indian Cultures in America, 1580–1640*. London: J. M. Dent and Sons, 1980.

Kupperman, Karen Ordahl, ed. *America in European Consciousness, 1493–1750*. Chapel Hill: University of North Carolina Press, 1995.

Landsman, Ned. "The Legacy of British Union for the North American Colonies: Provincial Elites and the Problem of Imperial Union." In *A Union for Empire: Political Thought and the British Union of 1707*, ed. John Robertson. Cambridge: Cambridge University Press, 1995, 297–318.

Laughton, John Knox. "Knowles, Sir Charles." In *Dictionary of National Biography*. London: Oxford University Press, 1882, 11:292–94.

————. "Martin, William." In *Dictionary of National Biography*. London: Oxford University Press, 1882, 12:184–85.

Laurie, Bruce. *The Life of Richard Kane: Britain's First Lieutenant-Governor of Minorca*. Rutherford, N.J.: Fairleigh-Dickinson University Press, 1994.

Lawson, Philip. *The Imperial Challenge: Quebec and Britain in the Age of the American Revolution*. Montréal: McGill-Queen's University Press, 1990.

Leach, Douglas Edward. *Flintlock and Tomahawk: New England in King Philip's War*. New York: Macmillan, 1958.

Le Blant, Robert. *Un Colonial sous Louis XIV: Philippe de Pastour de Costabelle, gouverneur de Terre-Neuf puis de l'Ile Royale, 1661–1717*. Paris: A. Margraff, 1935.

Leder, Lawrence H. *Robert Livingston, 1654–1728, and the Politics of Colonial New York*. Chapel Hill: University of North Carolina Press, 1961.

Lounsbury, Ralph Greenlee. *The British Fishery at Newfoundland, 1634–1763*. New Haven, Conn.: Yale University Press, 1934.

Lovejoy, David S. *The Glorious Revolution in America*. New York: Harper and Row, 1972.

Macinnes, Allan I. *Clanship, Commerce and the House of Stuart, 1603–1788*. East Lothian: Tuckwell Press, 1996.

MacNutt, W. S. *The Atlantic Provinces: The Emergence of Colonial Society, 1712–1857*. Toronto: McClelland and Stewart, 1965.

Malone, Patrick M. *The Skulking Way of War: Technology and Tactics among the New England Indians*. Baltimore: Johns Hopkins University Press, 1993.

Martijn, Charles A., ed. *Les Micmacs et la mer*. Montreal: Recherches Amerindiennes au Québec, 1986.

Martin, Calvin. "The European Impact on the Culture of a Northeastern Algonquian Tribe: An Ecological Interpretation." *William and Mary Quarterly* 3d. ser. 31 (1974): 3–26.

——. "The Four Lives of a Micmac Copper Pot." *Ethnohistory* 22 (1975): 111–33.

——. *Keepers of the Game: Indian-White Relationships and the Fur Trade*. Berkeley: University of California Press, 1978.

McCully, Bruce T. "Governor Francis Nicholson, Patron *Par Excellence* of Religion and Learning in America." *William and Mary Quarterly* 3d. ser. 39 (1982): 310–33.

McCusker, John J., and Russell R. Menard. *The Economy of British America, 1607–1789*. Chapel Hill: University of North Carolina Press, 1985.

McLennan, J. S. *Louisbourg from Its Foundation to its Fall, 1713–1758*. London: Macmillan, 1918.

McNeill, John Robert. *Atlantic Empires of France and Spain: Louisbourg and Havana, 1700–1760*. Chapel Hill: University of North Carolina Press, 1985.

Merwick, Donna. *Possessing Albany, 1630–1710*. New York: Cambridge University Press, 1990.

Millender, Michael Jonathan. "Transformation of the American Criminal Trial, 1790–1875." Ph.D. diss., Princeton University, 1996.

Miller, Christopher L., and George Hamell. "A New Perspective on Indian-White Contact: Cultural Symbols and Colonial Trade." *Journal of American History* 73 (1986): 311–28.

Moody, Barry Morris. "A Just and Disinterested Man: The Nova Scotia Career of Paul Mascarene, 1710–1752." Ph.D. diss., Queen's University, 1976.

Moogk, Peter N. "Reluctant Exiles: The Problem of Colonization in French North America." *William and Mary Quarterly* 3d. ser. 46 (1989): 463–505.

Moore, Christopher. "The Other Louisbourg: Trade and Merchant Enterprise in Ile Royale, 1713–1758." *Histoire sociale/Social History* 12 (1979): 79–96.

Morrison, Kenneth M. *The Embattled Northeast: The Elusive Ideal of Alliance in Abenaki-Euroamerican Relations*. Berkeley: University of California Press, 1984.

Murrin, John M. "Anglicizing an American Colony: The Transformation of Provincial Massachusetts." Ph.D. diss., Yale University, 1966.

Nash, Gary B. "The Failure of Female Factory Labor in Colonial Boston." *Labor History* 20 (1979): 165–88.

———. *The Urban Crucible: Social Change, Political Consciousness, and the Origins of the American Revolution.* Cambridge, Mass.: Harvard University Press, 1979.

Nietfeld, Patricia. "Determinants of Aboriginal Micmac Political Structure." Ph.D. diss., University of New Mexico, 1981.

Olson, Alison. "Hobby, Sir Charles." In *Dictionary of Canadian Biography.* Toronto: University of Toronto Press, 1966, 2:288–90.

———. *Making the Empire Work: London and American Interest Groups, 1690–1790.* Cambridge, Mass.: Harvard University Press, 1992.

Pagden, Anthony. *European Encounters with the New World: From Renaissance to Romanticism.* New Haven, Conn.: Yale University Press, 1993.

———. *Lords of All the World: Ideologies of Empire in Spain, Britain and France c. 1500–c. 1800.* New Haven, Conn.: Yale University Press, 1995.

Paquet, Gilles, and Jean-Pierre Wallot. "Nouvelle-France/Québec/Canada: A World of Limited Identities." In *Colonial Identity in the Atlantic World,* ed. Nicholas Canny and Anthony Pagden. Princeton, N.J.: Princeton University Press, 1987, 95–114.

Pargellis, Stanley M. "Winslow, John." In *Dictionary of American Biography.* New York: Scribner's, 1927, 20:396–97.

Parkman, Francis. *Montcalm and Wolf.* New York: Collier, 1966.

Pastore, Ralph. "The Sixteenth Century: Aboriginal Peoples and European Contact." In *The Atlantic Region to Confederation: A History,* ed. Phillip A. Buckner and John G. Reid. Toronto: University of Toronto Press, 1994, 22–39.

Patterson, Stephen E. "Indian-White Relations in Nova Scotia, 1749–61: A Study in Political Interaction." *Acadiensis* 23 (1993): 23–59.

———. "1744–1763: Colonial Wars and Aboriginal Peoples." In *The Atlantic Region to Confederation: A History,* ed. Phillip A. Buckner and John G. Reid. Toronto: University of Toronto Press, 1994, 125–55.

Paul, Daniel K. *We Were Not the Savages: A Micmac Perspective on the Collision of European and Aboriginal Civilizations.* Halifax: Nimbus, 1994.

Pearce, Roy Harvey. *The Continuity of American Poetry.* Princeton, N.J.: Princeton University Press, 1961.

Pencak, William. *War, Politics, and Revolution in Provincial Massachusetts.* Boston: Northeastern University Press, 1981.

Pencak, William, and Conrad Edick Wright, eds. *Authority and Resistance in Early New York.* New York: New York Historical Society, 1983.

Piers, Harry. "The Fortieth Regiment, Raised at Annapolis Royal in 1717; and Five Regiments Subsequently Raised in Nova Scotia." *Collections of the Nova Scotia Historical Society* 21 (1927): 115–83.

Pincombe, C. Alexander. "How, Edward." In *Dictionary of Canadian Biography*. Toronto: University of Toronto Press, 1966, 3:297–98.

Plank, Geoffrey. "The Changing Country of Anthony Casteel: Language, Religion, Geography, Political Loyalty and Nationality in Mid-Eighteenth Century Nova Scotia." *Studies in Eighteenth-Century Culture* 27 (1998): 55–76.

———."The Culture of Conquest: The British Colonists and Nova Scotia, 1690–1759." Ph.D. diss., Princeton University, 1994.

———. "A More Modest Proposal? British Imperial Policy in Ireland and Nova Scotia." In *States, Citizens, and Questions of Significance*, ed. John Brigham and Roberta Kevelson. New York: Peter Lang, 1997, 175–86.

———. "The Two Majors Cope: The Boundaries of Nationality in Mid-Eighteenth Century Nova Scotia." *Acadiensis* 25 (1996): 18–40.

Poirier, Michel. *Les Acadiens aux îles Saint-Pierre et Miquelon*. Moncton, N.B.: Éditions d'Acadie, 1984.

Porter, Roy. *English Society in the Eighteenth Century*. New York: Penguin, 1982.

Pothier, Bernard. "Acadian Emigration to Ile Royale After the Conquest of Acadia." *Histoire sociale/Social History* 3, 6 (Nov. 1970): 116–31.

Prebble, John. *Culloden*. London: Penguin, 1967.

Prins, Harald E. L. "Tribulations of a Border Tribe: A Discourse on the Political Economy of the Aroostook Band of Micmacs (16th–20th Centuries)." Ph.D. diss., New School for Social Research, 1988.

Pulsipher, Jenny Hill. "Massacre at Hurtlebury Hill: Christian Indians and English Authority in Metacom's War." *William and Mary Quarterly* 3d ser. 53 (1996): 459–86.

Ranlet, Philip. "Dudley, Joseph." In *American National Biography*, ed. John A. Garraty and Mark C. Carnes. New York: Oxford University Press, 1999, 7: 9–11.

Rawlyk, George. *Nova Scotia's Massachusetts: A Study of Massachusetts-Nova Scotia Relations, 1630 to 1784*. Montréal: McGill-Queen's University Press, 1973.

———. "1720–1744: Cod, Louisbourg and the Acadians." In *The Atlantic Region to Confederation: A History*, ed. Phillip A. Buckner and John G. Reid. Toronto: University of Toronto Press, 1994, 107–24.

———. *Yankees at Louisbourg*. Orono: University of Maine Press, 1967.

Raymond, William O. *The River St. John: Its Physical Features, Legends and History from 1604 to 1784*. Sackville, N.B.: Tribune Press, 1950.

Reid, John G. *Acadia, Maine, and New Scotland: Marginal Colonies in the Seventeenth Century*. Toronto: University of Toronto Press, 1976.

———. "Mission to the Micmac." *The Beaver* 70 (1990): 15–22.

———. "The Scots Crown and the Restitution of Port Royal, 1629–1632." *Acadiensis* 6 (1977): 39–63.

———. "1686–1720: Imperial Intrusions." In *The Atlantic Region to Confederation: A History*, ed. Phillip A. Buckner and John G. Reid. Toronto: University of Toronto Press, 1994, 78–103.

Remer, Rosalind. "Old Lights and New Money: A Note on Religion, Economics, and the Social Order in 1740 Boston." *William and Mary Quarterly* 3d ser. 47 (1990): 566–73.

Robichaud, Donat. *Les Robichaud: Histoire et généalogie*. Bathurst, N.B.: Private printing, 1967.

Roeber, A. G. " 'The Origin of Whatever Is Not English among Us': The Dutch-Speaking and German-Speaking Peoples of Colonial British America." In *Strangers Within the Realm: Cultural Margins of the First British Empire*, ed. Bernard Bailyn and Philip D. Morgan. Chapel Hill: University of North Carolina Press, 1991, 220–283.

———. *Palatines, Liberty, and Property: German Lutherans in Colonial British America*. Baltimore: Johns Hopkins University Press, 1993.

Rogers, Norman McL. "The Abbé Le Loutre." *Canadian Historical Review* 11 (1930): 105–28.

Rothman, David J. *The Discovery of the Asylum: Social Order and Disorder in the New Republic*. Boston: Little, Brown, 1971.

Roy, Muriel K. "Settlement and Population Growth in Acadia." In *The Acadians of the Maritimes: Thematic Studies*, ed. Jean Daigle. Moncton, N.B.: Centre d'Études Acadiennes, 1982, 125–61.

Sahlins, Peter. "Fictions of a Catholic France: The Naturalization of Foreigners, 1685–1787." *Representations* 47 (1994): 85–110.

Sauvageau, Robert. *Acadie: la guerre de Cent Ans des Français d'Amérique aux Maritimes et en Louisiane, 1670–1769*. Paris: Berger-Levrault, 1987.

Savelle, Max. *The Diplomatic History of the Canadian Boundary, 1749–1763*. New Haven, Conn.: Yale University Press, 1940.

Schutz, John A. *William Shirley: King's Governor of Massachusetts*. Chapel Hill: University of North Carolina Press, 1961.

Shannon, Timothy J. "Dressing for Success on the Mohawk Frontier: Hendrick, William Johnson, and the Indian Fashion." *William and Mary Quarterly* 3d ser. 53 (1996): 13–42.

Shoemaker, Nancy. "How Indians Got To Be Red." *American Historical Review* 102 (1997): 625–44.

Silverman, Kenneth. *The Life and Times of Cotton Mather*. New York: Harper and Row, 1984.

Sosin, Jack M. "Louisbourg and the Peace of Aix-la-Chapelle, 1748." *William and Mary Quarterly* 3d ser. 14 (1957): 516–35.

Speck, Frank. "The Eastern Algonkian Wabanaki Confederacy." *American Anthropologist* 17 (1974): 492–508.

Speck, W. A. *The Butcher: The Duke of Cumberland and the Suppression of the '45.* Oxford: Blackwell, 1981.

Steele, Ian K. *The English Atlantic, 1675–1740: An Exploration of Communication and Community.* New York: Oxford University Press, 1986.

———. "Surrendering Rites: Prisoners on Colonial North American Frontiers." In *Hanoverian Britain and Empire: Essays in Memory of Philip Lawson*, ed. Stephen Taylor, Richard Connors, and Clyve Jones. Rochester, N.Y.: Boydell Press, 1998, 137–57.

Sutherland, Maxwell. "Philipps, Richard." In *Dictionary of Canadian Biography.* Toronto: University of Toronto Press, 1966, 3:515–18.

Thériault, Léon. "Acadia from 1763 to 1990: An Historical Synthesis." *Acadia of the Maritimes: Thematic Studies from the Beginning to the Present*, ed. Jean Daigle. Moncton, N.B.: Centre d'Études Acadiennes, 1995, 45–89.

Upton, L. S. F. *Micmacs and Colonists: Indian-White Relations in the Maritimes, 1713–1867.* Vancouver: University of British Columbia Press, 1979.

Usner, Daniel H. *Indians, Settlers and Slaves in a Frontier Exchange Economy.* Chapel Hill: University of North Carolina Press, 1992.

Vaughn, Alden T. "From White Man to Redskin: Changing Anglo-American Perceptions of the American Indian." *American Historical Review* 87 (1982): 917–53.

Vickers, Daniel. *Farmers and Fishermen: Two Centuries of Work in Essex County, Massachusetts, 1630–1830.* Chapel Hill: University of North Carolina Press, 1994.

Walker, William, Robert Conkling, and Gregory Buesing. "A Chronological Account of the Wabanaki Confederacy." In *Political Organization of Native North America*, ed. Ernest L. Schusky. Washington, D.C.: University Press of America, 1980, 41–84.

Wallace, W. Stewart, ed. *The Encyclopedia of Canada.* 6 vols. Toronto, 1937.

Waller, G. M. *Samuel Vetch: Colonial Enterpriser.* Chapel Hill: University of North Carolina Press, 1960.

Walzer, Michael. *The Revolution of the Saints: A Study in the Origins of Radical Politics.* London: Weldenfeld and Nicolson, 1966.

Webb, Stephen Saunders. "The Strange Career of Francis Nicholson." *William and Mary Quarterly* 3d ser., 23 (1966): 513–48.

Weber, David J. *The Spanish Frontier in North America.* New Haven, Conn.: Yale University Press, 1992.

White, Richard. *The Middle Ground: Indians, Empires, and Republics in the Great Lakes Region, 1650–1815*. Cambridge: Cambridge University Press, 1991.

Wicken, William C. "Encounters with Tall Sails and Tall Tales: Mi'kmaq Society, 1500–1760." Ph.D. diss, McGill University, 1994.

———. "The Mi'kmaq and Wuastukwiuk Treaties." *University of New Brunswick Law Journal* 43 (1994): 241–53.

———. "26 August 1726: A Case Study in Mi'kmaq-New England Relations in the Early Eighteenth Century." *Acadiensis* 23 (1993): 5–22.

Wilson, Kathleen. "Empire, Trade and Popular Politics in Mid-Hanoverian Britain: The Case of Admiral Vernon." *Past and Present* 121 (1988): 74–109.

Withers, Charles W. J. *Gaelic Scotland: The Transformation of a Cultural Region*. New York: Routledge, 1988.

Index

Abbadie de Saint-Castin, Jean-Vincent d', 15

Acadians: families, 19, 23, 72, 81–82, 99, 101, 114–15, 120, 130, 134–35, 145–49, 152–53, 165–67; political organization, 22–23, 88, 92, 96–99, 104, 131, 144, 156; relations with British, 1–2, 7, 11, 14, 16, 18, 32, 40–41, 54–55, 57, 60, 64, 69, 71, 81–84, 87–105, 107, 111–14, 122–24, 129–30, 135–37, 140–57, 159; relations with French, 6, 22, 32–33, 41, 62–64, 88–91, 97, 99, 103, 107–8, 112–14, 122–24, 130–31, 137, 142–43, 156; relations with Mi'kmaq, 1–2, 19, 23–31, 60, 66, 70, 72, 81–84, 86, 87–91, 93–94, 97–98, 107, 111–14, 122–23, 125, 129–31, 135–38, 142, 146, 161; spiritual life, 60, 89, 91–92, 94–95, 98–99, 102–3, 113, 130; subsistence and economy, 19, 88–89, 112–13, 130

Act of Union. See Treaty of Union

Africans and African-Americans, 60

Agriculture, 13, 19, 41, 48–49, 59, 62, 84, 107, 112, 118, 137, 142, 147–48, 164

Algonkians, 14–15, 26, 31–32, 35, 36–37, 42, 60, 70, 71, 77–80, 82, 89, 96–97, 112, 125, 127, 140, 143, 150, 158–59, 161

Allegheny Mountains, 149–50

American Revolution, 165–66

Amherst, Jeffery, 158–60

Anderson, Benedict, 4

Andres, 84

Anglicans. See Church of England

Annapolis Royal, 1–2, 10, 12–13, 15–16, 18, 19, 22–23, 26, 32, 37, 40, 45, 55–62, 64, 66, 74, 78–79, 84, 88–90, 92–105, 107, 109, 111, 113–15, 137, 142

Anne, queen of England, 40, 50, 54, 87, 90

Antigonish, 65, 80, 92

Antoine, 84

Armstrong, Lawrence, 95, 97

Augustus, William, duke of Cumberland, 116

Azores Islands, 31

Babylon, 17

Barnstable Bay, 153

Barnstable County, 153

Basques, 24

Beaubassin, 19, 33, 37, 62, 83–84, 92, 97–99, 103–4, 114, 130–31, 142, 145

Beauséjour, 130–31, 135–36, 140–44, 149

Belcher, Jonathan, Jr., 145

Board of Trade, 47, 69–70, 76, 77, 87, 93, 120, 133, 142

Boston, 14, 16, 22, 36, 44, 45, 56–58, 81–83, 88, 102, 114, 127, 153

Boston Gazette, 110

British West Indies, 47

Brookfield, Massachusetts, 153

Bucks County, Pennsylvania, 150

Campbell, John, duke of Argyll, 55

Canada, 5, 22, 44, 47–51, 55, 64, 93, 99, 117, 130, 159, 165

Canso Island, 73–74, 77–79, 84–86, 88, 94, 97, 99, 106–11, 127–29

Cape Breton Island. *See* Ile Royale

Cape Cod, 153

Cape Roseway, 76, 81

Cape Sable, 31, 149

Carolina, 24

Cartier, Jacques, 24

Casteel, Anthony, 135–36

Catholics and the Catholic Church, 6, 13,
  15, 27–30, 32, 50, 59–61, 80–81, 85, 88–
  89, 91, 94–96, 98–99, 101–4, 106, 111,
  115–16, 120, 133, 137–38, 142, 160, 163

Cattle. See Livestock

Cayenne, 156

Charlestown, Massachusetts, 153

Charlestown, South Carolina, 152

Chester County, Pennsylvania, 150

Children and child-rearing, 79, 81, 101–2,
  107, 114–15, 130, 133, 134, 142, 145–49

Church, Benjamin, 33, 37

Church of England, 11, 18, 36, 50–52, 61,
  102–3, 110, 116, 133

Climate, 47–48, 58, 156

Coal, 60

Cobequid, 149

Colley, Linda, 3–4, 121

Colonial boundaries, 8, 35, 62, 64, 70–71,
  78, 97, 109, 117, 120, 122–24

Connecticut, 117, 149–50, 153

Cope, Jean-Baptiste, 9, 27–29, 65, 79–80,
  111, 123–25, 131–36, 141, 150–51

Cornwallis, Edward, 120–23, 125–30,
  133–34, 138, 158, 160, 162

Cotterell, William, 142

Courtship and sex, 19, 72, 100, 107, 114–15

Cumberland. See Augustus, William, duke
  of Cumberland

Darien, 42, 48

Daudin, Henri, 137–38

Davis, Mary, 101

Deerfield, Massachusetts, 36–37

Deportation proposals, 4, 49, 54, 87, 92–
  93, 112–14, 116–17, 138–39, 140–45, 160,
  162

Deputies and deputy system, 92, 94,
  99–100, 104–5, 111–12, 144

Deserters, 72

Des Friches de Meneval, Louis-
  Alexandre, 12, 16

Dikes, 19, 37, 114, 164

Disease, 30, 42, 58, 111, 114, 158, 162

Dogs, 33

Dominion of New England, 11, 16, 36, 50

Doucette, John, 79

Douglass, William, 118

Dudley, Joseph, 36–39, 44–52, 56

Edict of Nantes, 102

Education, 49–50, 72, 84, 99, 101–2, 115–
  16, 118–20, 133, 142

England, 36, 41–45, 50–54, 106, 110,
  116–18, 120, 158

Evangelicalism, 110

Evangeline: A Tale of Acadie, 165–67

Firewood, 60, 114, 137–38

Fishing and fishermen, 12, 14, 16, 18, 19,
  23–26, 31–33, 35, 37–38, 41, 47, 62, 64,
  70, 74–79, 81–86, 90, 106, 108–9, 112,
  124, 127–29, 134–35, 156, 163

"Foreign Protestants," 123–24, 129, 131–34,
  138

France and the French, 2, 3, 6, 8–9, 10–
  39, 41, 42, 45, 47, 62–65, 76–81, 87–90,
  91, 93–94, 97, 106–15, 117, 120, 122–23,
  129–31, 136, 140, 150, 156, 158, 160–62,
  165

French and Indian War. See Seven Years'
  War

French Protestants, 4, 24, 36, 102–4, 133,
  142

French West Indies, 62, 156

Fur trade, 19, 22, 24–26, 42, 47, 49–50, 73

Gaulin, Antoine, 65, 80–81, 92

General Naturalization Bill (1709), 54

George, 99
George I, king of England, 64, 84, 90
George II, king of England, 96, 143, 166
Georgia, 149, 152
Germany and the Germans, 117–20, 124,
    133–24, 141
Gibraltar, 55
Gift-exchange, 65–66, 73–74, 85, 127, 158
Glorious Revolution (1688), 10–11, 16, 42,
    68
Great Lakes, 158

Halifax, George Montagu Dunk, earl of,
    141
Halifax, Nova Scotia, 120, 122, 124, 126–
    34, 138, 144, 148, 158, 163
Harrison, John, 61
Hendrick, 52
Henri IV, king of France, 30
Hobby, Sir Charles, 44–45, 57–58, 60
Hollis-Pelham, Thomas, duke of New-
    castle, 110
Hopson, Peregrine, 134, 142
How, Edward, 85
Hudson River, 149
Huguenots. See French Protestants
Hunting, 23–26, 49–50, 134, 163
Hutchinson, Thomas, 159

Ile Royale, 2. 6, 7, 8–9, 24, 40, 62–64, 73–
    74, 77, 80, 88–90, 93, 97, 99, 106–9,
    111–14, 116–17, 120, 122, 124, 129, 140,
    150, 158, 160–61
Ile-Saint-Jean, 64, 140, 160
Ireland, 7, 24, 49, 57–58, 91, 142
Iroquois and Iroquoian peoples, 26, 42–44,
    52–54, 158–59, 161

Jacobitism, 56, 59, 108, 115–16, 160
James II, king of England, 10–11, 15, 36,
    42

Jedre, Jean-Baptiste, 81–83
Jedre, Paul, 82
Johnson, William, 159

King George's War. See War of the Aus-
    trian Succession
King Philip. See Metacom
King William's War. See Nine Years' War
Knowles, Charles, 116
Kupperman, Karen, 17

La Chasse, Pierre, 65
Lancaster County, Pennsylvania, 150
Land ownership, 26, 55, 65, 77, 84–86,
    101, 110, 116, 118–20, 122, 124, 126–27,
    134–35, 137, 142, 163
Language, 8, 23, 26, 27, 29 (caption), 38,
    66, 73–74, 87, 89, 94, 101, 104–5, 112, 115,
    136, 142, 156, 160, 163–65
La Tourasse, Charles, 13
Laughton, Captain, 31
Law, 1–2, 5, 69–72, 79, 81–84, 86, 88–101,
    103–5, 110–14, 116, 123, 137–38, 143–46,
    148, 162
Lawrence, Charles, 131, 141–45, 149
Le Clerq, Chrestien, 29 (caption)
Le Loutre, Jean-Louis, 99, 111, 125, 131,
    132 (caption), 136
Le Mercier, Andrew, 102
Liquor and wine, 94, 163
Livestock, 13, 19, 33, 49, 88, 93, 96, 107,
    112, 116, 150
Livingston family, 42
Livingston, Robert, 44
London, 44–45, 50–54, 87, 110
Longfellow, Henry Wadsworth, 165–67
Louis XIV, king of France, 15, 32
Louisbourg, 41, 62–65, 73, 79, 80, 88–89,
    99, 103, 107–8, 112–14, 117–18, 122, 124,
    129, 141, 158
Louisiana, 24–25, 165–66
Lunenburg, 133–34, 141

Maillard, Pierre, 29 (caption), 111

Maine, 14–15, 33, 76, 78, 127

Maligoueche, 80

Manchester, England, 116

Maps, 19, 62, 118

Marriage, 7, 19, 72, 101, 114–15, 117, 120, 137, 146, 165–67

Mary II, queen of England, 11, 13, 14, 36, 42

Maryland, 149

Mascarene, Paul, 102–3, 112, 118

Massachusetts, 10–39, 44, 51, 53, 56, 74–79, 81–83, 87–89, 97, 102, 107, 110, 117–18, 127, 140–41, 143, 149–50, 153, 159

Mather, Cotton, 15, 17, 18, 36, 44, 45, 56

Mather, Increase, 35

Membertou, 29–30

Meneval. See Des Friches de Meneval

Merchants and trade, 10, 12, 14, 16, 18, 22–24, 30–33, 35, 38, 41–44, 47, 54, 57, 59, 62, 73, 87–88, 93–94, 96–99, 101, 108, 112–14, 124, 129, 131, 142, 156, 163

Metacom, 31

Mews, James, 81–83

Mews, Phillip, 81–83

Mexico, 166

Michigan, 166

Migration, 7, 17–18, 19, 23–24, 40, 45, 47, 58, 61–65, 71, 77, 87, 92–93, 108, 116–20, 122, 124–25, 127–31, 137, 145–57, 160, 164–67

Mi'kmaq: families, 26, 72, 79, 81–82, 107, 130; political organization, 26–27, 71–72, 83, 86, 94, 122–23, 129, 134–35, 164; relations with Acadians, 1–2, 23–31, 60, 66, 70, 72, 81–84, 86–88, 93–94, 97–98, 107, 111–14, 122–23, 135–36, 138, 142, 145–46, 150, 161; relations with British, 1–2, 11, 14, 18, 31–32, 40–41, 60, 65–67, 68–86, 87–88, 93–94, 97–98, 107, 110–14, 122–31, 134–39, 140–41, 150, 158, 161–63; relations with French, 6, 24, 31–32, 41, 60, 62, 64–65, 73, 76–80, 95, 97–98, 108–11, 122–25, 129, 136–38, 143, 150, 162–63; spiritual life, 27–30, 32, 60, 164; subsistence and economy, 23–24, 67, 162

Millennialism, 15, 17

Minas, 19, 62, 84, 92, 97–99, 104, 114, 116, 130, 137, 145–49, 164

Mining, 49, 60, 84

Ministry of Marine, 22

Minorca, 55, 91

Miquelon, 140, 156, 163–65

Miramichi, 152

Missel, John, 81–83

Missions and missionaries, 6–7, 19, 22, 26, 27–30, 50–52, 59–66, 80–81, 84, 85, 91–92, 94–95, 98–99, 102–4, 111, 116, 118–20, 125, 133, 142, 160

Mississippi River and valley, 22

Monckton, Robert. 143–44

Montréal, 36, 51, 160

Moreau, Jean-Baptiste, 133

Morris, Charles, 142

Muse, Jo, 76, 81

Nantes, 156

Nationality, 3–4, 7–8, 22, 33, 36–37, 47–51, 54, 56, 67, 69, 71–73, 76, 88, 90–91, 95–97, 102, 104–5, 107, 109, 111–12, 115–17, 120–23, 131, 133, 138, 145, 156–57, 160, 165–67

Nebraska, 166

Nelson, John, 10

Netherlands and the Dutch, 4–5, 6, 18, 19–20, 25

New Brunswick, 8, 14, 26, 64, 77, 88–89, 96–97, 124, 140, 152, 164–65

New England, 6, 10–39, 40, 44–45, 49–50, 56–59, 62, 70, 74–79, 81–83, 87–89, 102, 106–11, 114–15, 117, 124, 127, 142, 145–48, 153, 159, 162–64

Newfoundland, 41, 44, 55, 62, 93, 163
New Hampshire, 117
New Rochelle, New York, 149
New York, 6, 18, 42–44, 48, 51, 149, 152
Nicholson, Francis, 50–56, 59, 61, 91
Nine Years' War, 10–35, 74
North Carolina, 149–50, 152

Oaths and oath-taking, 13, 14, 54–55, 57,
    61, 64, 71, 88, 90–92, 95–97, 104, 112,
    131, 142–45
Ohio River, 140–41, 158
Oregon trail, 166
Ozark Mountains, 166

Pain, Félix, 65
Panama, 42, 48
Pastour de Costabelle, Philippe de, 62
Pennsylvania, 117, 149–50
Perrault, 156
Philadelphia, 150, 165
Philipps, Richard, 68, 72–74, 77–78, 84–85,
    87, 91–93, 95–96, 98, 101–2, 161–62
Phips, Sir William, 12–16
Picot, Jeanne, 101
Piracy and privateering, 15, 16, 18, 31, 33,
    74, 81–83, 109
Pisiquid, 137–38, 149
Place-names, 7–8, 10, 19–20, 40, 55, 150,
    153 (caption)
Plunder, 13, 16, 45, 56, 109
Plymouth, 18, 37, 44
Political Economy, 47, 54, 59, 116, 118
Population, 17, 19, 22, 23, 31, 59, 64, 88,
    92–23, 96, 108, 118–20, 127, 149, 164
Port Royal. See Annapolis Royal
Portugal and Portuguese, 24, 31
Presbyterianism, 61
Prince Edward Island. See Ile-Saint-Jean
Puritanism, 12, 17, 18, 32, 36–39, 56, 107,
    110

Quarrying, 49
Québec, 12–13, 18, 22, 24–26, 44, 51, 95,
    150, 160, 165
Queen Anne's War. See War of the Span-
    ish Succession
Quitrents, 96, 98

Race and heredity, 3, 7–8, 19, 32, 47, 50,
    69, 71–73, 79, 81, 102, 107, 110–12,
    120–23, 129–30, 138, 158, 161, 167
Rhode Island, 117, 153
Roads, 84, 98, 130, 137
Robichaud, Prudent, 1, 7, 60, 64, 94–96,
    113
Robinau de Villebon, Joseph, 13
Roman Catholic Church. See Catholics
    and Catholicism

Saint-Castin. See Abbadie de Saint-
    Castin, Jean-Vincent d'
St. Croix River, 111
St. Domingue, 165
St. John River, 14, 19, 96–97, 100, 122,
    140–41, 149–50, 163–65
St. Kitts, 93
St. Lawrence River, 14, 17, 19, 22, 24, 51
Saint-Ovide de Brouillan, Joseph, 109
St. Pierre, 140, 163–65
St. Poncy, Claude de la Vernade de, 103–4
Salem, Massachusetts, 16
Savannah, Georgia, 152
Scalping, 33, 35 (caption), 79, 107, 110–11,
    122, 129–30, 150, 152, 158, 161
Scotland, 6, 7, 19–20, 36, 41–61, 67, 68,
    108, 115–16, 118, 120–21, 160
Seccomb, John, 163
Settlement projects, 45–46, 58, 62, 72, 74–
    77, 84–85, 87, 102–3, 108, 115–20, 122,
    124–26, 129, 131–34, 138, 142, 162, 164
Seven Years' War, 2, 8, 140–56, 158–65
Sheep. See Livestock

Shipbuilding, 49
Shirley, William, 109, 111, 114–18, 127, 137, 141–42, 145
Shubenacadie River, 65, 80, 92, 99, 111, 123, 125, 134
Slavery, 31, 60, 136
Smuggling, 44, 60, 88, 98, 124
Society for the Propagation of the Gospel, 51, 66
Soldiers, 12–13, 18, 22, 45, 49–50, 51, 56–59, 62, 79, 85, 89, 96, 100–102, 108, 110, 113–15, 117, 120, 135, 143–44, 146–47
Southack, Cyprian, 74–77, 81
South Carolina, 149, 152
South Sea Company, 87
Spain and the Spanish, 5, 15, 25, 106–7, 110
Spanish West Indies, 106
Staten Island, 149
Stuart, Charles, 115–16
Sugar, 47
Switzerland and the Swiss, 117–20

Teoniahigarawe. See Hendrick
Timber, 47, 49
Tory Party, 6, 41, 50, 53–56, 87
Tourangeau, François, 76
Treaties, native-British, 70, 79–81, 83, 86, 94, 123, 127, 134–37, 141, 162–63
Treaties, European: Aix-la-Chapelle (1748), 117–20, 122; Paris (1763), 156, 165; Ryswick (1697), 35; Utrecht (1713), 40, 41, 55, 61, 62, 64, 70–71, 76–77, 79, 89–91, 97
Treaty of Union (1707), 41–42, 47–48, 160

Ulster, 142
United States of America, 5, 165–66

Vetch, Samuel, 41–61, 65–67, 68, 76, 90, 121, 161–62
Vigneau, Jacques Maurice, 9, 23, 64, 98–99, 103, 113–14, 123–24, 130–31, 135–36, 141–44, 152–57
Vigneau, Joseph, 156
Vigneau, Marguerite, 135
Vigneau, Maurice, 64, 90
Villebon. See Robinau de Villebon, Joseph
Virginia, 149

Wabanaki Confederacy, 26, 27, 77–80, 140
Wales, 4, 59, 68
Walpole, Robert, 87, 93, 106
War of the Austrian Succession, 68, 86, 104, 106–17, 124, 129, 146, 162
War of Jenkins' Ear, 106–7, 110
War of the Spanish Succession, 35, 40–61, 74, 102
Whaling, 49
Whig Party, 6, 41, 45, 51, 54, 59, 68, 87, 93
Wicken, William C., 26
William III, king of England, 11, 13, 14, 36, 42, 68
Winaguadesh, Jacques, 84
Winslow, John, 143, 146–48, 165
Worcester, Massachusetts, 153
Wuastukwiuk, 96–97, 150

Acknowledgments

Like most books this one has been a long time in preparation, and I have acquired a huge cumulative debt of gratitude to dozens of individuals and groups who have helped me though the process of research and writing. The first person to mention is my friend and advisor John Murrin, who responded positively when I came into his office in the fall of 1992 and first mentioned my barely-formed idea of studying Nova Scotia. John has helped guide my work ever since, and by his own count he has read and reviewed three completely different drafts of this book. (I think the total may be four.) The other members of my dissertation committee at Princeton, Stephen Aron, Kathleen Brown, and Stanley Katz, have not been called upon quite so much, but each of them has left a mark on this work. I also gained valuable direction from my fellow graduate students, including the various members of the dissertation writers' group, and particularly Jacob Katz Cogan, Evan Haefeli, Gary Hewitt and Ann Little (a friend from the University of Pennsylvania).

After leaving Princeton I joined the history department at the University of Cincinnati, where my colleagues have been very supportive; Gene Lewis and his successor Barbara Ramusack have been as helpful as heads-of-department could be, and at least six of members of the department have read book-length versions of this manuscript, including Barbara, John Alexander, Roger Daniels, Wayne Durrill, Herb Shapiro, and Ann Twinam. Sigrun Haude, Maura O'Connor, and Willard Sunderland read shorter sections, but they all gave me valuable advice. Mona Seigel served as my indispensable liaison with the Bibliothèque nationale, and Man Bun Kwan gave me techinical assistance in the production of the manuscript. Maura convened a book-writers' group that included members of several of southeastern Ohio's academic communities, including Lynn Voskuil, Victoria Thompson, Karla Goldman, Katharina Gurstenberger, and Kathy von Ankum. Morgan McFarland, Kenneth Meyer, and Kelly F. Wright helped me with copyediting. I thank them all.

Since 1995 I have been active on the conference circuit, presenting papers containing material that has been incorporated into this book. I cannot name all the individuals who provided me comments or assistance at professional meetings, but I would like to mention two whose words of wisdom aided me greatly as I approached the task of writing: Charles Cohen (one of my former teachers at the University of Wisconsin) and William Pencak.

My research has been funded by the Taft Foundation at the University of Cincinnati, Cincinnati's University Research Council, the Canadian Embassy to the United States, the American Antiquarian Society, the American Society for Eighteenth-Century Studies, the Huntington Library, Princeton University and the Mellon Foundation. My thanks to them.

Sally Moffitt, the history librarian at Langsam Library in Cincinnati, provided me with important help, as did, of course, the staff of the interlibrary loan office and the secretary in the history department, Hope Earls.

One of the best perquisites of researching the history of Nova Scotia is that it gives the researcher a chance to visit the place. Over the years I have accumulated a collection of friends in Halifax and elsewhere in Canada who have provided me hospitality as well as challenging conversation. James D. Alsop, Maurice Basque, Donald Chard, Brenda Dunn, Naomi Griffiths, Elizabeth Mancke (who lives in Ohio, but belongs on this list), Barry Morris Moody, Daniel Paul, George Rawlyk, John Reid, and William C. Wicken were all generous with their time and happy to converse with me in detail about my work. Gillian Allen, Richard Twomey, Robert Ferguson, and Birgitta Wallace have been generous to me with professional assistance and in other ways, and they have made Halifax one of my favorite places on the continent.

Leonard Gaudet deserves my special thanks. He is among the numerous progeny of Jacques Maurice Vigneau, and he directed me to important material on his ancestor's life. Vigneau figures prominently in this book.

As I was searching for the right publisher for this project, D. H. Akenson, Roger Martin, Margaret Newell, and J. R. Pole aided me greatly and gave me necessary encouragement. But as soon as I met up with Richard Dunn I knew that I would be fortunate to work with him, the McNeil Center for Early American Studies, and the University of Pennsylvania Press. Richard's frank and direct advice led me to a radical restructuring of this book. He, Robert Lockhart, Alison Anderson, Mia Carino, Bruce Franklin, Cory Stephenson, and my two outside readers, Alison Olson and Ian K. Steele, allowed me to treat the preparation of the manuscript almost as a team effort. Without them the book would be very different, and almost certainly in several ways worse. (But of course I had the final word on the important decisions, and I take responsibility for everything wrong between the covers.)

My parents, John and Eleanor Plank, suffered a little, patiently, as they waited for the end of the writing process. But my wife-to-be Ina Zweiniger-Bargielowska endured more, as I obsessively revised, re-ordered, deleted, and rewrote paragraph after paragraph. Ina read the manuscript several times in postmodernistic, deconstructed and decontextualized snippets, yet she was almost always able to see where the overall project was heading, in order to give me advice on what to leave in and what to leave out. I cannot think of this book without thinking of Ina, but then again that is true of almost everything important in our lives. I met Ina three years ago at an academic conference a few miles below Niagara Falls. Three months later I met her daughter Sonja in Aberystwyth, a coastal town in mid-Wales. Since then Ina and Sonja have introduced me to a world of new landscapes (real and imaginary), with strange histories and mysterious futures. With them, life is wonderful. I will always be grateful.